BY THE SAME AUTHOR

The Other Nile
Travels in Nepal
Barcelona: A Celebration and a Guide

REBELS AND OUTCASTS

A Journey through Christian India

Charlie Pye-Smith

VIKING

VIKING

Published by the Penguin Group
Penguin Books Ltd, 27 Wrights Lane, London W8 5TZ, England
Penguin Books USA Inc., 375 Hudson Street, New York, New York 10014, USA
Penguin Books Australia Ltd, Ringwood, Victoria, Australia
Penguin Books Canada Ltd, 10 Alcorn Avenue, Toronto, Ontario, Canada M4V 3B2
Penguin Books (NZ) Ltd, 182–190 Wairau Road, Auckland 10, New Zealand

Penguin Books Ltd, Registered Offices: Harmondsworth, Middlesex, England

First published 1997
1 3 5 7 9 10 8 6 4 2

Grateful acknowledgement is made to Faber and Faber Ltd
for permission to reproduce lines from 'Didymus' by Louis MacNeice,
published in *Collected Poems* (1996)

Set in 12.5/15pt Monotype Baskerville
Typeset by Rowland Phototypesetting Ltd, Bury St Edmunds, Suffolk
Printed in England by Clays Ltd, St Ives plc

A CIP catalogue record for this book is available from the British Library

ISBN 0-670-85974-5

In memory of my mother, Margaret Anna Pye-Smith

Who has come here against you? Slow of speech
With trouble in his eyes and tarry hands
And no sophistication and no caste,
Who has come here armed with two plain crossed sticks
To flout your banyan riot of dialectic?
Is it a prince whose vein runs blue with magic?
Is it a sage whose water-divining mind
Will twitch to the smallest drop at the final nadir?
Is it a god who has more arms than yours,
More words, more shapes, more worlds, invincible avatar?
No; it is Doubting Thomas.

from 'Didymus' by Louis MacNeice

Contents

List of Illustrations

FIRST SECTION

SECOND SECTION

Acknowledgements

During the time I spent in India I met several hundred people who were involved with the Christian Churches. Some I deliberately sought out; others I met through chance encounters. I spent days with some, minutes with others. All, to a greater or lesser degree, helped to shape not only this book but also my own thoughts about our spiritual existence. I continue to see through a glass darkly, but I begin to discern patches of light where before there was none. My thanks go to all those listed below, many of whom I have written about, quite possibly to their embarrassment and consternation. India is not always an easy country for the traveller, but I was continually sustained by the warmth and generosity of those I met.

Shimla: Rev. Sunil Caleb, Shakti Chandel, Major F. Das, Dr K. N. Thakur Das.

Delhi: Fr Monodeep Daniel, John Dayal, Fr G. Gispert-Sauch, Fr Jose Kananaikil, Dr Amod Kumar, Fr Josey Kunnunkal, Dr V. S. Lall, Dr James Massey, K. P. Philip.

Bombay: Prianjali D'Costa, Fr Cleophas Fernandes, Rt Rev. Samuel Joshua, Pastor Jerry de Souza.

Pune: Tichnor Charles, the sisters at the Christa Prema Seva Ashram, Rev. Basker Onawale, Dr Neela Onawale and the staff of the Deep Griha society, parishioners of St Mary's church, Mrs Dinah Verghese.

Goa: Fr Miguel Braganza, Fr Cosme Jose Costa, Rev. Lagrange Fernandes, the sisters of the Holy Family convent at Sancoale, Fr George Nazareth, Fr Joaquim Loiola Pereira, Fr Ubuldo de Sa, Fr Willie d'Silva.

Mangalore: Fr Valerian Prashant Madtha, Gilbert Sequera.

Cochin: Rev. E. G. Korula, Rev. Dr Joseph Kureethara, Fr Xavier Palackal, Mr and Mrs Joseph Xavier.

Kottayam and Tiruvella: Fr K. J. Gabriel, Fr K. M. George, Sindhu Mary Jacob, Fr Jacob Kollaparambil, P. J. Kuriakose, Rev. A. C. Kurien, Rev. Dr D. Philip, Fr Thomas Philip, Fr John Thomas.

Trivandrum: K. P. Cheriyan, Rt Rev. Dr Joseph Mar Irenaeus, Commissioner Jillapegu Israel, Captain T. P. John, P. K. Johny, Fr Stephen Josemethachery, Rev. C. I. D. Joy, Fr Johny Lawrence, Fernandes Pereira, Fr Eugene Perreira.

Bangalore: Rev. K. U. Abraham, Shanti Gnanaoliva, all at the Mar Thoma Hoskote mission, Dr K. P. Mathai, Archbishop Alfonso Mathias, Sister Josephine Pauline and the Little Sisters of the Poor, Dr A. M. Prabakaran, Eddie and Cecilia D'Souza.

Madras: Rt Rev. M. Azariah, the inhabitants and staff at Balarama-puram leper colony, Rev. R. M. Dravyam, George E. Gregorian, Dr George Joseph, Professor George Koshy, Nalini Manuel and the staff at the Asha centre, Sister Getzie Mohan, the staff at the St Andrew's Kirk day-care centre.

Calcutta: Dr Reeti Biswas, Sarthak Roy Chowdhury, Dr J. T. K. Daniel, Mrs Luna Darta, Rt Rev. D. C. Gorai, Mrs Kusum Gupta, Dr Timotheus Hebrom, Rev. Dr R. Lalbiakmawia, Rev. David Luke, Rev. Subodh Mondal, Dr Amitavna Mukhopadhiya,

Charles Sarkies, Mrs Sumita Sen and the staff at the Cathedral Relief Service, Mr and Mrs Madhu Singh.

Shillong: Rev. P. A. Challam, Dr L. L. Cunville, Robert Cunville, Rev. Dr J. F. Jyrwa, Fr Sebastian Karotemprel, Dr George Kottuppallil, Rev. P. B. Lyngdoh, Rev. R. P. Lyngdoh, Fr Sngi Silvano Lyngdoh, Rev. Aziz Massey, Sandy Pariot, Rev. O. L. Snaitang, Rt Rev. Ernest Talibuddin, Rev. Dr E. R. Tongper.

Before I embarked on my journey I received valuable advice and many good contacts from Martin Heath of the United Society for the Propagation of the Gospel and Dr Andrew Morton of the Council for World Mission. Many thanks too to the friends who entertained me in India, especially Ranjan and Pinti Kamath, with whom I stayed in Bombay; my editor at Penguin Books, Eleo Gordon; David Davidar of Penguin Books in New Delhi; Mrs Bhagirath of the Indian High Commission in London; Annie Bowman; my wife Sandie, who joined me for a spell in south India; and all those whom I met on my travels but have not mentioned individually here – from the health workers in Sunder Nagari to trainee seamstresses in Cochin, from the men and women of Balaramapuram leper colony to the prostitutes' children in Bowbazar: these people, whatever their faiths, are the 'holy common people of God' whom this book is really about.

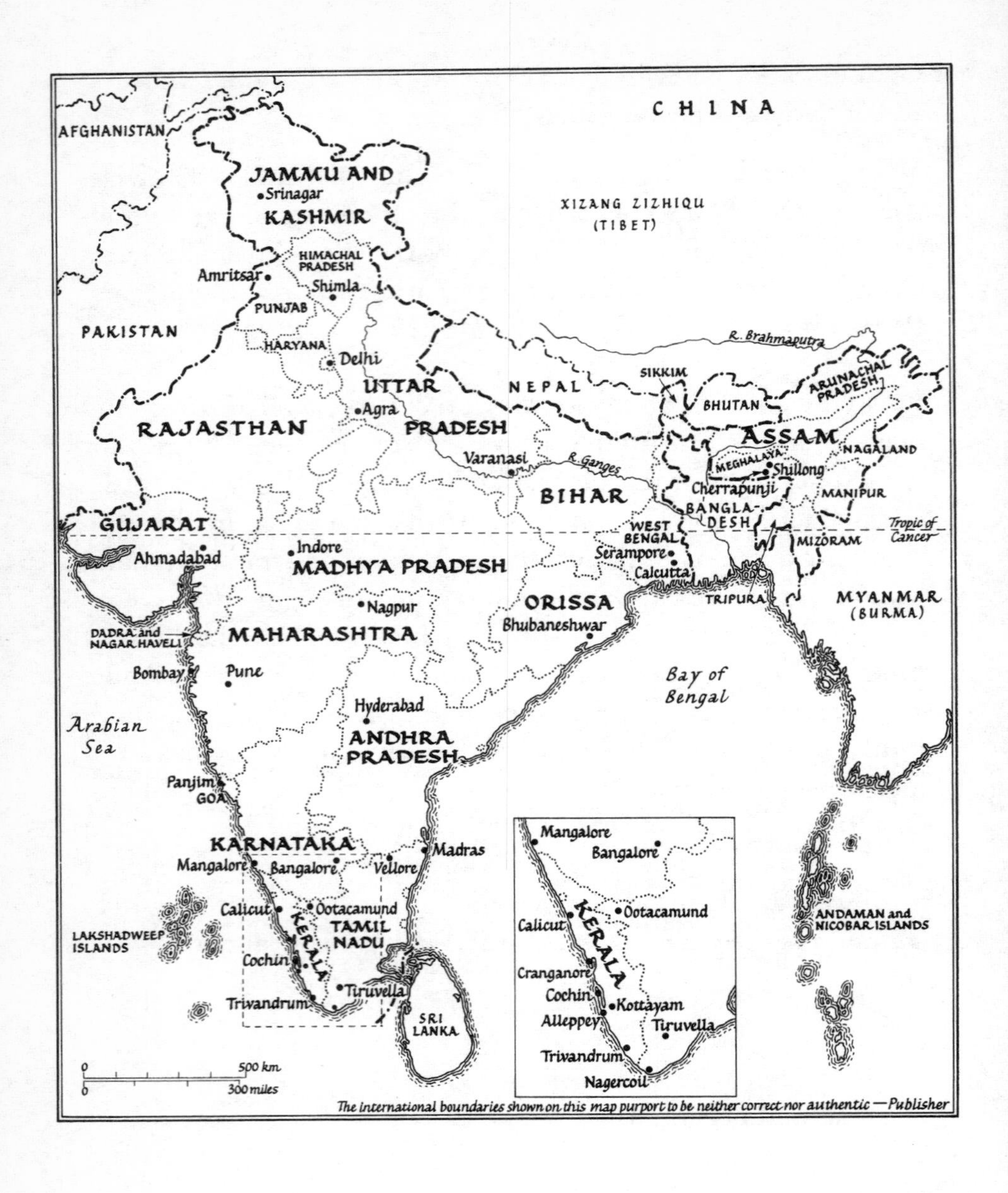
CHINA
AFGHANISTAN
JAMMU AND KASHMIR
Srinagar
XIZANG ZIZHIQU (TIBET)
HIMACHAL PRADESH
Amritsar
Shimla
PUNJAB
PAKISTAN
HARYANA
Delhi
R. Brahmaputra
UTTAR PRADESH
NEPAL
SIKKIM
ARUNACHAL PRADESH
BHUTAN
Agra
RAJASTHAN
ASSAM
NAGALAND
Varanasi
R. Ganges
MEGHALAYA
Shillong
Cherrapunji
BIHAR
MANIPUR
BANGLA-DESH
GUJARAT
WEST BENGAL
Tropic of Cancer
MIZORAM
Ahmadabad
Indore
Serampore
MADHYA PRADESH
Calcutta
ORISSA
TRIPURA
MYANMAR (BURMA)
Nagpur
DADRA and NAGAR HAVELI
MAHARASHTRA
Bhubaneshwar
Bombay
Pune
Bay of Bengal
Hyderabad
Arabian Sea
ANDHRA PRADESH
Panjim
GOA
KARNATAKA
Madras
Mangalore
Bangalore
Vellore
Calicut
Ootacamund
KERALA
TAMIL NADU
LAKSHADWEEP ISLANDS
Cochin
Tiruvella
Trivandrum
SRI LANKA
ANDAMAN and NICOBAR ISLANDS
Mangalore
Bangalore
Ootacamund
Calicut
KERALA
Cranganore
Cochin
Kottayam
Alleppey
Tiruvella
Trivandrum
Nagercoil
0 500 km
0 300 miles
The International boundaries shown on this map purport to be neither correct nor authentic — Publisher

CHAPTER I

The Raj on Its Knees

I was woken twice during the night: the first time by a troop of monkeys clattering across the tin roof of Prospect Lodge; later by the sound of a cloudburst. The pre-monsoon rains had begun to sweep fitfully across Shimla and the Himalaya, freshening the air and stimulating the release of an anarchic mixture of smells. Prospect Lodge was spectacularly situated on Jackoo Hill, high above Christchurch and the Mall; it was further still from the crowded alleys of Lower Bazar, yet the pungent smell of diesel fumes and rancid refuse rose up the hillside to mingle with far pleasanter smells: the sappy scent of deodar and pine; the earthy odour of horse droppings in the narrow street behind the lodge; the enticing smell of porridge and fried eggs waiting on the breakfast table. I dare say the monkeys contributed too to the olfactory pleasures of Shimla. They had certainly influenced its architecture: Prospect Lodge, for much of its history a holiday retreat of the nuns of St Steven's Community in Delhi, was neither handsome nor ugly, but the wire mesh that encased its creaking verandas and peeling window frames, and whose purpose was to keep the monkeys out, lent it the appearance of an over-sized chicken shack.

In fact, the whole of Shimla was infested by monkeys, and when they were not going about their daily business of procreating, suckling, grooming and scavenging, they were generally making a nuisance of themselves, swinging from the telegraph wires, scampering across the roofs and annoying the more timid members of the public. Some were even adept at snatching the handbags of unsuspecting females, then rifling through their contents like seasoned pickpockets. When I arrived I assumed that the countless broken windows in the government buildings that I passed on the climb up to the Mall were evidence of neglect or penury, perhaps both. No, the monkeys were to blame. Shimla's winters can be bitterly cold, and the monkeys, being creatures of some intelligence, smash the window panes and spend their nights indoors. No doubt it was their ubiquitous presence that prompted Sir Edwin Lutyens's caustic observation about Shimla (or Simla, as the hill station was called in the days before Independence): 'If I had been told it had all been built by monkeys, I would have said, what wonderful monkeys, they must be shot in case they do it again.'

Over breakfast I suggested to Dr Thakur Das, the church historian in charge of Prospect Lodge, that even though the monkeys could not be held responsible for Shimla's eccentric architecture, Lutyens's idea was not without merit; perhaps it would be cruel to shoot the monkeys, but at least they could be controlled with contraceptives. 'Oh, heavens,' he exclaimed, 'that couldn't possibly happen! Imagine how the BJP [Bharatiya Janata Party] would react.' For Hindus the monkey is the embodiment of the god Hanuman, and the hilltop temple high above Prospect Lodge, dedicated to Hanuman, was there long before the British came to settle the area in the 1820s. The BJP, a right-wing Hindu group and a powerful political force in the state of Himachal Pradesh, would no more countenance the introduction of birth control for monkeys than the Vatican would for humans.

After breakfast Dr Thakur Das accompanied me down the steep lane that led to Christchurch, a handsome Gothic building whose bell tower had dominated the hill station's skyline for the past 150 years. We arrived two or three minutes late for my appointment with Major Frederick Das, to whom Dr Thakur Das introduced me before continuing on his way into town. 'I was just about to leave,' explained Major Das without a hint of reproach. A small, wiry man, remarkably fit for his seventy-nine years, Major Das was courteous, charming and unmistakably military in both demeanour and dress. An umbrella was clamped to his side like a sergeant-major's baton, and he wore a beret and regimental tie. His grey trousers were sharply creased and the only hint of informality came from his orange suede shoes and yellow cardigan, from one of whose pockets poked a red, leather-bound copy of the New Testament. 'I have been coming here for over forty years,' he said as he took me by the elbow and led me towards an open side door, 'and I haven't missed a single service, except through absence or illness. It's all through God's grace, and He's blessed me immensely. Whatever I have asked for, I've been given.' The latest evidence of the Almighty's beneficence had arrived in the shape of an invitation to attend the Victory in Japan celebrations in London on the fiftieth anniversary of the conclusion of the Second World War. It would be Major Das's first visit to England and he was already, as he put it, polishing his medals in anticipation.

At first glance there was nothing to suggest that Christchurch was much different from countless Victorian churches to be found in the provincial towns of England. Perhaps the Gothic tracery was less ornate, the fabric in somewhat poorer repair, but Christ and the saints in the stained-glass windows were depicted as Europeans the organ had been made in London, and the inscriptions were all in English. However, this was no ordinary church: it had been built to serve a congregation whose members at one time ruled over one-fifth of the human race. In 1832, less than ten years after the first British-built house was erected among the deodar forests, Lord William Bentinck, the Governor-General of India, spent the summer months here, thus beginning a tradition that was to be formalized in 1862 when Simla became the official summer capital of the Raj.

As we walked up the aisle Major Das pointed to metal hoops fixed to the pews; these, he explained, were for the soldiers' rifles. The two front rows were devoid of rifle-holders, and discreet brass plaques indicated that they were reserved for their excellencies the viceroy, the commander-in-chief and the state governor. The last viceroy to worship here was Lord Louis Mountbatten. 'I met him in Kuala Lumpur,' said Major Das casually. 'In '45, I think. Or was it '46? He took the surrender of the Japs.' Major Das, like many of the men who had worshipped here, had spent a good deal of his life on the battlefield. He had seen action in Burma and Malaya during the war and he had been involved in both of India's skirmishes with Pakistan. The polished brasses suggested that he had been more fortunate than many. Brigadier General F. A. Hoghton, for example, was killed at Kut-al-Amarah on 12 April 1916, 'during the siege of that place by the Turks'. Mishaps and disease had also taken their toll: Arthur Bruce Wilson was killed by the accidental discharge of a gun in 1875; a local surgeon died 'after an illness of twenty-six hours'. Others had perished at sea on the long journey home, though there were a few who had died of old age, fulfilling the verse from Job that was inscribed on the plaque to Eugene James Earle: 'Thou shalt come to thy grave in a full age, like as a shock of corn cometh in, in his season' (5:26).

Over the years Christchurch has suffered its losses: several pinnacles were shaken off by an earthquake in the early years of this century, and the frescos around the chancel window, designed by Rudyard Kipling's father, have disappeared. A significant loss – and, according to Major Das, a relatively recent one – was the disappearance of the leather-bound volumes, some ten in all, that recorded the church's history. From these one might have been able to learn not only about the alterations made to the church but also about the attitudes of the vicars and congregations during the years of Empire. As it is, one is left with little other than anecdotes, although these in themselves can be revealing. In 1860 the vicar criticized the women in the congregation for wearing crinolines, which took up too much space; the following week they came in their riding gear. The church represented the ruling class at prayer, and the prayers of many, one suspects, had little to do with the true message of the Gospels: Simla was a monument to cultural élitism and hedonism, and indeed that is part of its charm. During Victorian times, when European women often far outnumbered men, colonels in the Indian Army regiments would not permit their subalterns to visit Simla for fear that they might seduce their wives, who had left for the hills unchaperoned. Adultery was to Simla what unnatural sexual licence was to Sodom. That, at least, is part of the mythology.

When we came out of the church Major Das suggested we go down to his club for a drink. The broad expanse of open ground outside the church was already full of tourists taking the morning air, and it seemed as though half of Punjab had fled the oppressive heat of the plains: young girls in pretty frocks, their lustrous hair tied in ribbons, played with coloured balloons while their turbaned fathers, many with bellies straining against their waistbands, sauntered beside their equally capacious wives as they admired the long views over the blue-green hills to the south. Ice-cream sellers were doing brisk business by the bandstand, below which a statue of Mahatma Gandhi watched over half a dozen ponies, Shimla's equivalent to beach donkeys. Public displays of affection are frowned upon in India, but an exception is made for the hill stations, and honeymoon couples held hands with the ardour of first-time lovers.

A flight of steps led us down to the Mall and we entered the Gaiety Theatre, the home of the major's club, the Shimla Amateur Dramatic Society. According to Major Das, the theatre was a miniature replica of the Albert Hall. A delightful, intimate little place, it was equipped with a VIP box, a press box and a small ballroom. Behind the boxes in the circle there were photos of past productions, including the 1987 staging of *See How They Run*: Major Das was listed below the cast as 'Backstage'.

The Amateur Dramatic Society's presidents have always been local battalion commanders, and the walls of the stone stairwell that led up to the club were hung with their portraits. Major Das gave a brief commentary as we passed them. 'This one was a Sandhurst man. He's dead. And this one, dead too. Now this commander – he was a nice chap. He's dead as well . . . This one's alive still . . .' In the bar a dozen or so men were chatting quietly among themselves or reading the morning papers. A few wore jacket and tie, but not enough for Major Das's taste. 'I'm afraid it's rather lost its decorum,' he said mournfully. 'Now it's just the old-timers like me who wear a tie. In the old days if someone from my regiment came in without a tie, I'd tell him to go and get one. In fact, the bearers used to turn people away if they weren't properly dressed.' In those days, new members were properly screened as well; nowadays anyone can join on a temporary basis.

By the time Major Das came to live in Shimla in the 1950s most of the British had left, and the Indian congregation of St Andrew's church, which had been built down by the Bazar in 1885 with Indian donations, had taken over Christchurch, leaving their old place of worship to be turned into a boys' school. 'When the British were here,' said Major Das, 'there were bearers outside the church to keep people away.' This was said without rancour: it was simply a statement of fact. By 'people' he meant Indians not of sufficient social standing to be considered worthy company for the British. In fact, at one time Indians were not even allowed to promenade on the Mall, whose fashionable shops were run by British merchants, and most lived in or near the Lower Bazar, 'a rabbit warren at an angle of 45 degrees', as Kipling described it. 'The dominant characteristic of British Simla,' suggested one local historian, 'was its contempt for all things Indian.' Contempt, one might add, for the canons of good taste too. Simla was designed as an evocation of the home country, but unlike classical Calcutta or Gothic Bombay, it was built in a kaleidoscope of conflicting styles. Some buildings look as though they were plucked from a Surrey high street, others from a remote Scottish moor or a quiet cul-de-sac in a Victorian seaside resort. The General Post Office is Wild West Swiss; Viceregal Lodge is austerely Elizabethan. Gorton Castle, at one time the government's secretariat, looks like a stage set for Gormenghast with its profusion of spires and turrets, while the design of the town hall behind the Gaiety Theatre was evidently inspired by the Arts and Crafts movement. The overall effect is not so much imperial as vaguely comic.

A portly man of great warmth and generosity, Dr K. N. Thakur Das could describe the most distant events in history with such perception and clarity that one wondered if he had witnessed them himself in an earlier incarnation. He had begun his working life as a mathematician and had later taught educational philosophy at Srinagar University in Kashmir. He had embarked on his new career as a church historian only in the early 1990s, when he retired from academic life and moved into Prospect Lodge. One morning, when we were sitting in his book-strewn study on the ground floor, the curtains drawn against a piercing sun, I remarked on the apparent popularity – judging by its widespread availability – of a book called *Jesus Lived in India.* This was a notion, he explained, that was plausible as far as the Muslim world was concerned; the Koran implied that Christ was brought down from the cross and revived. Dr F. M. Hussein, a director of archives in the Jammu and Kashmir government, had promoted the idea that Christ lived in Kashmir in a small pamphlet that drew its evidence from folk sayings and historical texts. Hussein and his associates claimed that there was concrete evidence too: a grave in the village of Khangar was inscribed with the words 'Isa (Jesus) Musa'. The Hyderabad-based Henry Martin Institute of Islamic Studies had considered the idea credible enough to be worthy of further investigation and Dr Thakur Das was a member of a team that was invited to look into the matter. 'Well,' he said in his quiet, lilting voice, chuckling at the memory, 'we used all sorts of techniques and examined all the sources. We even did carbon-dating on the grave, and we found that it was between 270 and 320 years old. There was no evidence, except in folklore, that Christ came to India.'

Many Indian Christians maintain that their religion was brought to India by the apostle Thomas in AD 52. One authority for this is St Jerome, who wrote that after the resurrection Christ 'dwelt in all places, with Thomas in India, with Peter in Rome, with Paul in Illyricum . . .' It would certainly have been possible for St Thomas to visit India – tradition has it that he landed by boat at Cranganore in Kerala – but there is no documentary proof. It has also been suggested that another apostle, St Bartholomew, visited north India, bringing with him the Gospel of St Matthew, which was the main text used by a sect of Christians in Punjab as recently as the nineteenth century. Some claim that the tradition of using St Matthew's Gospel, and none of the other books in the Bible, may have persisted through the centuries from St Bartholomew's time onwards. Dr Thakur Das would neither endorse nor refute such a claim, but he pointed out that early Christian societies, had they sprung up in north India shortly after Christ's death, might not have existed in a form that would be instantly recognizable to us today. 'In those times,' he said, 'Christianity was like a flower whose petals were just beginning to open.' Nestorian crosses from the ninth century have been found in Ladakh, in the high Himalaya, and there is no reason to suppose that Christians did not come this way long before then. After all, Alexander the Great had invaded what is now Pakistan, a little distance to the west, three centuries before the birth of Christ. The region had frequently been invaded from the west, and in the wake of the invaders had come the traders; it would be surprising if no missionaries had followed.

The small Christian community in the Shimla hills is of no

great antiquity, owing its origins to the arrival of the British in the early nineteenth century. In 1825 a military cantonment was established at Kotgarh, a hundred miles north-east of Shimla on the road to Tibet, and it was here that the first mission station was founded at the instigation of Major Boileau, the army commander after whom a suburb of Shimla is named, and Mr Gorton, a civil servant who was touched by the extreme poverty he witnessed. The early missionaries were shocked to discover that human sacrifice had till recently been practised, a young girl being annually offered to the demons in a cave near Kotgarh, and cases of infanticide involving the burial of live children were recorded as late as 1840. The practice of polyandry, of one woman marrying several men, was not uncommon, and the missionaries did their best to proscribe it. The Himalayan Mission set about the task of evangelizing the hill people, working primarily through the network of mission schools, the first of which was established in 1842.

The Christians also had a profound influence on agricultural life in the hills, thanks largely to the Moravian Brethren, a German group with close links to the Lutheran Church. 'They believed that the best way to bring people to Christ was not just through preaching,' explained Dr Thakur Das, 'but by following an exemplary lifestyle. They would colonize a place, live and toil with the people, and bring their skills and ideas to help them.' The Moravians set up a colony near Kotgarh and imported both tea and potatoes. Even now, nearly all the seed potatoes sown in northern India come from the areas where the Moravians introduced them. The Moravians had rather more luck with crops than souls, and by the 1880s they had made so few converts that they decided to move. 'But they never lost hope,' continued Dr Thakur Das. 'They became the Ganga Mission and they moved south in search of more fertile land in which to sow their beliefs.' Eventually, the Moravians reached Chota Nagpur in eastern India, and over a third of a million Christians there owe their faith to the small band of German missionaries who left the Shimla hills over a century ago.

So why, I asked, had the Moravians and others failed to evangelize the Himalaya with any great degree of success?

The strength of orthodox Hinduism was one important factor: converts were often persecuted by their families and forced to leave their homes. The British rulers, paradoxically, had also played their part in restricting the spread of Christianity. 'You've heard of the mass movements?' inquired Dr Thakur Das. 'Their heyday was from 1870 to around 1930, and they involved large numbers of people – whole families, castes, villages – converting to Christianity together. Well, one of the first of these happened after the Indian Mutiny of 1857. A faction of the Sikh Light Infantry was resting in St James's church in Delhi after they'd helped the British recapture the city. They came across Bibles and prayer books and they began to read them.' These soldiers were *dalits* – members of the oppressed classes – and they saw Christianity as a way of escaping from the caste system. 'Almost half the regiment became Christians when they returned to their base in Punjab,' continued Dr Thakur Das, 'and that caused panic among many upper-caste non-Christians.' In order to appease them, the British dissuaded missionaries from operating in certain areas and forbade Indian government officials from converting to Christianity. This was known as the 'concept of neutrality'.

For an Indian going about his business in the Bazar, or following his herd in the hills around Kotgarh, Christianity must have presented a confusing spectacle. On the one hand, there was the Christianity practised by the British rulers in the summer capital. 'I think the lifestyle they led was a turn-off to many Indians,' suggested Dr Thakur Das bluntly. 'It was the opposite of asceticism. The Indians saw practising Christians living lives of luxury, with trains of servants, and many couldn't understand why the British were always fighting wars if theirs was the religion of peace.' On the other hand, the people of Kotgarh had a better example to follow: the Moravians and the other early missionaries led simple, virtuous lives. However, the person who did the most to capture the imagination of the hill people – and his fame eventually spread to other parts of India and to Europe – was Sadhu Sundar Singh. The son of a Sikh landowner from the Punjab, he attempted to lead a Christian life in a recognizably Indian manner: instead of working within a Church, he became a wandering ascetic and teacher – in short, a Christian *sadhu*. He was baptized in 1905 at St Andrew's church at the age of sixteen, and he spent much of his short life preaching in the hills of northern India. He was last seen in 1929, when he set off across the Himalaya to Tibet, in those days a notoriously difficult country for foreigners to visit. On previous journeys his attempts to evangelize Tibetans had led to his persecution and imprisonment, and his task was made all the more difficult by the bitter cold. The vision that brought Singh to Christ was said to be similar to the one that St Paul experienced on the road to Damascus, and on his travels to Tibet he must have felt much as Paul did: 'We are fools for Christ's sake . . . To this day we go hungry and thirsty and in rags; we are beaten up; we wander from place to place; we wear ourselves out earning a living with our own hands. People curse us, and we bless; they persecute us, we submit; they slander us, and we try to be conciliatory. To this day we are treated as the scum of the earth, as the dregs of humanity' (1 Cor. 4:10–13).

Mrs de la Hay, Shimla's last surviving British resident, had a high opinion of the town's monkeys. 'Don't you love them?' she asked excitedly. 'They're just like humans the way they play with their babies.'

Mrs de la Hay was born shortly after the First World War. A year later her mother died in childbirth. She was educated in a local convent, then sent to school in England at the age of twelve. She returned after her schooling, married a doctor in the British

Army and remained till 1947, the year of Independence, when she and her family moved to England. Since 1970 she had made frequent visits to Shimla, and she had recently decided to settle here for good. Her present place of residence was a modest hotel near the bottom of the Mall, and from her room she could observe the monkeys clambering across the neglected façade of the tax office. She was extremely angry with Mrs Thatcher, whose policies, she asserted, had made life impossible for British pensioners, and she could never imagine living in Britain again. She loved Simla, as she still called the town, though everything she said was coloured with a deep nostalgia for an age that had long since passed. 'I beg you,' she said soon after we met, 'forget all these tourists, forget what you see – just imagine Simla as it was in the years when the British were here.' I couldn't, except in a caricaturish sort of way, though I understood what Mrs de la Hay meant when she said wistfully, 'The ghost of England still haunts Simla – or is it the other way round?'

The ghost of England is glimpsed, most obviously, in the churches and bandstands, in the pavilions and clubs, but it also manifests itself in more subtle ways: in idioms of speech that belong to earlier times – 'Are you fighting fit?' Major Das inquired of a brigadier at the club; in the solid breakfasts served in Prospect Lodge; and, in the case of Shakti Chandel, in his poetry.

Mr Chandel came across to Dr Thakur Das's study one mid-morning and invited me for poetry and tea in one of the large new houses that had been built almost directly in front of Prospect Lodge, and which partially obscured its view of the valley. He wore a clipped moustache, a blue blazer, grey trousers, black shoes and a coloured topi that was removed as we entered his front door to reveal a precisely circular bald spot. Since leaving the army – Mr Chandel had fought in both Indo-Pak wars – he had occupied two posts as a district commissioner in remote regions of the state and he was now the director of tourism for Himachal Pradesh. He was proud of his house, which he had designed himself, and he offered to show me around. Everything was in immaculate condition – the furnishings, the paintwork, the carpets, the tiling in the lavatory, the utensils in the kitchen – and I felt as though I was being given a guided tour through the pages of *House & Garden* or some such magazine. There was a debate about where we should sit, and eventually Mr Chandel decided on the bedroom, where we were served tea by his 'Gurkha johnny'.

'There's something in me that's mystical,' said Mr Chandel, who proceeded to talk of love and the soul, of happiness and frustration and other matters of concern to the poet. 'Please read this one.' He handed me a newspaper with a poem called 'Autumn'. Others followed: 'Winter', 'Fear and Hope', 'Hermit at the Door of Life'. Certain themes ran through all of them: a love of nature, a sense of melancholy and a predilection for archaic language – 'Why art thou sad?' began one poem.

'I hope you won't be insulted,' I said after I had read half a dozen of his poems, 'but they read like the works of a nineteenth-century Romantic.' I wondered aloud whether he had been influenced by Rossetti or Keats.

No, he replied, he was not in the least bit insulted; indeed, he took it as a compliment. Naturally he liked Keats, but he was more eager to talk about the poetry of Vikram Seth.

'I'm a humanist,' said Mr Chandel when I asked him what religion he practised, 'though I am not suggesting there isn't a power greater than us. Call it God, if that's what you want to call it.' He said that he admired Christianity, as he felt it possessed grace and dignity that were lacking in other religions, but he was greatly offended by the idea of celibacy. 'Why does your religion tell these poor nuns they cannot marry?' he asked. 'It's an injustice to their souls! You're denying their biological requirements. I mean, look at Dr Thakur Das. He has a family. Look at Dr Chandulal. He's got one too.'

Dr Anand Chandulal was the Bishop of Amritsar, and on a recent visit to Shimla he had taken Mr Chandel's poem 'Joys of

Life' as a text for a sermon. 'I also wrote a poem for His birthday,' added Mr Chandel, handing me a copy of the *Sunday Tribune* for 23 December 1994. 'Yes, that was a great honour for me.'

A week later, when I was in Delhi, I found myself in a long-established Christian monastery that one of the monks described as a meeting place for the wisdom of the East and the knowledge of the West. I had felt much the same about Mr Chandel and his bedroom. The bookshelves there were filled with English classics, and overlooking them was a bust of Gandhi and a statue of Buddha. There was a photograph of Rabindranath Tagore, the great Bengali poet and thinker, and a print of Lord Byron dressed in flowing Balkan robes. Mr Chandel was an artist as well as a poet, and above the large double-bed was a fine pencil drawing – a copy of a Victorian work, I imagine – of King Lear and Cordelia. I much preferred this to his poetry, although I didn't say so.

At times it is hard to work out whether it is England or Christianity that has had the greater influence on Shimla. In practice the two have often worked in tandem in the shape of the Anglican Church, which has established schools, hostels, homes for the poor and a variety of other institutions. The best-known of the schools, founded in 1857 and modelled on the English public-school system, is named after Bishop Cotton, a keen supporter of the Kotgarh mission. Nowadays nine-tenths of its pupils are non-Christians, but the headmaster is always a Christian and the school pays a tax of sorts to the Church. There may be fewer than 500 Christians in Shimla, out of a population of well over 100,000, but you can seldom walk anywhere for more than a few minutes without passing a reminder of the Christian presence. Beside the schools and the places of worship, which range from grand edifices like Christchurch to the Baptists' tin shack on the Mall, there are the YMCA and the YWCA, both colossal in size, and half a dozen cemeteries, all but one of which have been abandoned.

I had plenty of time to think about death, and the disposal of the dead, as I made my way down the hill to Kaylog cemetery. Once I had left the bustle of the Mall behind, skirted round Clark's – Mr Oberoi's first hotel – and descended past the Potato Research Institute, I found myself on narrow, mossy-banked lanes bowered with fir trees and punctuated with handsome bungalows whose occupants were taking mid-afternoon siestas on broad balconies. It had rained in the morning and the air smelt fresh and green; at last I was away from the noise of lorries and honking buses, and the only sounds came from the forest birds and my shoes slapping against the pitted tarmac.

On a previous visit to India I had met a Goanese woman, a Hindu, who professed disgust at the Christian preoccupation with death. No other religion, she pointed out, had as its symbol an instrument of torture – the crucifix; no other religion was so dominated by images of pain and suffering. To Christians, of course, Christ's death means everything: the principal theme of the New Testament is that God sacrificed his son to atone for the sins of mankind. St Mark talks of the son of man giving 'his life as a ransom for many' (Mark 10:45), and in St John's Gospel Jesus says, 'God so loved the world that he gave his only Son, that everyone who has faith in him may not perish but have eternal life' (John 3:16). At the eucharist, the main act of Christian worship, the priest reminds those present that by offering up his son, God made 'a full, perfect, and sufficient sacrifice . . . for the sins of the whole world'. Once the prayer of consecration – of which this forms a part – is complete, the believers are offered bread and wine, the body of Christ and the blood of Christ. Since the earliest times there has been debate among Christians about the precise nature of the offering: while the Roman Catholics, since 1215, have espoused the doctrine of transubstantiation – that is, the conversion of bread and wine into the whole substance of the body and blood of Christ (I once heard an Anglican friend of my mother redefine this as cannibalism) – the Anglican *Book of Common Prayer* is ambiguous, allowing communicants greater latitude in their interpretation of the eucharist. However, theological disputes do not make a jot of difference to the main message of the Bible, which is the message of the cross, of Christ's death.

There is no escaping death in India: if you don't see it in the streets, you will certainly read about it in the newspapers. One expects a nation of over 900 million people to experience death on a scale befitting its numbers, but India seems to be abnormally prone to accidents, civil mayhem and natural disasters. A bus plunges off a cliff in Maharashtra, killing fifty-seven; thirty-two rickshaw-wallahs die in Old Delhi after drinking illegally brewed spirit; seventy drown in a flood in Assam; a communal riot leaves scores dead in Ahmadabad. Murders, too, seem remarkably commonplace and are reported in the newspapers in the language of a cheap gangster novel, robbing all participants of dignity. Murderers commit 'dastardly deeds' and eventually, with a bit of luck, they are 'nabbed by the cops'. The more outlandish the death the better. While I was in Shimla a former member of the Youth Congress Party allegedly chopped up his wife and attempted to burn her body in the *tandoor* oven of a popular tourist restaurant in Delhi's Connaught Place. A couple of days later a twenty-eight-year-old man shot himself outside what the *Pioneer* called a 'posh colony'. In a suicide note he said he was taking his life so that his vital organs could be sold; he requested that the money raised be given to the chief election commissioner to pay for 'nation-building activities'. Despair and optimism in equal measure. 'After reading the suicide note,' said a police spokesman, 'the body was sent to the Institute of Medical Science', which just goes to show that police everywhere can speak in solecisms.

English-speaking Indians often avoid blunt language when referring to death, preferring to say that someone has passed away or expired rather than died. Yet such euphemisms seem strange, for Indians are refreshingly matter-of-fact when it comes to the business of dealing with the dead. If you go to the great Hindu city of Varanasi, you will witness a constant procession of bodies, each wrapped in a glittering chrysalis of silk or cotton, being brought down to the cremation ghats beside the Ganges; some come by taxi, others are wheeled down in cycle-rickshaws or transported on vegetable carts. Beside the water the bodies are burned on wood pyres, out in the open for all to see. In Shimla the contrivance that is used to take the recently dead back to their homes – for example, from hospitals – is an old vehicle with the words DEAD BODY VAN written along its side. Christians are buried rather than cremated, and in places such as Shimla, where there are no undertakers, bodies are washed, prepared and dressed in their Sunday best by members of the close family. Today Christians of all denominations end up in the same cemetery, Sanjauli, to which they are delivered in an ancient hand-pulled hearse. In the British days, a greater degree of pomp was involved, and before it fell into disuse in the 1920s the burials at Kaylog were often grand affairs.

When I reached Kaylog cemetery I immediately understood why Mrs de la Hay had failed to find the grave of her mother, one of the last people to be buried here. It was in a state of utter dereliction. There were several hundred graves ranged across three flattish terraces, but few had survived intact. Some had been strangled and shattered by creepers and the roots of trees; others had been toppled by vandals or perhaps by grazing cows. The surrounding wall had been plundered for its stone and the scuffed path that traversed the cemetery, linking two large houses with satellite dishes to the main road, was fringed by broken headstones, litter and human excrement. Despite all this the cemetery had a rustic charm – I could well imagine Mr Chandel writing a poem about it – and the dead, though long forgotten, did serve a useful purpose. In Shimla nearly every flat piece of land has been taken over for building: the cemeteries have helped to preserve pockets of green space and Kaylog is gradually reverting to a mature deodar forest.

Kaylog was used by the Anglican congregation that worshipped at Christchurch. Christchurch still exists; the Anglican Church in India does not, save in a few dissident pockets, for in 1970 six Protestant Churches – Anglicans, British Baptists, Brethren, Congregationalists, Disciples of Christ and Methodists – united to form the Church of North India (CNI). The individual Churches still tend to reflect their origins – for example, former Baptists pay less heed to the eucharist than former Anglicans; Baptists continue to practise adult baptism, while the Anglicans do not – and the marriage of the six Churches inevitably had its teething problems, both theological and material: while the Anglicans provided most of the property, the rest provided most of the Christians. Shimla's Protestants in the years before union were predominantly Anglican and well-to-do, while those of neighbouring rural Punjab, who were considerably more numerous, were largely Presbyterian and poor. The situation remains much the same today.

'Mine is definitely a very middle-class church,' said Rev. Sunil Caleb, whom I went to see one evening in the rambling vicarage above the Mall. Christchurch's presbyter was a slight figure, handsome in a boyish way, and he spoke with a quiet authority that belied his physical appearance. We sat in the cone of light cast by a bare bulb beside a monumental wooden desk, which was scarcely visible beneath an avalanche of books, newspaper cuttings and overflowing in-trays. 'I suppose you could say that they are rather lukewarm, but I do try to stir them up.' In addition to looking after his congregation of forty or so families at Christchurch, Rev. Caleb took services at St Michael's in the military cantonment. The Assam Regiment was based in Shimla, and there were many Mizos, Nagas and other Christian tribals from the north-east who attended the cantonment church. 'They're mostly Baptists and Presbyterians,' he explained. 'They are not very keen on the eucharist, but they expect a good sermon.

They come from a tradition which understands preaching and you can go on as long as you like as far as they're concerned.'

I wondered whether his church had become more Indian in character as the years had slipped by.

'No, not really,' he replied briskly, having obviously given the matter some thought. 'And, yes, it does bother me. I don't want the gospel, or our faith, to be alien to the people. But the most important thing is the language, not whether we go barefoot or sit on the floor rather than in pews. If we are using the language of the people, then we are a long way towards creating an Indian Church.' He added that the language of church services created serious divisions among some congregations in major cities like Delhi and Chandigarh. There the well-off generally attended an English service early on Sunday morning; this was followed by a service in Tamil for people from the south whom Rev. Caleb described as the semi-poor, and then by a Hindi service that was attended largely by the poorest Christians in the unforgiving heat of midday. The latter were understandably resentful. 'Thank God I don't have those problems here,' he concluded.

During these early days of my journey through Christian India I felt there was one question of paramount importance, regardless of one's personal beliefs: who is saved? Are non-believers destined to be eternally damned, as some Christians claim, or do they too have access to the Kingdom of Heaven? 'Some people say I'm wishy-washy,' said Rev. Caleb when I raised the subject, 'but maybe that's God's way. I preach the gospel I've received. Evangelical Christians like the Pentecostals are very definite. They are very sure about who is saved. I can only say that it's not my decision. "Vengeance is mine, saith the Lord." I believe that. I can't say for sure that the only ones who will be saved are those who are baptized in the Lord.'

Over dinner at Prospect Lodge that night – cooked as always by a delightful Hindu woman called Bunty – I asked Dr Thakur Das about his views on salvation. 'My belief,' he said, 'is that salvation is through the blood of Christ. But I don't like the way that evangelicals say to others: "You won't be saved." I'd like to say: "Christ died for everyone." Who am I to judge non-Christians? Christ talked of his love for all who travail and are heavy-laden; he didn't say for Christians who travail and are heavy-laden. My feeling is that the evangelicals tend to undermine the universality of Christ. You may not know Christ as such, but if you know truth, you come close to Christ.'

The other guest at Prospect Lodge was an American student of linguistics. 'I gave myself to the Lord when I was twenty-four,' she said in her Deep South accent when I asked her which Church she belonged to. 'I'm non-denominational. I'll go to any church as long as they preach the gospel.' I think that she had a pretty shrewd idea about who would and would not be saved, and though she never said so – and I didn't press her to tell me – I don't think she would have subscribed to the view held by Christians of a more liberal persuasion and expressed thus by C. S. Lewis: 'The truth is God has not told us what His arrangements about the other people are. We do know that no man can be saved except through Christ; we do not know that only those who know Him can be saved through Him.'

The linguist said that she would go to any church that preached the gospel, but the Scriptures, unlike computer manuals, are open to a wide range of interpretation; one person's gospel can be another's heresy. If it were otherwise, then there would be one Church rather than scores. Even modest little Shimla has seven churches serving different denominations. Beside the Church of North India and the Roman Catholic Church – which represent the majority of Christians – there are the Baptist Church (one faction of which did not join the CNI), the Seventh Day Adventists, the Evangelical Church of India, the Assembly of God and the New Life Fellowship. These last three Churches are all relatively recent in origin and are proving highly popular in India, as in many other Third World countries. They may object to being lumped together, but they do possess certain features in common. They place a strong emphasis on personal salvation; they often adopt charismatic forms of worship, such as speaking in tongues, and they practise prophecy and spiritual healing; they tend to be fundamentalist in their interpretation of the Bible and they believe Christ's second coming is close at hand. They are opposed to ritualistic forms of worship and hold no hope of salvation for non-believers.

'On the whole,' said Rev. Caleb, 'we all get along very well indeed in Shimla.' However, he was concerned about the increasingly overt influence of American fundamentalism in India. 'You can hear it on the radio,' he said. 'They have absolutely fixed ideas about what the Bible says. They'll take the Book of Revelation, for example, and they'll say: "Revelation says that this will happen, and this, and this," as though everything is pre-determined. This inevitably breeds fatalism. We had an environmental workshop recently and there was a woman there, a fundamentalist Christian, who said: "There's no point in worrying about trees, or the environment, because the Bible says . . ."' The presbyter's voice trailed off into the great empty spaces of his dark study and he shrugged his shoulders in resignation. 'I agree that we're saved through faith – not through good works – but we must express our faith through work. We must practise what we preach. After all, Jesus asked us to give our lives to other people.'

I asked him what he thought this meant in practical terms.

'I'd like the Church to be the conscience of the nation. We should be speaking out against such things as child labour. We should be siding with the poor. So long as the Church is running schools and hospitals for the élite, people are happy. If we start preaching against injustice, we'll come up against vested interests; then we're in trouble. But that's what we should be doing.'

Certain members of Shimla's élite had done very well, in

material terms, at the expense of the Church, and on my last afternoon at Prospect Lodge I was told a story by Dr Thakur Das that was to become depressingly familiar on my travels: disputes over property have riven the Church of North India, in general to its own detriment and to the benefit of others.

From the turn of the century until recently Prospect Lodge was used by the nuns of St Stephen's community in Delhi as a retreat. Some fifteen years ago the nuns felt that its upkeep was becoming too much for them and they were given permission by the executors, the Church trustees, to part with some of the adjoining land. According to Dr Thakur Das, the nuns had also been put under pressure: 'Local bigwigs told them that if they didn't sell the land, the government would requisition it. In fact, the government had declared it part of a green belt, so there shouldn't have been any new building here.' An eminent lawyer – he still lived close by – helped the bigwigs slither past legal obstacles and they acquired the land in front of the lodge for 137,000 rupees (approximately £3,000). This was outrageous, continued Dr Thakur Das, as the land, if it were to be used as building land, was worth many millions of rupees. The nuns had been either ill-advised or, more probably, not advised at all. The bigwigs began to build houses for themselves, each violating the regulations limiting their height to two storeys. Most now have four storeys; all obscure Prospect Lodge's view of the valley. Midway through construction the land immediately in front of the lodge began to suffer from subsidence: the nuns were forced to pay 140,000 rupees to repair the damage and build an ugly concrete terrace.

'The Church is one of the biggest landowners in India,' said Dr Thakur Das with feeling. 'But it's terribly inefficient. It seldom seems to know how to handle its assets properly. The tragedy is that the Church needs all the money it can get.' He pointed out that the average vicar could not afford to stay at Prospect Lodge at his own expense, even though full board and lodging cost a mere 30 rupees (less than 70p) a day. Their average monthly salary was around 1,000 to 1,500 rupees (£20–30), which was roughly what a coolie working on the roads would earn.

~

The trains out of Shimla were booked for over a week ahead, so I was forced to catch the night bus to Delhi. I left Prospect Lodge after dinner – I would miss the company and my simple room with its shabby furniture; I would even miss the sound of the monkeys clattering across the tin roof – and I made my way down the steep hill towards the town. When I reached Christchurch a porter from the vicarage appeared and took my rucksack; we struggled through the evening crowds on the Mall like elvers swimming against the tide, then descended sharply down an unlit footpath, the government buildings on either side looming above our heads like the rusting hulks of abandoned ships. The bus to Delhi took over eight hours and my notes record nothing out of the ordinary. We passed only one fatal accident, though there were several traffic jams caused by crashes. Once we were back in the plains the night air was furnace-hot; the man in front of me was sick several times; the children behind me were fractious most of the time. Beside these prosaic notes I also wrote: 'Forgot to ask Dr T. D. what he meant by the truth.'

CHAPTER 2

Heaven and Hell

I arrived in Delhi at the tail-end of one of the worst heat waves in living memory. The monsoons were a month late – it was now early July – and every day the temperature climbed to 105 °F or more in the shade. The nights, too, were uncomfortably oppressive, but there was a brief period, for an hour before dawn and a short time after, when it was possible to venture out without discomfort. On most mornings I would rise at five o'clock, drink tea at a roadside stall, then spend an hour or so walking the streets. Sometimes I wandered round New Delhi, past the Catholic cathedral to the secretariat, down magisterially impressive Rajpath to India Gate and then back to the YMCA by way of breakfast at the Imperial Hotel. But New Delhi, whatever the time of day, seemed an impersonal companion and I much preferred the intimacy of Old Delhi's narrow alleys. I would make my way past the sleeping bodies that lay about Connaught Place like shoals of fish trapped in time, then take a rickshaw to Chandni Chowk, where I would watch the world of the bazar, with its clutter of workshops and mosques, its food stalls and cafés, shake the sleep from its eyes as a blood-orange sun rose above the massive walls of the Red Fort.

In Indian cities one takes crowds for granted. There are certain places – in parts of Old Delhi, for example, or outside Bombay's Victoria Terminus – where a sweep of the eye encompasses, during the daily rush hours, a gulch of humanity that can be numbered only in tens of thousands. In Indian cities one expects to be jostled; one expects to share the broken pavements with businessmen, beggars, cigarette vendors, coolies, people of every class and profession, in every conceivable state of attire and disrepair. One's senses are continually battered by a Babel of sounds and a cornucopia of smells. Indian streets shimmer with colour and energy; they are sensuous, chaotic, frequently disgusting, but never dull.

However, New Delhi is not like this. It is the most un-Indian of cities and its streets reflect the character of the people for whom it was originally built, the civil servants who run the country. In 1911, at a Durbar attended by 562 maharajas, King George V announced that the capital of the Empire was to be shifted from Calcutta to Delhi, and within three months Sir Edwin Lutyens had been commissioned to design it. The intention was to create something that would coalesce with the great walled city of the Moghuls, Shahjahanabad, or Old Delhi as it is more commonly known, but in the end a policy of architectural apartheid prevailed and it is almost impossible to imagine two cities less alike in character than New and Old Delhi. New Delhi occupies 33 square miles; Old Delhi less than a quarter of the space. Within a few years of New Delhi's inauguration it had a population of 65,000 people; Old Delhi had five times that many people in its congested living quarters. Today the figures are much inflated, but the difference between New Delhi and Old Delhi is more pronounced than ever. When I first came to India, several years ago, I was briefly fooled into thinking that the capital was sedate, affluent and scantily populated: that is how New Delhi strikes the first-time visitor. On each subsequent visit I have seen more and more of Delhi's poverty, and it was this aspect of the capital that Dr V. S. Lall, the Church of North Indian's general secretary, was determined to talk about when I went to see him late one afternoon at his headquarters in New Delhi.

'You've heard all about the liberalization of the economy,

haven't you?' he asked as soon as I sat down to face him across a large desk whose neat piles of papers and stationery seemed to mirror the orderly world outside. 'You know, the policies promoted by the World Bank.' He explained that since 1991 the government had introduced a wide range of economic reforms. The old mix of Nehruvian socialism and Gandhian asceticism, with its emphasis on government intervention and self-reliance, had been deemed a failure. Now, partly at the instigation of the World Bank and the International Monetary Fund, India had liberalized its trading arrangements and opened its doors to the outside world. New policies had been formulated to slacken the grip of government and encourage private enterprise. Inflation had fallen, while foreign investment and industrial growth had rapidly risen.

Dr Lall was a large man with an imposing face dominated by a fine hooked nose. He had a grey moustache, and his hair, parted near one ear, was swept across the crown of his head to reach almost as far as the other. He looked like a Roman emperor and I could imagine him holding court in a *praetorium*. He produced a blank piece of paper and with a pen in his left hand drew a rectangle which he divided into three, cross-hatching the upper and lower segments. 'Up here,' he said, tapping the upper segment, 'are 200 million people. These are the wealthiest people in India – the industrialists, the landowners, the big traders – and they are the people who will interact with the economies of the outside world, buying, selling, trading . . .' He pointed to the middle of his diagram, which he had left blank. 'Here you have 500 million people. Bureaucrats, teachers, petty traders, people who are surviving but not without a struggle.' His pen slid down to the cross-hatching below. 'And here, at the bottom of the pile, are 200 million people. These are the poor, the destitute, the hungry.'

He leaned back in his chair, sniffed expansively and asked: 'So what will the new economic policies mean for these people? I will tell you,' he continued, leaning forward again and tapping his pen on the desk. 'This economic miracle that people talk about is not going to benefit the people at the bottom of the heap. Just think of the absorption capacity of the 500 million in the middle. If there's any fluid left over from the top 200 million, they'll absorb it all. There's not going to be any drip-drip-drip of wealth getting down to the poor. And that's where 80 per cent of my Church are – they are down there, at the bottom of the heap, far beyond the reach of economic miracles.' For the most part, he explained, the Christian poor were *dalits*, a term which meant 'broken' or 'oppressed' and which was now used to define not only the lowest rung of the Hindu caste ladder – the untouchables, as they used to be known – but also those who had sought to escape the stigma of untouchability by converting to other faiths.

I dropped by to see Dr Lall several times. He was generous with both his time and his knowledge and I enjoyed his energetic approach to life. I explained at the outset that I did not intend to spend long in Delhi. For one thing I had never warmed to the city in the way I had to, say, Calcutta or Bombay. For another, I felt that I could learn far more about Indian Christianity in provincial towns and the countryside. Christians probably amounted to around 1 per cent of Delhi's population – compared with 38 per cent in Goa, 21 per cent in Kerala, 94 per cent in Mizoram – and many of them were first-generation immigrants, bringing with them the ways of worship which they had learned in their rural, or provincial, homelands. Better to spend time at the foot of the tree itself, I reasoned, than with wind-blown seeds. If Dr Lall was dubious about the merit of this strategy, he was kind enough not to say so, but he suggested I visit half a dozen individuals whose experience would help shape my future travels. He was also keen that I spend my time in Delhi not among wealthy Christians, who were a minority, but among the poor, or at least with people who were trying to help the poor. He mentioned, in particular, Dr James Massey, an authority on Christian *dalits* and a *dalit* himself, and he also suggested I call on the Brotherhood of the Ascended Christ, a Protestant monastic order active among the poor, and St Stephen's Hospital, a Christian institution with a health programme in a slum in south Delhi. It was while I was with the doctors and nurses of St Stephen's that I began to understand his parting remark: 'You might find that you sometimes learn most about Christianity – and the Church – where it is numerically least influential.'

~

Dr Amod Kumar was a neatly built young man with sharp, delicate features, a sallow complexion and a voice so gentle that I had to strain to catch his words as the hospital bus juddered through Delhi's suburbs towards Sunder Nagari. It was Saturday – one of the three days a week set aside for the TB clinic – and besides ourselves there were eleven health workers on the bus. Dr Kumar explained that Sunder Nagari owed its origins to the slum-clearance schemes that Sanjay Gandhi initiated soon after his mother, Mrs Indira Gandhi, had declared a state of emergency in 1975. The beautification of Delhi involved, among other things, pushing the poor out of sight. Some of the urban refugees found themselves living in conditions superior to those they left behind; others, including many at Sunder Nagari, did not.

St Stephen's Hospital began its outreach programme at Sunder Nagari in 1981. 'It was very humble at first,' said Dr Kumar, 'just one or two hospital staff sitting in the shade of a tree and giving advice and help on a small scale.' After a while the slum dwellers offered the hospital a room; this became its dispensary. Gradually its activities increased: by 1989 the primary health-care programme catered for around 15,000 people. Today 55,000 people benefit from the programme and twenty-seven hospital staff operate from a new, purpose-built dispensary at the heart of the slums.

Shortly before we arrived we passed a large public hospital; set well back from the road, it towered above the suburbs that surrounded it. It was good for emergencies, said Dr Kumar, but the slum dwellers preferred to use St Stephen's Hospital and its dispensary. 'In general,' he said, shouting to make himself heard as we clattered on to a potholed side road, 'people consider Christian hospitals better – they think that there's more concern for the patients than in public hospitals. Christianity highlights the idea of care, of service. In the old days, most of the nurses at St Stephen's were nuns. Professionals often lack the devotional qualities they had.'

As soon as we arrived at the dispensary the health workers filed past the TB patients and climbed the stone stairs to the second floor, where they assembled in a large room cluttered with wooden desks and chairs. Dr Kumar handed a well-thumbed Bible to an obese young man who read a passage in Hindi. Another man then read a few more verses, and all joined in the Lord's Prayer, again in Hindi. Many of the staff left immediately afterwards to attend to the TB patients or begin their rounds, but a few stayed behind and followed Dr Kumar into his starkly furnished office. A poster with a picture of a noose and the words 'Aids is Incurable' was pinned on to a wall beside a metal cabinet. Another, listing the symptoms of plague, was more encouraging: 'Plague is Curable. DO NOT PANIC.'

Once Dr Kumar had discussed the morning's work programme he asked if I had any questions for his staff before they left. I wondered whether they were all Christians. No, said a young woman: of the fifteen people at morning prayers, nine or ten were Hindus. Did they object to using Christian prayers? 'All religions have the same ideas,' replied a young man, a Hindu. 'They're all searching for the truth. So why not?' Another man said that nearly all Hindus respected the Bible as a holy book. 'We should have respect for all religions,' said Dr Kumar, adding that he had often seen pictures of Christ in Hindu temples. As it happened there were no Christians in Sunder Nagari: 60 per cent of the people were Hindus and the rest were Muslims.

The health workers filed out of the room and Dr Kumar explained that each was responsible for 5,000 people – adults and children – and visited twenty-five households a day. He or she took note of any health problems, weighed the young children, examined pregnant women and gave advice on hygiene and family planning. Dr Kumar picked up a folder at random and read out the details. 'This one's fairly typical. There are ten people in the family, living in one room. There's no running water and no sanitation – just an open sewer outside. Here it says a child suffering from malnutrition was taken to the public hospital: LAMA – that means left against medical advice.' So far none of the children in this family had died. This was mildly surprising. The average rate of infant mortality in Delhi is 32 per 1,000. In Sunder Nagari it is 83 per 1,000. 'This sounds bad – and it is,' said Dr Kumar, 'but it's better than it was when we came.' In 1983 it was about 100 per 1,000; in other words one in ten children died before its first birthday.

'Deaths are very common here,' said Dr Kumar as we headed for the stairs. 'You go into a shack where a child has died, and when you ask what happened, the family will say: "Oh, he just died." They accept death. You have to probe to find out why a child has died.' From the top of the stairs we could see over the slums. The sun was high in a cloudless sky and the unpaved street below us shimmered in the heat. A naked child appeared from the one-storey concrete dwelling opposite the dispensary, squatted on the doorstep and shat. 'There's a lot of superstition,' continued Dr Kumar. 'Recently four children died in one area of the slums. Their families all say that they were hit on the head by mud pots. I don't think for a minute that that happened. But what did?'

I followed Dr Kumar down to the ground-floor crèche. During the weekdays, he explained, over seventy children were looked after at the dispensary. They came from what he described as disastrous backgrounds; they were the ones most at risk of neglect or abuse. They came in the morning and were delivered back to their families in the evening. The dispensary provided them with clothes, a midday meal and informal teaching. A woman who had come with us on the bus sat on the floor with nine children, most around four or five years old. They were drawing pictures with crayons, some with surprising competence and flair. 'She's a wonderful woman,' said Dr Kumar, motioning towards the helper. 'The children adore her.'

In the room next door there were twenty younger children. 'When Mahesh came six months ago, he was a year old and he only weighed 2.1 kilos,' explained the doctor as he picked up a tiny child. 'He looked like a little monkey.' He still did: large eyes stared glumly from a haggard face and a scanty crop of hair rose vertically from the crown of his head; his limbs were thin and fleshless and he looked less than half his age. 'We first came across his mother when she had TB,' continued Dr Kumar. 'We didn't know about the cruelty then. We just knew the children were undernourished.' When staff at the dispensary suggested they help by taking one of the woman's six children into the crèche, the mother resisted, claiming that she herself had received poor treatment for TB. Then Mahesh became very sick and was admitted to the public hospital where his mother had also been taken, in labour with her seventh child. This time the mother relented and agreed to let Mahesh go to the crèche. 'Normally we only take one child from each family,' explained Dr Kumar, 'but this time we have had to take three.' He looked across the room to a boy and girl who sat beside one another. 'That's Mahesh's brother. His father beat him so badly that he broke his hand. And, not long after, his sister came in covered with blood. Her mother had hit her across the face with an iron bar.'

Dr Kumar handed Mahesh back to a female helper, whom he clung to fiercely. There was nothing he could do, he explained wearily, about the abuse. 'I've talked to the father, and he just says, "I get so frustrated . . ." If I went to the police, they might take the children away, but then they'd be orphans. Where would they go? It'd only be worse. We can't withdraw children from their environment. They have to face reality. But at least we can give them a few hours of happiness each day.' Except on Sundays, when the dispensary was closed. Mahesh's condition was gradually improving, but he was still losing weight between Saturday afternoon, when he was returned to his family, and Monday morning, when he came back to the crèche.

It was approaching midday when we walked around the slum. Soon the monsoons would arrive and the narrow streets, already seams of squalor, would liquefy into rivers of sewage that would penetrate the slum dwellers' shacks, most of which were stitched together with bits of old tin and cardboard, hessian bags and scavenged wood. Considering the dreadful conditions and the overcrowding, many of the children looked clean and well cared for; some of the girls wore pretty dresses and their black hair was tied with coloured ribbons. There was plenty of industry too: one family squatted outside its shack making *bindis*, the decorative marks worn by women on their foreheads; another family was sifting through a pile of rags, sorting them into recyclable waste.

'You know that famous line of one of the Moghul rulers?' asked Dr Kumar as we headed back to the dispensary. 'I think he was talking about Kashmir. He said: "If there's a heaven on earth, it's here, it's here, it's here." Well, I sometimes feel that if there's a hell on earth, it's here, it's here, it's here. All the social evils are here – drunkenness, violence, sexual abuse, incest.'

Not that Dr Kumar was unremittingly gloomy. During their time in the slums, the health workers had brought about marked improvements. In one year alone, 1993, the dispensary dealt with over 28,000 individual visits; in 1995 over 250 patients were receiving free treatment for TB; and health education had led to a decline in such common ailments as child diarrhoea. In recent years the staff had used dance and drama to highlight problems such as alcoholism and domestic violence, and Dr Kumar and his colleagues had recently established an adult literacy programme. Female literacy for Delhi stood at an average 68 per cent, yet in Sunder Nagari only 11 per cent of women could read or write. A more literate population, argued Dr Kumar, would be a healthier one: he expected the campaign to increase female literacy to 80 per cent.

Early that morning, when I arrived at St Stephen's, I had spent a few minutes with the hospital's chief administrator, Mr K. P. Philip. He spoke with unabashed piety, much as I imagine Protestant missionaries must have done in the last century. That evening, he said, Christian members of staff would pray continually from six p.m. to six a.m. in the stone chapel beside the administration block. On Fridays he and three senior members of staff, including the director – 'a very prayerful man' – met for Bible study and prayer. How, I inquired, did the non-Christians at St Stephen's, around half the staff, feel about the hospital's overtly Christian outlook? He thought about this for a while, then said: 'Some have mixed feelings, I suspect. Some feel neglected. But many of the Hindus appreciate working in a Christian institution.'

This was certainly true of Dr Kumar, who felt that he had achieved much through the morning prayer sessions. 'When I say that prayers have helped,' he said, 'I don't mean in the sense of divine intervention. It's the psychological aspects of prayer that have helped us.' When Dr Kumar had arrived two years earlier he found that the staff were saying the prayers but not listening to their message. 'I began to challenge them, to ask them what they thought the readings were about. If there were verses that seemed particularly relevant, I tried to explain them.' He fell silent for a few seconds, then continued: 'It happens so often. For example, Jesus said, "I am a shepherd and I care for lost sheep." Well, the staff here were very angry with Mahesh's parents, who'd even told them, "You're spoiling our children." So I said, "Listen, the whole family are lost sheep. We must go after them all." And we did go after them, time and again, before they let their children come to us. Then there's another time when Jesus said, "I care for my sheep like a shepherd, not like a hired servant." So I've told the staff that we should be like that. We should really care for the people – not just see it as a job. When I came here there were a lot of little conflicts; people were very time-conscious. Now they aren't. Today should be a half-day, but the staff will all be back here tonight to put on a street play.' Dr Kumar admitted that as a Hindu he would have liked to include readings from other religions at the morning prayer session, but the hospital's constitution was explicitly Christian and he didn't wish to rock the boat.

On our way back to town he told me about a young woman from the slums who had recently visited him at his home in the hospital compound. His home, he explained, was nothing grand, but his son had a room to himself, and there were separate rooms for eating, cooking and sleeping. 'She could scarcely believe her eyes,' he said. 'She simply had no idea people could live like this. She assumed that all families lived crammed into one room, just as they all do in the slums.'

I left Dr Kumar at the hospital and took a taxi back to the YMCA. Rather than head through Old Delhi, we skirted round it, but the roads were still thick with traffic and our progress was fitful. The Ambassador was decked out like a floozy's bedroom, with pink fluffy material obscuring the surrounds of the dashboard; a variety of cheap knick-knacks – a plastic vase with plastic flowers, glinting transfers of gods and gurus, a contrivance with flashing bulbs – further enlivened the gaudy décor. At the traffic lights men in *dhotis* with aluminium platters of sliced coconut pressed their wares on the occupants of waiting vehicles, while beggars shuffled between headlights and tailgates like wraiths from another world. Teenage boys were swimming and splashing in the Yamuna river, briefly glimpsed between the rusting, bent-bumpered buses which spewed oil-black vapour trails along the freeway, while high above, in the opaque blue sky, kites wheeled effortlessly over the Red Fort and the riverside slums, their eyes scouring the world below for butchers' waste or perhaps a dead dog. Sunder Nagari was hell, and so was this, not so much in terms of the poverty –

though it was here, lying in rags below the half-built flyovers, scavenging barefoot among the crowds at the interstate bus terminus – as its disconnectedness. The ugly and the exquisite, the transient and the everlasting, the mundane and the bizarre: they were jumbled together with Dadaesque incongruity, each unrelated, it seemed, to anything other than itself. The taxi window became a diorama framed in fluffy pink, and across it glided a church with a florid classical dome; a pair of eunuchs luridly made up as women and cackling haughtily from a horse-drawn cart; a vat of bitumen bubbling like treacle; a man without legs on a wooden trolley with wooden wheels; a uniformed policeman, smoking, his arms flapping like semaphores; two women with long black pigtails and beautiful faces, both carrying books; a Moghul wall with crenellations like tulip flowers; a truck carrying crates of Coca-Cola . . .

When I first met Dr Lall he asked me how I found the YMCA. Simple but perfectly adequate, I replied. 'You think that's simple?' he asked incredulously. 'Why, that particular YMCA is almost five-star!' True, it had a swimming-pool and hot and cold running water, but it was run more along the lines of an army barracks than a hotel. However, I looked at it very differently on my return from the slums. I ate a simple lunch in the canteen, then retired to my room, where I listened to Alastair Cooke's *Letter from America* and ball-by-ball commentary on the Lord's test match. Dr Lall was right about the YMCA: it was, when seen in the light of Sunder Nagari, an oasis of five-star comfort.

~

From 1498, when the Portuguese explorer Vasco da Gama arrived on the south-west coast, to 1947, when the British left India, the subcontinent's history was largely one of coming to terms with foreign influence. Vasco da Gama had been sent east by the King of Portugal, or the 'Lord of the Navigation, Conquest and Commerce of Ethiopia, Arabia, Persia and India', as a papal bull expansively referred to him. In practical terms, as da Gama told a local Hindu ruler, he had been sent for Christians and spices, conversions and trade. In 1510 the Portuguese took control of Goa, and soon afterwards the Sultan of Gujarat ceded the settlement of Diu. While the Portuguese consolidated their grip on these and other coastal territories, the northern regions of India fell to Moghul invaders from Central Asia. Babur, a descendant of Timur and Genghis Khan, proclaimed himself Sultan of Delhi and Agra in 1525 and later defeated the Rajput rulers to the west. He was followed by his son Humayan and Humayan by Akbar, the greatest of all the Moghul emperors.

By the time Akbar came to the throne in 1556, at the age of fourteen, Christianity was well established in Goa, which by then had scores of churches and a seminary with over 3,000 students. Akbar took a great interest in spiritual affairs, and in 1580 he invited a party of Jesuit priests from the seminary to attend the court at Fatehpur Sikri, the fabulous city which he had built near Agra. Being a man of liberal and eclectic disposition, Akbar also invited Muslim and Hindu scholars, Jains and Zoroastrians to debate religious matters. The Jesuits were keen to convince Akbar that he should become a Christian, and their optimism grew as the months passed. They were allowed to establish a chapel where they could freely teach the gospel; one of them became tutor to Akbar's second son; and Akbar soon made it clear that he preferred the Jesuits' preaching to that of the Muslim mullahs. Two years after the Jesuits' arrival, and to the chagrin of all, Akbar decided to establish an entirely new religion, which he called Din Ilahi, a mongrel faith that borrowed elements from all the mainstream religions except Islam. He declared himself head of this new religion, and the Jesuits returned to Goa. A second Jesuit mission was similarly unsuccessful, but a third – known as the Agra mission – attended the court from 1595 to 1803. The priests undoubtedly had an influence on Moghul art – they introduced elements of chiaroscuro and perspective into painting, and Akbar and his son adorned palaces with images of saints and angels – but they made few converts.

Over the years thousands of Christian missionaries – Jesuits, Anglicans, Moravians, all sorts – were to experience failure and rejection in north and central India, where today fewer than one person in 200 is Christian. The historian Paul Johnson suggests that had Asia been successfully Christianized between 1550 and 1900, during the great period of European influence, twentieth-century history would have been dramatically different, 'and indeed Christianity itself must have been radically changed'. There were two main reasons for its failure to catch on over much of India and Asia. For one thing, Christianity did not penetrate areas where the great Eastern religions of Hinduism, Buddhism and Confucianism were already well established. For another, the Christianity imported to India by European missionaries from the sixteenth century onwards was a Western version of the faith. The Christian Churches, whether Catholic or Protestant, were often perceived by the subjugated peoples as an integral part of the imperial force, and Christianity – in Johnson's words – failed to acquire an Asian face. This is starkly apparent in most of Delhi's grander churches, which were built during the days of the Raj.

According to *The Penguin Guide to the Monuments of India*, the Cathedral Church of the Redemption in Lutyens's New Delhi is redolent of Palladio's Il Redentore in Venice; the Sunday service, however, was unmistakably Anglican and English. Whatever could be sung by the celebrants – including the Nicene Creed and the lesson – was sung, and sung in the tuneless manner familiar to anyone who has attended High Anglican services presided over by unmusical vicars in England. The sermon began with the Fall and proceeded to the Sermon on the Mount, with brief excursions to visit the Prophet Isaiah and John the Baptist. Its theme was 'Love thy persecutor'. The congregation, referred to frequently by the preacher as 'my dear friends', numbered about a hundred and looked anything but persecuted. These were not the Christians at the bottom of Dr Lall's social heap; they were the prosperous middle classes and they had arrived in their new Maruti cars rather than on foot or by rickshaw. The men, I guessed, were mostly professionals; their women were dressed in expensive saris and fashionable frocks, and several teenage girls even wore mini-skirts. The communion wine was not the supermarket *vin ordinaire* favoured by churches in England but cherryade or a close relative.

There are two cemeteries within a mile or so of Connaught Place, and I visited both on Sunday afternoon. Neither would have looked at all out of place in England, though they served, or had served, very different communities. Paharganj cemetery occupied a large expanse of land behind Nehru Bazar, not far from New Delhi railway station. I approached the cemetery through a small arch and walked towards a group of men and women, who sat silently in the shade provided by an avenue of scruffy trees. Off to their left the ground was scattered with coffins, some half-made, others ready for business, and I could hear the coffin-maker tapping away inside a shed. To my right were three abandoned vehicles, one of which was an ambulance stripped of its wheels. It was not until I reached the open coffin – it contained a woman of late middle age – that I realized that this was a funeral party. The cemetery was a sad sight. Rubbish was scattered around its periphery, the paths were unkempt and many of the graves lay hidden beneath a tangle of weeds. A young couple sat by a headstone – the family name was Greene – from which they had hung a garland of marigolds. The man lit a couple of incense sticks and the sickly smell followed me past a handsome clump of cannabis bushes and back towards the main gate. There were no grand monuments here, and many graves were marked simply with a small wooden cross on which was written roughly, in white paint, and generally in English, the name of the deceased and the date of death.

Prithviraj cemetery in New Delhi, closed for burials since 1991, had served a wealthier class of Christian. Half a dozen staff were assiduously watering the flower beds and weeding the paths and there was a high-class florist at the entrance. The graves were altogether more substantial than those in Paharganj. Some had little statuettes and ornate crosses and many had pithy epithets written below the names of the dead. Elizabeth Roach had 'Fought the Good Fight'; Violet Henry was now 'Safe in the Arms of Jesus'. All the same, they were curiously uninformative. The only ones I could find that alluded to the professions of the dead were those belonging to nuns, monks and missionaries, who had been allotted a special section of their own. Nor did any of the graves mention where the dead had been born. I don't suppose this matters much, but one of the problems with surnames is that they obscure people's racial origins. Was Mrs A. P. Stephens English or Indian, or perhaps a mixture of the two? And what about Natalie Wright and Maurice Steele?

My taxi-driver, a Muslim, disliked these cemeteries, but his humour improved when we arrived at Vailankanni, Our Lady of Health, a Catholic church near Prithviraj. He said it was a good place; Hindus and Muslims as well as Christians came to the church to pray and ask for divine favours. A pity, he added, that we hadn't come on Saturday, which was the main day of pilgrimage. Many of those who came to this spiritual wishing-well had their heads shaved; once relieved of their locks, they threw them into the Yamuna river and offered them to God – or to the gods, this custom owing more to Hinduism than to Christianity. This particular Sunday there was no barber in attendance, but several families were sitting on the marble floor, mumbling prayers and gazing at the riotously over-decorated altar. A crucifix with a red light bulb was suspended above the altar table, which was crammed with brass vases of plastic and paper flowers and many burning candles. A man was selling incense and cheap icons at a stall near the door, and there were several wooden cabinets filled with rows of plastic saints and garish pictures of biblical scenes.

Tacked on to the walls, strung from every pillar and propped against the cupboards and the altar were pictures of Christ. From an artistic point of view the only representations of any merit were Dali's *Crucifixion* and Michelangelo's *Pietà*. The rest were either sentimental European – with Christ as a soppy-looking, blond-haired romantic – or Indian kitsch, although even the latter depicted Christ not as a Middle Eastern Jew, which he was, but as a pale-skinned European.

In the courtyard outside the church two ancient female beggars sat quietly beside a shrine to the Virgin Mary, while a crippled man with a broken pair of spectacles dragged himself about on his haunches sweeping away fallen leaves with a cane brush. I presume he was a permanent or at least a semi-permanent fixture, for he had parked his hand-driven invalid chair inside the gate. The chair was festooned with pots and pans, old clothes, plastic bags, a garland of dead flowers and an assortment of cheap trinkets. I suspect the old invalid was the closest thing Our Lady of Health had to a sexton, and I wondered if he appreciated the irony.

Was the Christiantity practised here, at Our Lady of Health, Christianity with an Asian face? Or was it, rather, a syncretic mix of religions, a sort of modern-day version of Akbar's Din Ilahi? Evangelical Christians would undoubtedly claim the latter; most Catholics – and presumably the Church hierarchy – would argue that this church was an example of acculturation, of Christianity adapting itself to local customs.

~

I had determined at the start of my journey that I would concentrate on the Protestants – and especially those belonging to the Church of North India – when I travelled around the north, and leave my investigations of the Catholic Church to its original point of entry into the country, which was Goa and the south-west coast, even though there was a good population of Catholics in Delhi and a very large one in Bombay. However, I did pay a brief call on Father Gispert-Sauch, a Catalan Jesuit who had arrived in India in the 1950s and remained in the country ever since. A fit-looking man with thick greying hair and angular, chiselled features, he spoke English with a pronounced Catalan accent. I was later told that he spoke several Indian languages – Hindi, Gujarati, Marathi, I think – with the same Catalan accent.

'When I came to India,' he said, as we sat down to eat lunch at the Vidyajyoti seminary, 'there were missionaries from Italy, Sweden, France, South America, Germany and many other countries here. But that changed in the Fifties and Sixties. Nearly all the foreigners have left and the priesthood is almost entirely Indian now.' Of the 130-odd Catholic bishops in India, all were Indian. Ninety per cent of the priests were Indian, as were 98 per cent of the Catholic sisters. The Catholic Church in India, suggested Father Gispert-Sauch, was far more Indian in nature than the Catholic Church in South America was South American.

Did this mean that Christianity had acquired an Asian face, something that it had lacked before?

'That depends where you look,' replied Father Gispert-Sauch. 'In Bombay, in Goa and Mangalore the Church is very European still. You will find that the Catholics are very Portuguese in their devotions. But the tribal Churches are very Indianized. We have encouraged them to keep some of their tribal customs and to compare their own myths about creation with the biblical myths, with the Genesis story.' He talked about a feast which the Catholic students in Delhi organized for the 10,000 tribal Catholics from Chota Nagpur who had come to the capital for work. The feast was not specifically Christian, but it helped the Catholic tribals maintain their links with those who had retained their own spiritual traditions.

I told Father Gispert-Sauch that I was astonished by the European character of the Christian art that I had seen so far. He said that people were used to these images, were comfortable with them: 'I'm not sure it matters much. God is a divine being. He's beyond terrestrial identification.' However, during the past twenty years or so some Indian artists had sought to depict Christ and the Virgin Mary in a more Indian guise, and institutions like the Vidyajyoti seminary had commissioned work from them. Before I left Father Gispert-Sauch showed me the small chapel whose altar wall had been painted by Jyoti Sahu, a renowned symbolist who lived in an ashram of Christian artists near Bangalore.

Many years before the creation of New Delhi, and not long after the Indian Mutiny, a group of English Protestants, concerned about the imperial nature of the Anglican Church, made a conscious attempt to establish a Christian community that would respect Asian mores and beliefs. The inspiration for this community came from Brooke Foss Westcott, Professor of Divinity at Cambridge University, and Thomas Valpy French, an Anglican missionary in Agra. They set up the Cambridge Brotherhood, whose direct descendant, the Brotherhood of the Ascended Christ, is to be found a few minutes' walk from Vidyajyoti seminary.

The Brotherhood's home, 7 Court Lane, looked quintessentially English. A stone structure of little beauty, it reminded me of the austere Edwardian villas that are found on the outskirts of towns like Bradford and Huddersfield. The illusion of Englishness persisted when I was shown into the library, a stately if somewhat gloomy room at whose centre stood a table strewn with magazines as cerebrally diverse as the *Spectator* and the *Dalesman*, the *Guardian Weekly* and the *Garden*. I half expected a woman in a white coat to announce that the dentist would see me now. Instead I was received by Father Monodeep Daniel, a youngish man with a fine head of thick black hair and a pleasant, amused manner. He said I had come at a very quiet time. Father Amos Rajamoney, the leader of the religious community – the term 'monastic order' is considered old-fashioned now – was away, and the two British members of the community, Fathers Stuart and Weathrall, were on leave in the UK. This left two ordained priests and a lay brother. If I wanted to see the work carried out by the Delhi

Brotherhood Society in the slums and with street children, I would have to come back in a fortnight's time.

There was an oil painting of Westcott above the fireplace and Father Monodeep talked about the early fathers' determination not to import a patrician, Eurocentric brand of Christianity. 'The West has much to learn from the East,' wrote Westcott in a letter to French, 'and the lesson will not be learned until we hear the truth as it is apprehended by Eastern minds.' Westcott had a vision of Delhi as a place where the great faiths would meet, mingle and learn from one another, much as philosophers and scientists did in Alexandria in the third century BC. However, an essential prerequisite for such a meeting – a strong Church – did not exist. The local Christians, the few that there were, had little in common with the Hindu and Muslim intellectuals of the city, and consequently the members of the Brotherhood found themselves fully occupied in building up the Church, administering to congregations and teaching in Christian schools. Nevertheless, they never lost sight of their original aim, which was to work towards the day when the Indian Church would be run by Indians rather than by Europeans.

The cities, suggested Father Monodeep, were not the places to find Christianity with an Asian face: here, in Delhi, the Protestant Churches were similar to those in the West, both in appearance and in forms of worship. When I visited the countryside, and especially the tribal areas, I would discover Churches that were much more strongly Indianized. However, even in the cities, certain Indian traditions had percolated into Christian worship. 'In north India,' he explained, 'we have a tradition of singing *bhajans*. These hymns come from the tradition of *bhakti*, or devotion. For Hindus, it is devotion to Krishna; for us Christians, it is devotion to Christ. This is one of the Indian traditions which Christians have adopted.'

I had first heard of the Brotherhood when I visited the London headquarters of the United Society for the Propagation of the

Gospel, an organization whose links with the Brotherhood went back to the last century. Martin Heath, the USPG's co-ordinator, described their work among the mainly Muslim immigrants of squatter colonies as something that sprang straight from the New Testament: 'It is unconditional love in action,' he said admiringly. I repeated this to Brother Monodeep, and he replied by saying that even in the very early days of its existence, the Brotherhood never saw itself as a proselytizing agent. 'When we go into the slums,' he said, 'we go on the community's terms and conditions. We have no hidden agenda.' Much of the Brotherhood's social work had been concentrated on Shahid Nagar, a slum area with a population of around 50,000. There was just one Christian family, as far as Father Monodeep knew, and there had been no conversions. Besides providing practical help in the slums – mainly through health and training schemes – the Delhi Brotherhood Association, the organization set up by the fathers, used street dramas to alert slum dwellers to such problems as child labour, drug addiction, environmental pollution, plague and, most notably perhaps, communal violence. In 1992 many thousands of people were killed in riots between Hindus and Muslims following the destruction of a mosque at Ayodhya by Hindu militants. Shahid Nagar was a potential flashpoint, yet it remained calm: the Brotherhood defused tension by putting on their street dramas pointing to the follies of communal violence and by getting Hindu and Muslim leaders to talk to one another.

After a while we were joined by one of the Brotherhood's seven lay companions, men who work outside the monastery but join in its spiritual life whenever they can. A chemistry teacher from nearby St Xavier's College, he arrived while we were discussing communal violence. The main participants are nearly always Hindus and Muslims, but Father Monodeep felt that all religions had been hijacked at one time or another for political reasons, including Christianity. Earlier in the year two Christians in Pakistan, one a teenage boy, had been found guilty of blasphemy against Islam and sentenced to death. When news of the court verdict reached Assam, in north-east India, several Muslims were burned alive in their homes. 'And that was done by Christians, by Baptists,' concluded Father Monodeep. 'And it was done in the name of Christianity.'

The chemistry teacher listened to this, then said: 'Indian Christianity is moving to the right. There's a lot of uncalled-for influence from the American evangelicals. Their main programme seems to be to divert our minds from issues of social justice.' He called this 'briefcase theology' and he said its practice was fuelled by Christo-dollars. Besides paying for Indians to train as missionaries in the States, and paying their families annual salaries, the evangelicals made good use of the airwaves and there were many evangelical radio programmes, written in the States but broadcast in local Indian languages.

Father Monodeep had studied at an evangelical seminary which preached that salvation could only come to Christians, but he had subsequently scrutinized the Scriptures in greater detail and changed his views. 'I can't be exclusive,' he said simply.

'So you believe it's possible for Muslims, Hindus, whoever, to reach paradise?' I asked.

'If there is one!' he replied with a broad grin.

Before I left, Father Monodeep gave me a tour of the monastery: in particular he wanted me to see the modern paintings done by Indian Christians. One was a depiction of the Passion by Jyoti Sahu, with Christ in a *dhoti* encased by the crucifix. A gloomy painting by an artist called Bairagi showed the ascended Christ over a roofscape of Delhi, and another oil painting depicted the Virgin Mary in a sari. The painting I liked most portrayed John the Divine, the author of Revelation, floating above the sea with his feet on an eagle. It was, as Father Monodeep said, a very mystical work and thoroughly Asian in character.

Over the last few days the temperature had begun to drop to around 90 degrees in the shade, and when I left the monastery the sky was grey and sunless. I decided to walk back towards Old Delhi, and before long it began to rain: it was a hot, diffuse rain, pleasant to walk in, yet deceptively wet, and by the time I reached Kashmir Gate I felt as though I had been embalmed in sodden cotton. I spent some time trying to flag down passing taxis, but they were all full and I took shelter in St James's church. It lay some distance back from the road, surrounded by a drought-stricken lawn, with a small graveyard enclosed by iron railings off to one side. The church was built in the shape of a Greek cross and surmounted by a large dome supported by baroque buttresses. The man who commissioned it was Colonel James Skinner, a portrait of whom was casually propped on a chair at the rear of the church. In his person the East and the West had met in the most tangible way possible: his mother was a Rajput, his father a Scotsman. In the early years of the last century Colonel Skinner had raised his own cavalry regiment, known as Skinner's Horse, or the Yellow Boys after the colour of his men's uniform, and he conceived the idea of the church while he lay wounded on the battlefield. He promised God that if he was spared, he would build a church as testimony of his faith in the Christian religion. This may have come as a surprise to God, for Skinner had been promiscuous with both his beliefs and his body. He had already built a mosque for his Muslim wife and a temple for his Hindu wife, though by the time work on the church began, in 1826, he had dispensed with the services of his twelve concubines.

While I waited for the rain to cease I studied the memorials that lined the walls of the church. There were several to men who died during the Indian Mutiny of 1857, including the principal of Delhi College – one who feared God and eschewed evil – and an Indian doctor, Chimman Lall. Converted to Christianity in 1852, Dr Lall had fallen 'a martyr to his faith on the day of the massacre of the Christians in Delhi'.

The 1857 uprising of rebel troops within the British-run army was sparked off by a rumour that new rifle cartridges – which in those days had to be bitten prior to loading – had been greased with cow and pig fat. To Hindus the cow was sacred; to Muslims the pig was polluting. Christian missionaries were already agitating against the Hindu caste system; now, it seemed, the authorities were openly attempting to defile their faith. The uprising was eventually quashed, but not before both sides had suffered great losses and behaved, at times, with unspeakable barbarity. Nobody would claim that this was a religious war, yet it was religious beliefs, and the threats to faith, that had caused the flames of dissent to splutter and ignite.

The memorials in St James's church told a confusing story of conquest, sacrifice and forgiveness, and they seemed to highlight a profound dilemma faced by Christians of all times. On the one hand they are required to love their neighbours, to act as peace-makers, to forgive their enemies – 'Lord, lay not this sin to their charge,' entreats the inscription on Dr Chimman Lall's plaque – while, on the other, they are required actively to evangelize, to proclaim the rightness of their own beliefs and, some would say, the wrongness of others. At one end of the spectrum I could see the Brotherhood of the Ascended Christ and the health workers from St Stephen's Hospital; at the other end, the racially superior Bible-thumpers who were partly responsible for creating the ill-feeling that led to the Mutiny – and to the death of good men like Dr Chimman Lall. During the next few weeks, on my travels in and around Bombay, I was to come across divisions within the Christian community that were every bit as acute as those I had begun to glimpse here.

CHAPTER 3

The Enemies Within

'Just look what life's like for most people in Bombay,' said Bishop Samuel Joshua. 'They spend three hours or more commuting each day, and eight hours at work. It's a struggle to survive and the last thing that they want to do is think about the finer points of theology. They want a living God who speaks to them. A God they can pray to when they're hungry, when they're lonely. And that's exactly the sort of God the evangelicals are giving them.'

Had I met the bishop on a train or in the street, rather than in his mansion beside St John's church in leafy Colaba, I might have taken him for a doctor or a biology lecturer at a university. A neat man in his sixties, with a close-cut grey beard framing a broad, handsome face, he spoke beautiful, precise English. By upbringing an Anglican, he had mixed feelings about Church union: the denominations that now made up the Church of North India had been severed from their ancestral roots and he missed the feeling of belonging to a world-wide Anglican community. He talked about corruption within the church administration, about the social status of the 20,000 members of his diocese – most were *dalits*, or poor, or both – and about the diffuse nature of the Christian community in India. There were fewer Sikhs than Christians, he said, but they were concentrated in one area, the Punjab, and there were some among them who were prepared to take up arms for their ethnic cause. The Muslims also tended to be militant. Consequently the government took more notice of these minorities than it did of the Christians. 'We are scattered,' he said, 'except in Kerala and the north-east, so we're not a cohesive force. And of course our teachings tell us to be non-violent, to accept suffering.' However, Christianity does have a militant wing, loosely termed evangelical, and I expected the bishop, like most I had met so far, to view it with disdain, if not disapproval. He was, after all, a liberal in outlook.

'Yes,' he agreed, 'my own attitudes are liberal, and they are carefully thought out. But while we boast of our liberal theology, it has had little effect outside the conference room.' He paused to gauge my reaction, then said: 'The fact is that this liberalization of theology is feeding only the intellectuals, and the only thing many of them are committed to is being liberal. It's not feeding people spiritually. That's why many are turning to the evangelicals. Their preachers are Old Testament types. They have a deep sense of commitment, and people want their effervescence.'

Didn't he feel threatened by them?

'No, I don't,' he replied briskly. 'So far we haven't lost many people to the evangelical Churches. But in any case, my attitude is that if people are leaving the mainstream Churches and going to them, that's fine; they're still Christians. If I do have a concern, it's about their theology. But if my world view isn't convincing, then people will naturally go elsewhere.' He said he admired the evangelicals' zeal and their willingness to send missionaries to remote areas where they were often the object of intense hostility. 'But then,' he added, 'the Church doesn't grow unless it's persecuted.' It was true, as some of the evangelicals' critics argued, that they did little in the way of social work, but they did look after their own people with love and diligence. If a child was sick, or needed a place in a new school, the pastor and laity would rally round and help, and those who joined the evangelical Churches had a strong sense of community, of belonging, something that was often lacking in the larger congregations of the established Churches.

Before I left, the bishop gave me the name of a pastor in the New Life Fellowship – the most evangelical of the evangelicals, apparently – and said: 'You must go and see these people. This is where the future of Christianity lies in India.'

It was a sentiment, I reflected as I walked out into the muggy dusk, that seemed jarringly at odds with the stately Victorian world of the old British cantonment. Bishop's House might have come straight out of the pages of *Barchester Towers*, although Trollope would have done something about the unkempt garden, which was wrapped around the building like a bedraggled stole around a dowager's neck. The gracious spire of St John's church, built as a memorial to those who fell in the first Afghan War, rose above the crown of an ancient banyan tree, and for a fleeting moment I imagined I was a witness to an earlier and more confident age. The illusion was short-lived: a battered bus ploughed a slushy furrow through pond-sized puddles and within a few minutes a taxi had deposited me in the vibrant chaos of downtown Bombay.

Superficially, Bombay is entirely lacking in artifice. Mobile phone in one hand, glass of imported scotch in the other, it struts the western seaboard like a high-class hooker touting for trade. It can be a cruel, heartless city, in pockets ostentatiously affluent, often unremittingly poor, but Bombay has many faces, not all of which are painted in lurid colours. Plucked from the jumble of memories from several visits, over several years, I recall in particular setting out on foot along Marine Drive in the hour before dawn. Gradually the lights on the black hump of Malabar Hill softened and faded, as though in imitation of the stars above, and high-rise buildings swam out of the dark like giant pencils, their façades growing whiter by the minute, to be reflected in the pale, pellucid blue of the bay, as flat and still as a Canaletto seascape. On another occasion, at the end of a long trip, I arrived at Marine Drive at ten o'clock in the evening to catch the ex-servicemen's bus to the airport. The bus was late and the night-watchman at an American bank invited me to shelter from the rain while I waited. He gave me a cigarette and as we smoked we studied in silence the trickle of passers-by. First came a group of young men, arms raised against the rain and jackets pulled over their heads like monks' cowls. Then came a beggar woman with a baby in her arms, followed by two bare-footed girls who were chatting jauntily despite the rain and the late hour. As they passed, a horse and cart came by; one of the girls rushed after it and leapt up to grab hold of the axle. When the cart disappeared from sight, several minutes later, she was still swinging between the wheels, and her mother and sister trudged far behind, unmoved, as though this was the most natural thing in the world.

Memorable, too, are the dusks in Bombay, and never more so than during the monsoon months. On one occasion, shortly before I met the bishop, I wandered into St John's church in bright late-afternoon sunshine and left, half an hour later, in a cloudburst. I flagged down a taxi and asked the driver to drop me at a Chinese restaurant near the Taj Hotel. The taxi had no windscreen wipers and the driver was forced to navigate by instinct rather than by sight, which is why we ran into a flood on Strand Road. The engine gave a strangulated gurgle and water came swirling in over the floorboards. I paid off the driver and waded, knee-deep, towards the Taj. The Gateway of India loomed out of the grey, slanting rain like a Norman keep, and the scene reminded me of those grim towns with crumbling boarding houses and tacky esplanades that punctuate the north-east coast of England: Saltburn-by-the-Sea, for example, or the classier end of Hartlepool.

It was on an evening such as this that I went to see Pastor Jerry de Souza of the New Life Fellowship. His flat overlooked the seafront at Bandra, one of the city's smarter suburbs, and I arrived as the sun was sinking in a pool of crimson.

'Welcome, brother,' he said as we shook hands.

Pastor de Souza was a stocky character, around my age or a

little younger, with a luxuriant moustache, a fleshy face and a direct, open manner. He began by telling me briefly about his Church, which had been founded in 1968 by two New Zealand missionaries. By 1980 it had only a hundred or so members here in Bombay, but since then it had grown rapidly. 'We sought the face of the Lord in prayer and fasting,' said Pastor de Souza, his voice confident and declamatory, 'and God spoke to us and told us to look outward, to start house groups in the city.' In Bombay there were now over 1,500 house groups, or house churches, each with between seven and fifteen members, and 250 celebration centres where anywhere between thirty and 500 believers came together to worship. The New Life Fellowship had congregations in every state of India now, although Pastor de Souza said that Bombay remained the spiritual gateway to the country.

'Why do you say that?' I asked.

'Over three decades,' replied the pastor, 'different people are telling us that. Not long ago a woman came from overseas and she stayed with us here. When she went into the bedroom she had a vision. She saw a map of India with a light burning brilliantly over Bombay, and the light spread out all over India.' The New Life Fellowship, he continued, had attracted a great range of people: Hindus, Muslims, Catholics, Anglicans, Jains, Buddhists; high-caste and low-caste, rich and poor. Actors from the Bollywood film world had been drawn to the Fellowship and a house church had even been established among a community of eunuchs. 'We are looking for India to become a Christian country,' said the pastor. This confident claim was accompanied, appropriately, by a loud crack of thunder. Golden tendrils of lightning momentarily threw into sharp relief the black trunks and wind-whipped fronds of the palm trees in the garden, and the pastor rose to secure a flapping window. When he returned to his seat I asked him how he would describe his Church.

'Evangelical and charismatic. Very charismatic. Being charismatic is being spirit-filled. It means we are flowing in the gifts of the spirit.'

Charismatic Christians believe that they can have the same experiences, and receive the same gifts, as the first Christians did on the day of Pentecost, and their guiding text is found in the Acts of the Apostles: 'The day of Pentecost had come, and they were all together in one place. Suddenly there came from the sky what sounded like a strong, driving wind, a noise which filled the whole house where they were sitting. And there appeared to them flames like tongues of fire distributed among them and coming to rest on each one. They were all filled with the Holy Spirit and began to talk in other tongues, and the spirit gave them the power of utterance' (Acts 2:1–4).

Being charismatic, continued Pastor de Souza, means being baptized in the Holy Spirit. Unlike the traditional baptism by water, the sacramental right that admits a person into the Christian Church, baptism in the Holy Spirit is something altogether more participatory. Its outward manifestation is speaking in other tongues, in a language previously unfamiliar to the speaker. Charismatic services begin with a direct confession to God, either in silence or aloud, and with songs of praise, which are a celebration of the 'Victory of the Lord'. After the songs, the congregation then 'moves in the gifts of the spirit'. On rare occasions someone may be touched by the gift of prophecy. 'But more often,' said the pastor, 'we have forthtelling. This means that God's word is being spoken by humans. The human element delivers in obedience to the word of God.' He raised his finger to emphasize the point: 'Divine sovereignty – human responsibility.'

'And what does God say?' I asked.

'He exalts the congregation to lead a good life. He tells us to be holy.'

The Acts of the Apostles and St Paul in his first letter to the Corinthians list nine gifts of the spirit, which include, among other things, speaking in tongues, prophecy, exorcism and the power to perform miracles. Pastor de Souza said that he himself had often laid hands on sick people and cured them of their illnesses. Recently he had visited a Fellowship group in Goa, in the town of Margao, and he and his brothers and sisters had prayed over a woman who had a cancerous lump in her breast. She writhed on the floor for a while, then went into the bathroom; there she discovered that the lump had gone, something which was subsequently confirmed by a doctor. 'I also cured somebody of AIDS,' continued the pastor. 'Right here in this house.'

This struck me as being an altogether superior class of miracle and I asked whether it had been reported in the newspapers.

'No,' he said, 'we don't publish miracles – it would be like casting pearls before swine.' He added that members of the New Life Fellowship had recently raised three people from the dead in the state of Andhra Pradesh.

Like many members of the charismatic community in India, Pastor de Souza had been brought up as a Roman Catholic. However, when he was twenty-one he began to read the Bible – something that in the past Catholics were discouraged from doing – and he said that he soon realized that there was no authority in the Gospels, or elsewhere in the New Testament, for many Catholic beliefs and practices. He took exception – as, indeed, do all the Protestant Churches – to the Catholic assertion that the Pope is Christ's Vicar on Earth; and in reading the Bible he also saw that there was no authority to justify the veneration of the Virgin Mary, or praying through the saints, or praying for the souls in purgatory. He decided to abandon the traditions and rituals of Rome in favour of a religion that based its beliefs and actions solely on the word of the Bible. 'It's not tradition, but it's proof,' he intoned. 'It's not rituals, but it's the reality of a revelation. It's not religion, but it's relationship.' The pastor's language was strangely liturgical for someone so averse to the idea of formal liturgies, and there were times when I felt I was part of a much larger audience, of the ecstatic sort, for example, that he might address at the Fellowship's celebration centres. It was clear that he was unwilling to enter into theological debate or to admit to any spiritual uncertainties. When he said that his Church believed every single word that was written in the Bible, I suggested that it contained many contradictions and that there were inconsistencies even within the three synoptic Gospels.

'No,' he said tersely, 'there are no contradictions – not once you've studied the Bible properly.'

I asked him how he felt about Darwinian theories of evolution.

'Before Darwin died,' he replied, 'he admitted that his theories were hogwash. He may have repented just before dying. Who knows, he may have been saved.'

The Fellowship, as one would expect, has firm views on the subject of salvation. 'Anyone who repents and is born again in the Lord can be saved,' explained the pastor.

What was repentance?

'A change of mind leading to a change of heart leading to a change in direction.'

'How about the Hindus?' I inquired. 'Can they be saved?'

'There's no excuse for anyone who isn't born again in the Lord. The Bible's quite clear about that. Romans 1.' Presumably the pastor was referring to those verses in Paul's letter to the Romans that attack idolatry. 'They boast of their wisdom, but they have made fools of themselves, exchanging the glory of the immortal God for an image shaped like mortal man, even for images like birds, beasts, and reptiles. For this reason God has given them up to their own vile desires' (Rom. 1:22–4).

India was a long way from becoming a Christian country, said Pastor de Souza, but there were far more Christians than the authorities were prepared to admit. Government statistics suggested that there were 720 million Hindus in India, 100 million Muslims, 20 million Christians, 18 million Sikhs and 6 million Buddhists, though in the last decennial census, taken in 1991, religious allegiances were not recorded, as they had been on previous occasions. Pastor de Souza pointed out that even Mr L. K. Advani, the leader of the BJP, a political party that wished to turn India into a Hindu state, had admitted that only 50 per cent of Indians were truly Hindu. The confusion stemmed from the Constitution defining Hinduism by what it is not, rather than by what it is. Anyone who is not a Christian, a Muslim or a Parsi is considered to be a Hindu. Consequently, Buddhists, animists and atheists are all counted as Hindus. However, Pastor de Souza was also convinced that there were many more Christians than the statistics implied. He said many people who practised Christianity were loath to admit it, either out of fear of reprisals from Hindu militants or because their official status as Hindus enabled them to take advantage of government benefits – for example, positive discrimination for *dalits* in job allocations – which did not apply to Christians.

When I rose to leave I held out my hand to shake the pastor's. Much to my astonishment, he clasped it firmly, closed his eyes and proceeded to pray for my salvation, my enlightenment, my safety and even for the success of this book. I am not used to this sort of thing, but it was kind of him to be solicitous, and I am inclined to think it is better to be prayed for vigorously than not at all.

It was still raining hard when I left, and by the time I found my taxi I was soaked to the skin. The journey to Powai, the northern suburb where I was staying with friends, should have taken no more than an hour at this time of the evening, but it took twice as long, as trouble on the railways, and the closure of lines to the northern suburbs, had forced the city's commuters on to the roads. It was partly their own fault. That morning a group of commuters, exasperated by the perennial inefficiency and the chronic overcrowding of Bombay's trains, had descended on to the platform at Thane to remonstrate with the station master. It was a steamy day and the fans in their carriages had broken down. While the commuters were voicing their displeasure, the train moved out of the station without them. They waited for the next train, and when that was cancelled they went on the rampage: thirteen carriages were set on fire, and damage to trains and the station was put at 50 million rupees (£1 million). The newspapers were quick to point out that the rioters, of whom there were several thousand, were not professional thugs; for the most part they were middle-class office workers who had simply lost patience with the transport system.

I was now beginning to understand more clearly what the bishop had meant when he said that the city's commuters were not looking for erudite theology so much as a living God who speaks to them – and, presumably, a better train service. By the time I arrived at Powai I felt as though I had been doubly battered: on a prosaic level by the noisy, fume-laced journey; on a higher plane by the vigorous preaching and immutable beliefs of Pastor de Souza. At times I found the pastor's fondness for snappy aphorisms tiresome, but he spoke a language that many would find exhilarating. It was a language that seethed with intolerance for other religions and conjured up a world of demons and sin, of miracles and divine utterances. It was a language that sprang from the warmth of the heart rather than from the cooler realms of reason, and it was a language, above all, that stressed the immediacy of God. No need to pray through the Virgin Mary or ask favours of obscure saints in the classified advertisement columns of newspapers. The evangelicals, as the bishop said, brought God right down into the living-room.

Towards the end of my Indian journey, by which time I had come across a great range of denominations and sects, I spent a day with a pastor in the Church of God, whose stronghold is the Khasi Hills, to the north of Bangladesh. 'Some people see me as a liberal, but others think I'm a fundamentalist,' he said when I asked him to describe his theological views. 'Then again there are some who claim I'm very evangelical, but others think I must be ecumenical, as I'm on good terms with the Catholics and the Anglicans.' But how did he see himself? 'Actually,' he replied, 'I don't like any of these labels. I want to bring people together; labels drive them apart. But if I had to choose one for myself, then I'd call myself a post-evangelical.'

I had some sympathy with the pastor's reluctance to be typecast, and I had tired of the way in which evangelical Christians used 'liberal' as a term of abuse, and liberals, likewise, used 'evangelical' pejoratively. However, the terms 'evangelical' and 'ecumenical' do provide a convenient shorthand to describe the two main poles of contemporary Christian thought. The term 'evangelical' was originally used to describe the Protestant Churches after the Reformation in recognition of their claim that their beliefs were based solely on the teachings of the Bible. Evangelicals still see the Scriptures as the only source of authority, but the term nowadays has wider connotations. Evangelical Christians place a strong emphasis on personal conversion – on being born again – and they proclaim their faith at every possible opportunity. Many believe, like Pastor de Souza, in the inerrancy of the Bible, and they generally disapprove of inter-faith dialogue and calls for greater unity among the Christian Churches. Toleration and respect for other faiths, and for Christians of different denominations, are the hallmarks of the ecumenical movement, whose liberality is an affront to many evangelical groups. The ecumenical movement dates, in terms of recent history, from the World Missionary Conference held in Edinburgh in 1910. This and subsequent gatherings led to the founding of the International Missionary Council and later the World Council of Churches, which now counts among its members most of the established Protestant denominations of the Western Church, some of the Eastern Orthodox Churches and over 200 smaller Churches in the developing world. The ecumenical spirit has manifested itself, most obviously, in the organic union of various Protestant denominations – for example, to form the United Reformed Church in Britain, and the Churches of North and South India – and in the dialogue that the Churches have established with people of other faiths. It was this yearning for dialogue that led to one of India's most intriguing religious ventures: the founding of a Christian ashram in Pune. If the New Life Fellowship represents evangelical Christianity at its most extreme, then the Christa Prema Seva Ashram can claim to do the same for the ecumenical movement.

I arrived in Pune, some four hours by train from Bombay, late in the afternoon, checked into a businessmen's hotel near the station and headed off on foot in search of the town centre and a place to eat. The sun had recently set, but swallows and house-martins were still swooping above the pantiled roofs in search of insects, while the first bats of the evening – pipistrelles, I think – fluttered among a spaghetti of telegraph wires, picking off moths and beetles that flapped untidily around the street lamps. Below, the broken pavement was crowded with office workers, women shopping and people doing their *pujas* outside little Hindu temples where flickering candles illuminated stone idols and sent their shadows wobbling about the walls in a curious dance. I passed a row of fine old villas whose upper floors had spacious balconies with classical columns and ornate architraves, then turned down a narrow street whose tall, terraced buildings appeared to be in two minds about whether they were dwellings or warehouses. Many had shops and stores on their lower floors – a Muslim sat cross-legged among huge sacks of rice and lentils; a barber applied black dye to a grey-haired head – while above, on the long balconies, elderly men smoked and weighty women, their broad bosoms resting on the balustrades, exchanged gossip like a conspiracy of crows.

To wander at random through a small Indian city in the early hours of the evening provides a degree of pleasure that would be greater still if it were not for the annoyance of buses and lorries juddering their way along streets designed for bullock carts and donkeys, hand-pulled rickshaws and the occasional elephant. A century ago these streets would have smelt of cow dung, donkey breath and the spicy produce of the country, of the sweat of coolies and the scent of perfumed women. Today the smells are of diesel and petrol fumes, of burning refuse and human waste. Indians are fastidiously clean in their homes, but few have much respect for public space: there were plenty of public latrines in Pune, yet they were poorly patronized and I passed a well-dressed gentleman, who should have known better, emptying his bladder against a wall that carried the slogan DON'T LET PUNE PERISH. The two rivers that meet in the city were doing precisely that – perishing in a biological sense, at least – and slums and industrial development had gobbled up much of the surrounding countryside. 'The whole ecology's buggered up!' said an Irish-Indian whom I met at St Mary's. He took me to see the old war cemetery in the northern part of the city, and he kept pointing to shanties or factories and saying: 'When I was a boy, those were fields and forests.' All the same, patches of green have survived, most notably in the old cantonments and in the well-wooded parks dotted along the river banks. There are also many smaller plots of wooded land, one of the loveliest being in the possession of the Christa Prema Seva Ashram, although its survival, both as a religious institution and a physical entity, was now in doubt.

I was met at the gates of the ashram by a stocky, square-shouldered woman in her seventies. She had close-cropped grey hair, listed to one side when she walked and spoke with a pronounced German accent. Her name was Melita. No, she said, she wasn't one of the sisters, and Sister Brigitte, the ashram's *acharya*, or guru, had gone to Bombay to protest to the Charity Commissioners about the activities of the Bombay Diocesan Trust Association, which was threatening to evict the sisters and develop the land for housing. If I wanted to meet Sister Brigitte, I would have to return another day. In the meantime she would show me around.

The ashram was situated in beautiful grounds. Towering trees cast their shade over a small chapel and bougainvillaea clambered up the sides of a one-storey, horseshoe-shaped building that contained a library, the sisters' rooms, kitchens and another chapel. The rooms overlooked a garden at whose heart was a pond dappled with lotus flowers. Near the entrance to the ashram was an old stable block that had been converted into guest rooms, and it was when we reached here that Sister Bridget appeared. I had always pictured nuns as austere-looking females with billowing habits, starched wimples and unscented skins as dry as parchment. Sister Bridget could not have been further from the stereotype. She wore a pink patterned smock, loose-fitting cotton trousers and sandals, and she was very pretty, with a thick crop of grey hair, a serene smile and a most convivial manner.

'You must be Polish,' she said airily as she approached, a young Alsatian straining on the lead that she held in her left hand.

'No, he's a writer,' explained Melita. 'From England.'

'Ah, we're expecting a Polish yoga chap,' replied Sister Bridget. 'Shall I take over, Melita?'

As she led me around, Sister Bridget told me a little about her life and about the ashram. Soon after she left school she had entered an enclosed order of Anglican nuns in Norfolk, remaining there for seven years. Later she had moved to the Convent of St Mary the Virgin at Wantage, in Oxfordshire. Her mother superior had sent her to the ashram for six months in 1993, and she had recently returned, this time for a year. She was happy in the ashram, but she was a sculptress and she missed her studio at Wantage. She had brought a few chisels to Pune, and she had done several small pieces, which she said she would show me later.

The ashram had originally been established in 1929 by an

Anglican father, Jack Winslow, as an order for men. The rules that he laid down for life in the ashram still apply today. The ashram, he wrote, 'has within it both Indian and non-Indian members, who together form a spiritual family of perfect equality and fellowship, bearing witness to the world of the unity that is in Christ'. Then, as now, the ashram sought to explore other religious traditions, and particularly Hinduism. 'In its work and study,' wrote Father Winslow, 'it approaches with reverence and sympathy the great non-Christian systems of religion, seeing in Christ the One who came not to destroy the other faiths of mankind, but rather to be the fulfilment of man's spiritual quest. And while holding fast to the whole truth as it is in Jesus, it seeks to interpret that truth through the characteristic terms of Indian religious thought.' Over the years the ashram attracted many important religious thinkers, including Mahatma Gandhi. For a variety of reasons, the men's ashram was eventually dissolved and the buildings and gardens fell into disuse. However, in 1972 the Anglican Bishop of Bombay, who was also chairman of the custodial managers, the Bombay Diocesan Trust Association, agreed that the ashram could be reopened as an ecumenical venture for Christian women. At the time of my visit the core community consisted of three sisters who belonged to a Roman Catholic order, the Society of the Sacred Heart of Jesus, and three from an Anglican order, the Community of St Mary the Virgin, or the Wantage sisters.

Before lunch Bridget took me to see Sara Grant, one of the Catholic sisters and until 1992 the ashram's *acharya.* A frail woman with piercing blue eyes and the strong features of a Scottish aristocrat, she sat with her feet tucked beneath her in a chair overlooking the garden. 'I'm like a long-playing record,' she said, smiling, when I pulled up a seat beside her, and for the next hour I felt as though I was being treated to an informal lecture delivered by someone who was intellectually brilliant – she had taught moral philosophy and metaphysics at Bombay's Sophia College – yet not entirely satisfied with the ways of the world or her present predicament.

'The whole tragedy of the missionary endeavour,' she said when I asked about her view on other faiths, 'was that Christianity was seen as being at war with Hinduism. The devil was supposed to be inhabiting all the temples. Of course, the missionaries couldn't understand the iconography . . . You can't blame them, though; that's how they saw it then.'

Sister Sara went on to talk about the influence of the Second Vatican Council, whose deliberations between 1962 and 1965 led to great changes in the way the Roman Catholic Church perceived other faiths and other Christians, whom it now called 'separated brethren'. In 1854 Pope Pius IX had insisted that there was no hope of salvation outside the Catholic Church: '*extra ecclesiam nulla Salus*'. Over the years Rome became less dogmatic in this assertion and Vatican II went so far as to suggest that other religions were worthy of both recognition and celebration. Vatican II also led to the use of vernacular language in worship, instead of Latin, and to a new liturgy, and it encouraged the hierarchy to adopt a less authoritarian attitude towards the Catholic laity. 'After Vatican II,' explained Sister Sara, 'some of us decided that we should make a deeper study of certain aspects of Indian and Hindu culture.' She learned Sanskrit and wrote a doctoral thesis on a ninth-century Hindu theologian. Later she published several works that attempted to find common ground between Hindu and Christian thought, including a collection of scriptural texts, *Descent to the Source*, which she offered 'to all those who are both haunted by the disunity and conflict that tear mankind apart, and strongly drawn to a prayer "too deep for words"' (Rom. 8:26). I was intrigued to see that she had avoided problems of copyright by making her own translations from the original Sanskrit and Greek.

Sister Sara described the ashram as a crossroads of the spirit: its fundamental purpose was to show that the gospel could be lived in any culture and many of the customs associated with traditional Hindu ashrams were practised here. Members and visitors were expected to dress modestly and help in the daily chores of running the ashram; regular periods were set aside for meditation, prayer and discussion; meals were vegetarian and eaten cross-legged on the floor, using fingers rather than knife and fork; and the sisters dressed in Indian clothes rather than European habits. However, what really distinguished the ashram from other Christian institutions was its willingness to borrow and learn from other spiritual traditions, something that might have led to its being anathematized in earlier times. 'From the outset,' said Sister Sara, 'we have tried to cater for experiment. We feel that it is legitimate to use non-biblical Scriptures in Christian worship.'

Sister Bridget suggested I join her and a few others – Sister Sara was too frail to come – for pre-lunch prayers, and she led me into a small room that was bare save for a brass cross in one corner, a bowl of flowers with a lighted candle and an Orthodox icon of the Virgin and Child. After a period of silence there was a brief chant – from the *Bhagavad-gitā*, I think – and then one of the sisters offered the lighted candle to all those present. Each symbolically took the light with outstretched fingers and transmitted it to his or her forehead. Hindus would recognize this practice as *arati*, the honouring of gods with the offering of flowers and the waving of a lamp.

A dozen people came to lunch, including several guests who were studying yoga at the renowned Ayyengar school nearby. The meal was preceded by a brief reading from a Sufi mystic and a sung grace. We ate in silence. Afterwards I climbed up to the roof with Sister Bridget and she showed me photographs of some of her sculptures. They ranged in size from large figurative pieces that now stood in various English churches to tiny Dadaesque creations made out of bits of scrap. Sister Bridget was not an intellectual, but she had a warm, inquiring mind and I suspect that she was unshockable. One of her sculptures portrayed an agonized Christ – 'You know,' she said, 'Christ as the fool in Corinthians.' She let out a ripple of laughter: 'It scandalized some of the other sisters!'

The following day I returned to the ashram at seven o'clock for the eucharist, which was held in the octagonal chapel in the garden, a beautiful building whose wire-mesh walls were decorated with various religious symbols: the Hindu swastika, the Star of David, the crescent of Islam, the ying and yang of Taoism. The priest, who came from a nearby CNI church, sat on the floor beside a painting of St Francis of Assisi and a brass platter that held the sacrament and some flowers. The rest of us sat in a circle on rush mats. Those present included Sister Brigitte, who had returned from Bombay, Sister Bridget, Melita, two Indian sisters, one of whom sang beautifully, an Irish trainee priest fully equipped with ginger beard, pony-tail and pressed-peat crucifix, and a Japanese girl who was soon to be baptized. The service began with the singing of a *bhajan* in Hindi; otherwise it was conducted in English, using the liturgy of the Church of North India. One of the Indian sisters read a passage from the Scriptures and the priest read a lesson about tax collectors and sinners, then gave a brief address on the subject. It was not so much a sermon as a meditation and afterwards he invited comments. Sister Bridget suggested that Christians could learn from other faiths; Sister Brigitte reported that her meeting with the Charity Commissioners in Bombay had gone reasonably well. Holy Communion followed and the brass platter with the consecrated wine and chapati was handed around the circle.

The words which the priest says when he consecrates the bread and the wine, and which recall Christ's celebration of the Last Supper in an upstairs room in Bethany the night before his trial and crucifixion, have come down to us, scarcely changed, since they were first used in the early Church: 'Take, eat: this is my body which is given for you: Do this in remembrance of me . . . Drink ye all of this; for this is my Blood of the New Testament, which is shed for you and for many for the remission of sins.' These or similar words you will hear at every Christian eucharist, whatever the denomination, and yet it is hard not to feel that in many churches it has become little more than an elaborate piece of theatre, a Restoration parody of what must have been a simple supper. What, I wonder, would people who had never been inside a church make of the pomp and ceremony that are favoured by many denominations? What would they make of the bishops and priests arrayed in gorgeous vestments, the deacons swinging antique censers, the bizarre processing and arcane rituals? Would any of this remind first-time visitors of that large upstairs room and the roughly hewn table with its thirteen diners, many of them peasants with callused hands and the demeanour of men who had spent their lives pulling fishing nets, or ploughing, or walking barefoot through village markets? I doubt it. On the other hand, if these visitors were to spend some time at the Christa Prema Seva Ashram, I believe they would get a much truer picture of Christian beliefs and ideals. At the very least they would be beguiled by the atmosphere of spirituality, by the simple beauty of the chapel and by the sound of Indian cuckoos and bulbuls singing in the trees outside. But the ashram offers more than a memorable aesthetic experience. Religious institutions are often places of dogma; this is a place of inquiry.

After breakfast I introduced myself to Sister Brigitte, who looked two decades younger than her eighty-odd years. She was tall and lithe and she had an angular face that reflected a ferocious intelligence. During our brief conversation we touched on many subjects – the Vatican's attitude to family planning and the meaning of the Virgin Birth; Hindu Scriptures and the interpretation of miracles – but the issue that was uppermost in her mind had nothing to do with religion. Some time ago the Bombay Diocesan Trust Association, the custodial managers of the ashram site, had sold some land that used to be part of the garden; this had been turned into a bus depot and the constant drone of engines was a reminder of its presence. Now the trust wished to sell off another plot of land immediately in front of the main buildings. The trustees had told the Charity Commissioners in Bombay that the land was derelict and that they wanted to build houses for poor Christians. 'The Commissioners,' said Sister Brigitte sniffily, 'had said, "Yes, jolly good." But it's not true! The trust wants to sell the land to a builder who will construct seven- or eight-storey luxury flats.' Land prices in Pune, she added, were extremely high.

Once the sisters in the ashram realized what the trust intended to do, they took the decision to build the garden chapel: however corrupt the planning system in India, it was highly unlikely that an official would dare sanction the destruction of a religious building. Neither the trust nor the builders, who periodically came to measure up the land, had been deterred by the sisters' opposition to their plans. Indeed, the previous evening three cars had arrived with a group of fifteen or so men who had come to view the land. The warden of the hostel outside the ashram's gates confronted the men, apparently with a considerable display of belligerence and some ripe language. He noticed that one of the Ambassadors was a VIP car with dark windows and he asked who was inside it. 'If you knew who was in there,' came the reply, 'you'd shrink into the ground with terror.'

My stay in Pune coincided with the 170th anniversary of St Mary's church. The celebratory service was a grand affair, as indeed was the church, a stately building typical of its period and full of memorials to the soldiers who had worshipped here, including one who had participated in the Charge of the Light Brigade. The Bishop of Kolhapur, dressed like a bird of paradise in golden mitre and glittering cloak, gave a lengthy sermon that included the following observation, which I transmitted verbatim into my notebook: 'Despite government of India making Taj Mahal white as possible for all to enjoy, I tell you this' – and here he raised a hand in a regal gesture – 'one day, Taj Mahal will crumble away, fall down, but Lord's message will last for ever!' The service began and ended with a great deal of pomp, and there was much injudicious use of the censer, which caused one member of the choir to pass out in mid-hymn. The celebrations attracted considerable attention in the local press and the city's dignitaries were well represented. Anyone who knew little about the affairs of the Church of North India in Pune would have thought, judging from these celebrations, that it was in rude health. That it was not had much to do with the Bombay Diocesan Trust Association.

I had first heard about the perfidious behaviour of the trust when I visited Bishop Samuel Joshua. He mentioned, when I was admiring Bishop's House, that certain members of the trust had entered into a deal with a property developer, which, had it gone through, would have entailed the demolition of Bishop's House and the erection in its place of high-rise residential flats. The bishop went to the high court, which put a temporary stop to the proceedings. 'I've received all sorts of threats because of this,' he recalled blithely. 'Murder, electrocution . . .' Since then the trustees had held their meetings without the bishop, although he was still technically the chairman. They stood to make considerable profits from the sale of Bishop's House and they continued to press their case in the courts throughout the 1980s. 'It's as though your bodyguards are shooting you,' said the bishop. 'For half my time, I'm a half-baked lawyer. I can't afford the solicitors' fees, so I'm always having to appear in court myself.'

Before Church union in 1970, each of the denominations that were to join the Church of North India had its own trust to look after its property. For example, the United Church of North India – which comprised Presbyterians and Congregationalists – had the United Church of North India Trust Association, which was set up in 1924. The Anglican diocese of Bombay had the Bombay Diocesan Trust Association, which began life in 1928. Ideally, at the time of union, the various trusts should have handed their properties over to a new body of trustees, but it was to be another seven years before the Church of North India Trust Association was established, and while most of the old trusts relinquished their properties, the Bombay Diocesan Trust Association refused to do so. It continues to act as custodial manager of former Anglican property, not only in the present CNI diocese of Bombay, which is relatively small, but throughout the former Anglican diocese of Bombay, a vast area which extends as far south as the state of Karnataka and which includes Pune.

'The relationship between the Church and the Bombay trust broke down,' continued the bishop. 'The old Church – the Anglican Church – was no longer there to appoint trustees, so the trustees began to hand-pick themselves. They seemed to develop a lust for power.' They even claimed that there was no constitutional relationship between the CNI and themselves, as they were an Anglican trust, not a trust of the Church of North India.

The trust appealed against the high-court decision that blocked the development of Bishop's House, and in 1992 another court took the view that it had no jurisdiction over the issue and that decisions about the project should rest not with the courts but with the Charity Commissioners. 'Well, they're corrupt and in league with the builders,' said the bishop bluntly, 'so the trustees were delighted.' Fortunately, the municipality had recently designated St John's church and Bishop's House as heritage sites; this meant they could not be sold, demolished or despoiled. 'At least, that's the position technically,' added the bishop, 'but in India anything can happen. Bribery is rampant and even justice can be bought off.'

And if justice can be bought, so can hired thugs, as the girls of St Crispin's home discovered in 1984. The home looks after and educates 400 girls, many of them orphans or the offspring of parents too poor to look after them, in a pleasant district north of the river in Pune. When the home's forerunner, a boys' school, was established by the Society of St John the Evangelist, a monastic order in Oxfordshire, the site was surrounded by jungle and marshland. There were frequent malaria epidemics and the school was eventually closed down, but it reopened as a home for destitute girls, run by the Wantage sisters, in the 1950s. Since then the home and its grounds have been engulfed by the spreading suburbs, and in 1984 the Bombay trust decided to take advantage of escalating land prices by selling off 15 *guntas* (approximately 1,500 square feet) of land to a local builder. The builder, a Mr Mehta, is said to have paid 40 lakh rupees (£80,000 at current prices), a portion of which allegedly ended up in the trustees' pockets. The manager of the home, Tichnor Charles, whom I met one morning shortly before he left for Bombay to pursue his struggle with the trust, went to Pune civil court as soon as he learned of the 1984 sale and obtained an injunction restraining the builder from proceeding with the construction of residential flats. Mr Mehta made his displeasure clear by sending round a lorry-load of thugs. More than a hundred girls joined in the battle. The younger ones collected stones and rocks, which the older girls used to pelt the thugs, many of whom were armed with sticks and crowbars. Twenty-five girls were injured, one seriously; many of the thugs were injured too.

Mr Charles was away in Delhi at the time. 'I flew straight to Bombay as soon as I heard the news and was back here by nine thirty the next morning,' he recalled. 'I got a very rousing reception. Some of the girls said, "Don't you worry. We'll fix those guys."' A few months later another lorry-load of rough characters pulled up at the gates, but they left as soon as they saw Mr Charles. 'I recognized one of them,' he said. 'He was a farmer whom I'd helped on a small dairy project, and a bit later I bumped into him on MG Road. He told me that they'd come to give me a thrashing. Luckily they realized who I was first.' He added that Mr Mehta had recently been imprisoned for breaking into a shop which he claimed to own, but presumably did not.

Over the years litigation against the Bombay trust has cost St Crispin's over 200,000 rupees (£4,000), money which this admirable institution can ill afford. However, Mr Charles was convinced that he would eventually win the case, that the builder, who still had a watchman on the site, would be forced to retire and that St Crispin's would continue to do what it has always done, provide an education, and the possibility of a decent career, for girls who would otherwise have been destined for a life of poverty. The fate of the ashram, sadly, is less certain. The dispute with the trustees had caused such distress that midway through 1996 the Society of the Sacred Heart decided, with the agreement of the Convent of St Mary the Virgin, to withdraw Sister Sara and the other Catholic sisters. The convent also announced that it could no longer guarantee to maintain its presence beyond the end of 1997: this, it hoped, would force admirers of the ashram within the Church of North India to fight for its survival.

The day before I left Pune I was taken to see the work of the Deep Griha Society in the Jyoti slum. In a curious way, it was a relief to escape the institutional squabbles of the Church of North India and see the practical work of a Christian organization. Jyoti was a typical Indian slum with some 20,000 people living in an organic patchwork of tin-roof shacks; long queues of women waited at the standpipes; naked children scrabbled in the dirt alongside scavenging pigs and goats. I was introduced to a delicately beautiful young woman in a pink sari who was in charge of an AIDS project. Five per cent of the women in the slum were prostitutes, and many were in their early teens; nearly half were HIV-positive. 'If the women can't control their husbands,' said the AIDS worker, 'then at least they can get them to use condoms.' Over a fifth of the men in the slum were habitual drunks who frequently subjected their wives and families to violence. A recent survey found that schoolboys were regular clients of the prostitutes and that during exam times there was a sharp slump in the sex business. Besides its work with prostitutes, Deep Griha ran health centres in three slums and over fifty pre-school classes for children between three and five years old; it also organized coaching for truant children and ran about 200 adult literacy classes.

Deep Griha, which means 'lighthouse', was set up twenty years ago by a formidable couple whom I first met at St Mary's 170th anniversary service. Dr N. D. Onawale said that she and her husband, Rev. Basker Onawale, had had a mountain-top vision; God had guided them. 'Yes,' agreed Rev. Onawale, who was now the principal of the United Theological Seminary, 'we weren't sure how the organization would develop, but gradually God led us. It was His plan and we feel that He has been working through us.'

His language had an evangelical ring to it, but Rev. Onawale said that Deep Griha had never intended to make Christian converts of the Hindus and Muslims with whom they worked in the slums. 'Christ's love is in us,' he said, 'and that love should be seen in action.' Indeed, he was unhappy about the growing influence of certain evangelical groups, especially those who came from outside India. He disliked their exclusivity and self-righteousness. 'Some are working with the poor,' he said, 'but ultimately what they want to do is pour water on people's heads.' They appealed, in particular, to women and to people whom he called emotional types. 'They are often very negative. They talk about Christian love, yet they don't have it themselves. They talk about the non-material way of life, yet they accumulate material possessions.' He added, with a grin, that groups like the Assembly of God and the New Life Fellowship were becoming very rich.

Rev. Onawale was hoping to establish within the seminary an inter-faith conference centre. 'The earliest missionaries asked us to keep away from people of other faiths,' he explained. 'It was as though they were protecting a child from a disease. But a child must grow up. He must be tough both physically and spiritually if he's to survive in the real world. In the same way, we shouldn't cocoon Christians from people who believe in other religions. In the modern age we are travelling in the same train – Christians, Hindus, Muslims. There should be a dialogue between all these faiths.' Rev. Onawale had already set up several meetings between religious leaders, and to one of these he had invited the Rashtriya Swayamsevak Sangh (RSS), a militant Hindu group whose members had recently stepped up their attacks on Christian institutions and church leaders.

CHAPTER 4

The Roman Conquest

Throughout India Mahatma Gandhi's 125th birthday was celebrated, out of deference to his memory and to the sensibilities of temperance-minded Hindus, by a day of prohibition. On any other warm, post-monsoonal evening the streets of Panjim in Goa would have hummed with the chatter of strolling families, the bars would have been full and the concrete benches in the square below the great balustraded staircase that zigzagged up to the Church of the Immaculate Conception would have been occupied by courting couples, old ladies resting their legs and groups of men discussing business and politics. Tonight the square was almost deserted, the bars and liquor shops were closed and I was forced to wash down my *massala* pomfret, eaten at a formica-topped table in a modest café, with a glass of mineral water. After supper I made the long climb up the ill-lit laterite stairs to the church. It was a moonless night, yet there was just enough light to see that the great baroque façade, a pure pearly white when I had last visited Panjim a couple of years earlier, had been streaked a dirty grey by the rains. A bush grew from a crack at the base of the belfry and clumps of weeds sprouted around the showy towers on either side.

'You want a drink, friend?' inquired a slow, slurred male voice that seemed to come from a thicket of scrub at the side of the church. As it happened I did, if only to celebrate my return to Goa. A figure detached itself from the gloom and swayed uncertainly towards me, a raised hand revealing in silhouette a small bottle.

I declined the offer and made my way back down the stairs.

'Which country, please?' called the drinker, punctuating the question with a series of fruity belches.

When I reached the square the sound of singing drew me down a side street where some forty people were gathered in front of a large cross that was embedded in an alcove between Progress School – a squat building with a wooden balcony running around the second floor – and Chicky-Chocky, a fast-food restaurant. The alcove appeared to belong to Ganja Printers, whose sign hung above the closed door beside it. The cross was garlanded with flowers, framed by two leafy bamboo branches and illuminated by dozens of candles whose wax flowed down the wall on to the pavement below. A elderly man with grey hair played the violin in front of the cross. The music was sad and reflective, at times gypsyish in its cadence and rhythm, and it reminded me of the melancholy tunes you once heard in late-night bars in ports like Lisbon and Barcelona in the days when men with violins were still welcome in such places. Beside the violinist stood a young man who acted as cantor for the litany, which was in Latin. Some people had sheets of paper with the words to the litany, but many of those present, including a barefooted coolie who sat on the pavement where I stood, knew the words by heart. The litany concluded after more than an hour with a prayer, chairs were brought out into the street and I fell into conversation with Desmond, the owner of Chicky-Chocky restaurant. Litanies such as this, he explained, were peculiar to Goa. They were often family affairs, or they brought together people living in the same street or quarter, and one could see similar gatherings, in front of wayside crosses and shrines, all over the Catholic districts of Goa. He led me forward to inspect the cross and we were joined by another young man who claimed that it had miraculous properties. It appeared to have been made of moulded plaster and it had been given a thick coat – dozens of coats, more likely – of silver paint. There was a crucified hand in raised relief on the crossbeam, a chalice on the upright and a small depiction, naïve in style and execution, of Christ ascending into heaven. The rest of the alcove was painted matt black and spangled with gold stars.

Desmond was articulate and well educated, and like many Goans he had travelled widely. He had spent time in Bombay and he had worked in Paris and Munich. 'I won't make a fortune here,' he said when he reflected on his return to Goa, 'but this is the most beautiful place in the world.' It was true, he continued, that Goa was beginning to change. Real-estate values had risen sharply, corruption was creeping into business and politics and the commercialization of Goa's coast was proceeding too rapidly. However, Desmond had no time for those who claimed that tourism was going to ruin the state.

While we were talking a gang of small boys and girls distributed plates of rice, curry and sliced white bread. We were also offered glasses of *feni*, a powerful spirit made out of cashew, an important crop in Goa.

'Goa,' said Desmond with pride, 'is the only place in India where this could happen today.'

I wondered aloud what the police would do if they found people drinking alcohol on the streets.

'The police?' he said. 'Why, they'll probably come and join in soon.'

'First we pray to God,' a priest told me later, 'and then to Bacchus – that's the Goan way.'

Goa is a *mestico* state – part Portuguese, part Indian – and it possesses the charms of both races with few of the faults of either. Its capital, Panjim, is small, clean, quiet and virtually beggarless. It may not possess many buildings of great architectural merit, but the overall effect is thoroughly pleasing. Replace the palms with plane trees and you could easily imagine that you were in a small town on the Mediterranean coast. On previous visits I had always stayed at the Hotel Mandovi, a vaguely Art Deco building whose front rooms had fine views across the river after which the hotel was named, palm-fringed on the far bank and, in the late afternoons, the highway for scores of trawlers returning to land their catch in the congested harbour a few minutes' walk upstream of the hotel. The harbour had been shifted to the other side of the river since my last visit, and the Mandovi had doubled its prices, so I was forced to search for cheaper lodgings, which I found in Fontainhas, the old Latin quarter clustered around the baroque chapel of St Sebastian. From the Panjim Inn, an old family home with four-poster beds, creaking fans and its own art gallery, it took me no more than half an hour to walk anywhere in town, and whichever way I wandered I found the same hybrid mix of colonial Portuguese and contemporary Indian. Four hundred and fifty years of Portuguese rule have left their mark on more than Goa's architecture; in their manner of dress – the men in sober suits, the girls in frilly flamenco frocks – and in their unhurried approach to life, the Goans often seem more Latin than oriental.

It is said that if you throw a stone in Goa, you are sure to hit a coconut tree, a pig or a de Souza. If it is not a de Souza, it will be a Fernandes or a Pereira or a Costa. On my first morning in Panjim I returned to the Church of the Immaculate Conception and found Rev. Lagrange Fernandes in a musty office to the side of the building. He told me that I should go immediately to Bishop's House. As I made to leave he asked me if I knew Swiss Cottage in London. He had spent some time there, although he was more familiar with southern Europe, having been educated in Rome and Coimbra, an old university town in central Portugal.

It took a quarter of an hour to climb up the wooded hill to Bishop's House, which commanded long views across Panjim's roofs, the river Mandovi and the coconut groves beyond, and I was immediately led into the office of Father Joaquim Loiola Pereira, who ran the Diocesan Centre for Social Communication Media. He was good-looking in a flashy way and very helpful, although I was rather put out when he suggested I return to Pune to visit the Catholic seminary, the largest of its kind in India. During the course of our conversation he answered several telephone calls: in one he spoke a mixture of English, Portuguese, Konkani – the local language – and Marathi, at times changing from one language to another in mid-sentence. He said I should visit the diocesan seminary at Rachol, where he himself had done his theological studies, and the Pilar seminary in Old Goa, where he suggested I meet Father Cosme Jose Costa, a leading authority on Goan Catholicism. He warned me that Father Cosme had a speech impediment and that I might find him difficult to understand on the telephone. He had, but I didn't and we arranged to meet that afternoon. The drive to Old Goa was brief and enchanting, despite the recent proliferation of roadside billboards advertising pesticides and toothpaste, new condominiums and American cigarettes. Farmsteads were dotted among the rice paddies like small ships bobbing in a sea of green, and every now and then we passed a whitewashed church.

Father Cosme was having a siesta when I arrived at the seminary, and he shook the sleep from his eyes as he invited me into a room that contained a single bed and a desk whose surface was partially hidden below books and papers. There was a cheap icon of the Virgin Mary and a plate of pebbles and seashells beside the desk lamp. The books on the shelf above the desk were mainly in English, but there were several volumes in Italian, Latin and Portuguese. A wiry man with a greying beard, Father Cosme had a wry sense of humour and a fondness for anecdotes and good stories. I think he naturally enjoyed the act of talking, even though he appeared to masticate his words, much as one would a tough piece of meat, before he was able to expel them.

Roman Catholic popes, he said as soon as I sat down, had been directly or indirectly involved in the affairs of Goa for almost 500 years. In 1493 Pope Alexander VI defused the rivalry between the two great maritime powers, Spain and Portugal, in a series of papal bulls. He recognized the rights of Spain, following Columbus's discovery of America the previous year, to trade with lands across the Atlantic and he encouraged its king 'to bring to Christian faith the people who inhabit these islands and the mainland . . . and to send to the said islands and to the mainland wise, upright, God-fearing, and virtuous men who will be capable of instructing the indigenous peoples in good morals and in the Catholic faith'. The Pope drew a line down a map of the world from one pole to the other, to the west of the Azores. Spain was to take the spoils to the west, Portugal those to the east. In 1497 Vasco da Gama rounded the Cape of Good Hope and opened up the sea route to India and the east. Thirteen years later Alfonso de Albuquerque successfully laid siege to the town of Gova, or Old Goa. The Muslim soldiers who defended the city either fled or were massacred. They left behind their wives, most of whom had had the sense to bury their gold and their jewellery before the Portuguese arrived. Now that they found themselves either widowed or abandoned, they were obliged to seek the protection of the invaders. Eight hundred Muslim women converted to Christianity, retrieved their buried treasure and married Albuquerque's soldiers and sailors. 'Albuquerque wrote to the King of Portugal,' explained Father Cosme, 'saying, "I've got 800 families. Their children will be your future ministers, priests and civil servants."' Their offspring were *mesticos* and over the centuries they tended to marry among themselves. Father Cosme thought there were probably no more than ten *mestico* families left in Goa; most took up residence in Portugal, Britain and North America when Goa won its independence and became part of India in 1962.

The Portuguese conquest of Goa was staggered over two centuries. In 1510 Goa Islands, the present-day *taluka* of Tiswadi encompassing the once great city of Old Goa, Panjim, the Mandovi estuary and the immediate hinterland, fell to the Europeans. By 1543 the neighbouring *talukas* of Bardez and Salcete had come under Portuguese control. These three *talukas* made up the Old Conquests, and they became a great centre of Christianity: the Franciscans opened a house in Old Goa in 1510 and the Jesuits arrived in 1542, to be followed by the Dominicans in 1548 and the Augustinians in 1572. By the time these last arrived the Old Conquests had been Christianized: temples and mosques had been destroyed, Hindu priests expelled and non-Christians banned from government service; those Hindus who did not wish to convert had been forced to sell their property and move into the adjacent territories, which were known as the New Conquests when they later came under Portuguese control. Under a papal bull of 1553 the diocese of Goa was given jurisdiction that extended over the Catholic communities from South Africa to Japan; in 1557 Goa became an archdiocese and in 1572 the Archbishop of Goa was recognized as the Primate of the East.

Today most of Goa's Catholics live in the Old Conquests, while the New Conquests are predominantly Hindu, reflecting still the diaspora of the sixteenth century. 'In my opinion,' said Father Cosme, 'the pulling down of the Hindu temples only harmed the cause of Christianity.' The last temple was destroyed in 1541 and between then and 1560, when the Inquisition arrived in Goa, the great army of priests and monks made few new converts. Ironically, it was this brief and troubled period in Goa's history that saw the arrival of one of the greatest missionaries of all time. Goa will for ever be associated with St Francis Xavier, not least because his ravaged body lies in Old Goa's basilica of Bom Jesu and attracts a constant stream of pilgrims, in addition to the million or more who attend the public exposition of his relics every ten years.

Xavier was one of the first members of the Society of Jesus, the order founded by Ignatius Loyola in Paris in 1534 and officially recognized by the Pope in 1540. This new order was established primarily to spread the word of Christ across the world; the Jesuits took a vow of obedience to the Pope and agreed to undertake whatever missions he wished. 'Within the next hundred years,' wrote the historian Stephen Neill, 'Jesuits were to lay their bones

Champion
OATS

Previous page: Flower-seller, Panjim market, Goa. Flowers such as marigolds play a colourful part in religious ceremonies, and women frequently wear garlands of heavy-scented jasmine in their hair.

Top left: Kaylog cemetery, Shimla. During the days of the Raj, the British ruled over a quarter of the world's population from Simla, India's summer capital. Simla is now Shimla and most of the old Christian burial places have gone to ruin.

Top right: Christa Prema Seva Ashram, Pune. When the Christian sisters realized that the notorious Bombay Diocesan Trust Association intended to sell their garden to a property developer, they built a small chapel among the trees. Planning officials are unlikely to sanction the destruction of a religious building.

Bottom: Jyoti is one of many slums in Pune where the Deep Griha Society, a Christian organization, is working on health and education programmes.

Above: In recent years efforts have been made to give an Indian flavour to church architecture. St John's in Merhauli, Delhi, was built in a synthesis of Islamic and Hindu styles.

Below: A crèche run by St Stephen's hospital outreach programme in Sunder Nagari, Delhi. Over seventy children, many the victims of neglect and abuse, spend their weekdays at the dispensary, whose staff provide medical care for 55,000 slum dwellers.

Top: Goa is studded with Portuguese baroque. The Church of the Immaculate Conception has dominated Panjim, and the lives of her people, since the time of St Francis Xavier. Founded in 1541, it was rebuilt in 1619.

Bottom left: The Chapel of St Sebastian in the picturesque Fontainhas Quarter, Panjim.

Bottom right: Rachol Seminary, established by Jesuits in 1606, had one of the first printing presses in India. It remains a great centre of Christian scholarship.

Top: Father Miguel Braganza and village boys outside the church at Carambolim, a few miles from Old Goa. The first Goan to be ordained as a priest served here. Built around 1552, this church, like many in Goa, is sorely in need of repair.

Below: The porters in Panjim harbour protect their heads with plastic trilbies. The fishing communities were among the first to be converted to Christianity in Goa.

Top: Praying for the Blessed Virgin Mary, who was scheduled to appear at 2.50 p.m. on this particular Saturday. The small boy behind the cross is said to speak to her daily.

Bottom: Father K. M. George, principal of the Old Seminary, Kottayam. There are some 2 million Orthodox Syrian Christians and 600,000 Syrian Orthodox Christians in Kerala. The Old Seminary serves the former. They trace their spiritual origins back to the arrival of St Thomas in AD 52.

Above: Rickshaw-wallah, Kottayam.

Right: The 'Persian Cross' in Valiapally church, Kottayam. According to legend, this was one of seven crosses carved by St Thomas. In fact, it dates from around the seventh century.

Overleaf: India's coral strand: on the road leading south from Goa to Mangalore.

in almost every country of the known world and on the shores of almost every sea.'

Xavier was sent to India both as a representative of the King of Portugal and as the Pope's apostolic nuncio. It took his ship thirteen months to sail from Portugal to Goa, six of these being spent in Mozambique while they waited for favourable winds. He arrived in Goa on 6 May 1542 to find a magnificent city endowed with great churches and monasteries and inhabited largely by Europeans and *mesticos*. Though notionally Christian, they were leading loose and lascivious lives, and Xavier did what he could to instil Christian values in the inhabitants of Old Goa. He would gather large crowds, which he then led to a church to listen to his preaching, by walking around the streets, ringing a bell and declaiming: 'Faithful Christians, friends of Jesus Christ, send your sons and daughters and your slaves of both sexes to the Holy Teaching, for the love of God.'

Five months after his arrival, Xavier was on the move again. He travelled south to the tip of India and there, on the Coromandel Coast, he worked among the Parava fishermen who had converted to Christianity six years earlier. 'They were mostly pearl fishermen,' explained Father Cosme, 'and they had been terribly exploited by the Muslims, who'd bought their pearls at a low price and sold them exorbitantly. One day a quarrel broke out between a Muslim and a Parava, and the Muslim cut off the ear of the fisherman's wife – she was wearing a pearl earring. The Paravas went to the Portuguese, who offered them protection providing they became Christians. So they converted *en masse*.' Xavier found 10,000 Paravas who had received no Christian teaching or pastoral care since their baptism. He immediately baptized their unbaptized children and set about teaching the gospel. Other Jesuits followed in his wake and by the end of the century there was a resident father in each of the sixteen Parava villages. Xavier returned briefly to Goa, then made his way in 1545 to the Moluccas and Indonesia, where he established new missions. He returned to India in 1548, revisited the Paravas and Goa and set out the following year for Japan. He came back to India again in 1552, spent but a few months in the country and then sailed east once again, this time in the hope of evangelizing the Chinese. He fell ill before he reached the mainland and died on Sancian, an island off the coast of China, in 1552.

Xavier is remembered as much for his work in the field of education as for his remarkable success in planting new missions. 'He had a vision of an indigenous priesthood,' reflected Father Cosme, 'and he fought vigorously to encourage it.' While Xavier was in Japan, he heard news that Anton Gomez, the director of St Paul's seminary in Old Goa, had dismissed all the Indian students. 'Gomez felt that the priesthood was not meant for dark-skinned people,' explained Father Cosme. 'Xavier was horrified. It was as though his dream had been shattered.' Xavier returned to India and when he landed in Cochin he received a letter telling him that he had been made the Society of Jesus's first provincial of India. He immediately dismissed Gomez from the seminary. 'Xavier said he was a rotten fellow,' said Father Cosme with an approving nod. He added that the first Goan priest was ordained in 1568, although no religious order accepted an Indian within its ranks until 1680. Control of the Catholic Church remained in Portuguese hands until Independence; it was only then that the archdiocese was placed in the care of a Goan archbishop.

On several occasions during the course of the afternoon I attempted to steer Father Cosme towards modern times. We had begun with the events of the early sixteenth century and it had taken two hours to reach the closing years of the seventeenth. My prompting always elicited the same reaction. 'Wait,' he would say, 'there is another story you must hear first.' He told me about his village, Aldona, whose people had agreed to convert to Christianity in 1569 providing they be allowed to continue such local customs as the wearing of *dhotis* and saris. 'One of them was burned at the stake for this during the Inquisition,' he remarked, 'and many fled south to Mangalore.' He talked about the suppression of foreign religious orders by the Portuguese between 1835 and 1928 and about the birth, in the late nineteenth century, of his own indigenous order, the Missionary Society of St Francis Xavier. But the best story of all he kept for last. 'Soon I must go up to the major seminary,' he said, referring to the grand buildings on the hilltop above us, 'but I tell you one more story.' He gave me a crooked, lopsided smile, then said: 'I am a miracle boy.'

In 1929 Father Cosme's mother gave birth to a premature son, who died within six hours. It was discovered that she had a defective womb. The following year she bore a daughter, who survived despite a difficult pregnancy and birth. She then had three miscarriages, but this did not weaken her resolve to bear a son. One of her sisters – she had ten in all – suggested she pray to Father Joseph Vas, the Goan missionary who helped establish Christianity in Ceylon in the seventeenth century. This she did. Within two months she had conceived again – thanks to Father Joseph Vas. In the fourth month of the pregnancy she had a massive haemorrhage. Further haemorrhages followed and in the sixth month her husband tied her to a bed and took her in a *caminhao*, a country lorry, to see Goa's leading gynaecologist in Panjim. 'He said there was a 99 per cent chance that mother and baby would die,' explained Father Cosme, adding, with his crooked smile, 'but 100 per cent are both living and well till now.' His mother's many sisters and relatives gathered around her bed and stormed heaven with their prayers after placing a picture of Father Joseph Vas on her body. The haemorrhage stopped and she gave birth to a tiny baby. 'I weighed two and a half pounds,' said Father Cosme proudly. The doctors, already astounded at the unexplained cessation of the haemorrhage, assumed that the child would die. He did not, although his development was fraught with difficulties. 'I couldn't walk till I was four and I couldn't talk till I was five,' recalled the priest. 'Even then I had a severe stammer till I was seventeen and I couldn't hold my head straight till I was twenty.' He cured his stammer by shouting across the countryside from the roof of the seminary with pebbles beneath his tongue.

In 1990 the case history of Father Cosme's birth was submitted to five doctors in Rome by the Congregation for the Beatification of the Saints. The doctors declared that the sudden cessation of his mother's haemorrhage, and his birth without recourse to a Caesarian operation, could not be scientifically explained. The theologians of the Congregation informed the cardinals, who met the Pope. On 6 July 1993 Pope John Paul II signed a decree that paved the way for the beatification of Father Joseph Vas.

Religious extremists, whether Christian, Hindu or Muslim, invariably feed off the astringent diet of one another's prejudices. Militant Hindus tend to define Christianity in terms of its worst excesses – the Inquisition, for example, and the burning of temples and heretics – and are blind to the message of love and forgiveness that is central to the gospel. Likewise militant Christians prefer to define Hinduism by the activities of its extremists, citing the destruction of the Ayodhya mosque, the sporadic attacks on churches and nuns, the practice of bride-burning; they are inclined to forget that to be a good Hindu – in the words of one Catholic journalist I met in Delhi – 'is to be tolerant, honour the cow, honour Brahman, honour learning and observe the rituals of the faith'.

The journalist was John Dayal, the editor of one of Delhi's daily newspapers and the author of *For Reasons of State*, a critical study of the 1975–7 state of emergency under which Mrs Indira Gandhi suppressed all political activity in India. Since then Dayal had taken a keen interest in the rise of Hindu nationalism, which had been most obviously embodied in the political and electoral success of the BJP, which at the time of my journey formed the main opposition to the ruling Congress Party and held the reins of power in several states. The BJP has close links with the overtly militant RSS, an organization that came into existence in 1925 to promote the view that India should be run for Hindus by Hindus. The RSS, one of whose members murdered Mahatma Gandhi, looks upon secular, Westernized Hindus with almost as much contempt as it does Muslims, and, according to Dayal, it now sees Christians as a legitimate target too. Together with the BJP and the Vishnu Hindu Parishad (VHP), the RSS poses a serious threat to secularism and, possibly, democracy. Dayal considered the RSS's regular training programmes for young people as symptomatic of its illiberal and violent ethos. 'They might say they're teaching an Indian version of aerobics,' he said, 'but they're not. You only have to look at the attack-and-rescue games they play – it's always a Hindu woman being rescued from Muslims – and the hand-to-hand combat they teach, to understand what they are really about. Even if a young person doesn't join the RSS or the BJP afterwards, he'll have received a training which is based on violence against minorities. He'll be inculcated with a philosophy of aggression.'

I did not expect to come across the RSS or, for that matter, any other Hindu group in Panjim. Christians far outnumbered Hindus, and during the time I spent there I saw no more than half a dozen Hindu shrines and only one temple, which was hidden behind a modern building on the outskirts of town. On the other hand, wayside crosses and statues of the Virgin were everywhere to be seen, and each district had its own Catholic church.

One evening, sitting with a beer in the Panjim Inn, I idly mentioned to its owner, Ajit Sukhija, my desire to meet a representative of the RSS at some point during my travels.

'I think I know the secretary here in Goa,' replied Mr Sukhija, who seemed to know everyone of consequence in the town. He picked up the phone in his office, lit a cigarette and dialled a couple of numbers. Eventually he got through to Subhash Velingkar and explained that I wanted to meet him. 'So that's fixed,' he said as he put the receiver down. 'He says you're to meet him at the rally tomorrow evening – he'll be on the speakers' platform.'

I thanked him and asked what he thought about the RSS.

'As far as I can see, they're sensible chaps,' he said. 'Very sober. Office types. Mind you, they look a bit silly when you see them on their early-morning parades, waving their flags.' Coming from Mr Sukhija, this amounted to fulsome praise. He was charmingly rude about most people and most religions: he considered Christianity to be very primitive and he thought of himself as an intelligent humanist.

At six o'clock the following evening I duly made my way over the little footbridge that crossed the mangrove-fringed Ourem river to the sports ground where the rally was being held. Several thousand people were already gathered in front of the speakers' platform and late-comers were being ushered into the grounds by young men wearing orange bandannas. Many of these stewards had impressive moustaches and they looked as though they had just stepped out of a gangster film. I soon realized that I would be unable to reach the platform; in any case, it was obvious that the secretary of the RSS would be busy convening the rally.

When I read the speeches, reported without comment in the local newspaper the next day, I was thankful that I had left before they began. The principal speaker was a woman from the VHP who had achieved some notoriety earlier in the year. In April Sadhvi Rithambara had been arrested in Madhya Pradesh for making inflammatory statements. 'Mother Theresa is a magician,' she had told a crowd of supporters. She had followed this remark, more controversially, with the claim: 'Even if a single Hindu is converted, the Christians will be wiped out.' Soon after her arrest Hindu activists took to the streets and sparked off a riot. All of this took place in Indore, a town where a Catholic nun had recently been murdered, allegedly by a gang that included a BJP leader.

Ms Rithambara was in her best rabble-rousing form in Panjim. She castigated the government for failing to erect a temple on the site of the Ayodhya mosque, which had been demolished by Hindu zealots in 1992. She claimed that Independence in 1947 was simply a transfer of power from 'white British' to 'black British', which must have sounded curious, if not unintelligible, to the Goans, who had never come under British rule; and she delivered a vague diatribe against the Congress Party for allowing multinational companies to 'invade' the country. Most worrying of all, she suggested that India should take over Pakistan and Bangladesh. This, she said, would teach Mrs Benazir Bhutto a lesson for repeatedly stating that Pakistan was incomplete without Kashmir.

I asked a Jesuit priest, fleetingly met the day after the rally, whether he was worried about Hindu militancy. He motioned towards the Church of the Immaculate Conception and said: 'The self-assertion of Christians is just as terrifying for Hindus as vice versa. Up there you'll hear Catholic priests saying that all Goa should be made Christian.' On the one occasion that I did attend mass, the priest said precisely that in his sermon. Another priest I spoke to – a teacher at Rachol seminary – said that although he was disgusted by the 'rabid' views of the RSS and their fellow travellers, he shared their fears about the country's moral decline, which he attributed in part, as they did, to foreign cultural influences. 'I shudder to think what will happen in the future,' he said. 'Just look at all the Western things on Star Television. Boy meets girl and the next thing you know they're in bed together!'

Those who worry about India's moral decline often refer to the corrupting influence of satellite television, although from what little I have seen I am not convinced that programmes made by the foreign channels are more likely to deprave the young than the programmes made for local television. There is certainly more in the way of boy meets girl, and promptly beds her, on the satellite stations than on local television, but this is gentle fare compared to what goes on in Indian movies, which are shown not only on television and in cinemas but also in that unspeakably dreadful means of transport, and one which I had so far avoided on this journey, the video-bus. In popular Indian movies murder, street mayhem and torture are blended with a frothy mixture of music and romance; violence against women is commonplace and graphically depicted. I would have thought that movies such as these were far more likely to have a malign influence on impressionable minds than, say, *Baywatch* or *Inspector Morse*, both of which I saw on Star TV while in Pune. In terms of the dissemination of news and information, satellite stations like BBC World and CNN are able to keep the Indian public far better informed about sensitive issues within their country than their own television stations, which are state-owned and subject to censorship.

Ten years ago few people in India owned a television; now most homes have one, and as you drive along the city highways you will see that many slums are gently simmering beneath a haze of aerials. When I was in Pune Dr Onawale of the Deep Griha Society said she was particularly worried about the video-nasties which children watched nowadays. She mentioned, as an aside, that she knew of one woman in the slums who always panicked when it rained in case the water came through her flimsy roof and damaged the television. 'Why not buy a decent tin roof instead of the TV?' asked Dr Onawale in a plaintive voice, adding: 'But then that's the priorities of today for you.'

In her speech at the Panjim rally, Ms Rithambara made a fervent appeal 'to all the youth of this land to be proud of the nation and work tirelessly to liberate it from the clutches of foreigners and their agents'. By this she probably meant foreign companies investing in India, rather than tourists and travel agents, but it is the activities of the latter which are of greater concern to Goans, whose beaches are now visited by over 1.5 million foreigners a year. On a previous visit to Goa I had discussed the impact of tourism with members of the Jagrut Goenkaranchi Fouz (JGF), the Vigilant Goans' Army. They claimed that tourism was damaging the state, and they had plenty of evidence which seemed to support this contention. Villagers in Saligao, they said, were receiving a mere one hour's water a day as their groundwater supplies were being used to sustain the lawns of the Taj Hotel and fill the swimming-pools of several others. Many hotels, including the American-owned Ramada, had broken the state's environmental laws by building within 200 metres of the sea. Sand dunes had been bulldozed, palm groves felled, turtle nesting sites destroyed. Tourism was also seen as a cultural pollutant. Erstwhile fishermen, toddy-tappers and rice farmers had become flunkies and waiters; local girls had turned to prostitution; and some young Goans had adopted the drug-taking habits of their Western peers.

Much of what the JGF claims is true, but there are two important factors which the critics of tourism choose to ignore. The first is that tourism has helped raise the standard of living of a great many people in Goa, and especially those living along the coast. Many young people would rather be taxi-drivers, waiters and guides than peasants eking out a living on the farms and plantations where their forebears lived and worked. Critics also tend to blame the tourists for the environmental damage caused by hotels and the related infrastructure. This is unfair. It is up to the state government to ensure that businesses abide by Goa's environmental laws. Tourists cannot be blamed for either the avarice of the developers or the corruptibility of government officials.

~

The only tourists I saw in Panjim were those who stayed at the Panjim Inn, although I fancy they would have called themselves travellers. Most were middle-aged and morose – two lone women looked like the victims of broken marriages, or psychotherapy, or possibly both – and it was a great relief when four exceptionally pretty Sri Lankan students turned up for a couple of days and filled the rooms with their good-natured chatter and tremulous laughter. On most evenings I would eat out at a restaurant in town, then return to the Inn to sit with a book and a beer on the veranda, listening to the chirruping of geckos and sometimes to the sound of thunder or the hard drilling of rain on the street outside. However, on one evening I decided to call at Jesuit House, a drab building which overlooked the municipal gardens, a few minutes' walk from the Church of the Immaculate Conception. I climbed up several flights of stairs and came to a grille which separated the upper floors from those below. I rang the bell and was let in by the warden, a timorous-looking man with spectacles. He led me into a large room where an elderly man sat in a comfortable chair with his eyes closed and his hands resting on a domed stomach.

'This is Father Ubuldo,' said the warden as he nudged the priest awake.

Father Ubuldo de Sa gazed at me through thick pebble glasses, took a hearing aid from his trouser pocket, fixed it to his ear and adjusted the volume. 'What do you want?' he asked in a loud voice. 'You want to stay?'

I explained that I already had somewhere to stay and I told him briefly about the purpose of my visit to India.

'You're very welcome,' he barked. 'Where are you staying?'

'The Panjim Inn.'

'How much are you paying?'

'Three hundred rupees a night.'

Father Ubuldo was horrified at the extravagance.

There were around thirty Jesuit priests in Goa Province, eight of whom were based here. At present, said Father Ubuldo, they were all out, but he expected Father Willie d'Silva to return soon. 'You can talk to him then,' he said in his guttural accent. 'Willie's a very erudite fellow. Very intellectual. He's been to Calcutta.

He's been to Cuba. He's been to Germany. He's very fluent in German.' One of the other fathers ran a master's course in business administration, and Father Ubuldo was in charge of spiritual work. He gave sermons in churches and schools, took mass for the nuns at the nearby convent and heard confessions. 'This morning,' he said, 'five priests from here – I was one of them – heard the confessions of 1,000 boys, 200 each. It took four hours. Nine o'clock to one o'clock.'

He glanced over his shoulder towards a large table which had been set for dinner. 'You will stay for dinner?' he asked.

I explained that I had already eaten.

'Then come another night. Are you Catholic?'

'No,' I replied. 'Anglican.'

'You don't have confession.'

'No.'

'So what do you do to prepare yourself?'

After some thought I said that Protestants simply prayed direct to God for forgiveness if and when they felt inclined. I asked him whether he thought people always told the truth at confession.

'And why not?'

'Perhaps they're too ashamed of their sins.'

'If someone comes to confession, I am inclined to believe that they will tell the truth,' replied the priest. 'And we are not judges. If a man comes and says that he masturbates every day: what to do? I don't' – he leaned forward in his chair, his eyes bulging in mock horror. 'No, we show tranquillity. If a man says he's murdered his wife, I don't' – and he repeated his gesture of surprise. 'It's not as though we then say to the confessor, "Oh, sir, you told me terrible sins!" You see, we have to ask the confessor for permission to speak.'

'And if a man tells you that he has murdered his wife, you wouldn't tell the police?'

'Of course not,' he replied. 'Are you married?'

'Yes.'

'What does your wife do?'

I told him.

'How big is your house?'

'Quite large.'

'Two bedrooms?'

'Four.'

'What do you eat for breakfast? Bacon? Ham? Porridge? Toast?'

I laughed, but before I was able to reply Father Ubuldo had continued his interrogation. 'And for lunch every day you eat steak?'

'No,' I said. 'Too expensive.'

Father Ubuldo was very deaf, even with his hearing aid, and I had begun to adopt the same staccato mode of speech as the priest himself, stripping the language down to its bare essentials.

'How much?' he asked. 'How much is good steak?'

'Five pounds a pound,' I replied.

Father Ubuldo was fascinated by numbers and money and brand names. He wanted to know how much nurses, doctors and priests earned in England, and the price of foodstuffs and hotels. He was particularly impressed by the fact that Anglican vicars earned over £10,000 a year. 'Here,' he said, 'a priest gets 500 rupees a month. Some places only 300 rupees.' I could see now why he was so shocked that I was paying that much a night at the Panjim Inn. 'But he gets extras too,' added the priest. 'He'll get 30 rupees for a mass, and food and lodging are free. Laundry too.'

The warden returned with some tea and biscuits.

'Drink,' insisted Father Ubuldo, pointing to my cup. 'In 1962 things were very cheap here. You could get a litre of scotch for 11 rupees. Can you imagine?' He shook his head wistfully at the memory. 'Indian whisky does not come up to standard of Johnny Walker. Or Black Label. Or Red Label. Or Dimple. You agree?'

Father Ubuldo had joined the Society of Jesus as a young man, attracted to the order by the life and example of St Francis Xavier. 'I took a great liking to him as a boy,' he explained. 'He came from an intellectual family and he studied at the Sorbonne in Paris. He was a professor – MA, first-class.' Father Ubuldo spoke of the saint's compassion and of how he ministered to the sick and dying on a long boat journey from Portugal to India. He told me about his support for St Paul's seminary in Old Goa, which in those days had 3,000 students from across the Eastern world, and about St Francis's visits to the Paravas and his work in Japan. 'During his stay in India, he converted 400,000 people,' reflected Father Ubuldo. 'At least, that's what they say.' In fact, Father Cosme had suggested that St Francis converted no more than 15,000 people and it is clear from the letters that he wrote to his superior, Ignatius Loyola, that he became disheartened by the difficulties of converting Hindus. The Japanese were far more receptive to his message.

What happened to St Francis after his death is almost as remarkable as the events of his life. It is a story taught to every Christian child in Goa, and it evidently had a profound effect on the young Ubuldo. St Francis had made it known during his travels that he wished his bones to be returned to Goa after his death. He died on 3 December 1552, and his companions immediately buried him in a coffin which they filled with quicklime. They expected the quicklime to dissolve the flesh and leave the bones. Ten weeks later they exhumed the body to discover that it was as fresh as when it was buried. 'It was incorrupt,' explained Father Ubuldo, 'and when they accidentally cut the flesh with a spade, blood came out.' It took two years to bring the body back to India – it was briefly buried again in the Moluccas – and it was received with great pomp when it was handed over to the Jesuits in Old Goa. The vicar-general stuck his finger through a hole in the side of the abdomen and said he could feel intestines; the thighs and torso were still fleshy.

The Catholic obsession with relics led to the body being

vandalized, both by the authorities and by individual pilgrims. In 1614 the lower right arm was chopped off and sent to Rome, where it is preserved in a reliquary in the Church of Gesù. Three years later the rest of the arm and the shoulder were cut off, divided into three and dispatched to the Jesuit colleges in the Moluccas, Cochin and Macau. In 1620 the intestines were removed and sent to various places, including Japan. The coffin was opened for public kissing on feast days and whenever visitors of importance came to Goa; bits and pieces of the saint were periodically pilfered. A Portuguese woman bit off his toe, which, according to one source, remains to this day in the possession of her family in Lisbon. However, Graham Greene wrote in the *Illustrated Weekly of India* in March 1964 that he saw a toe – perhaps it was a different one – when he visited the relics in the early 1960s: 'It seemed a grim, apocalyptic place, Old Goa, with the shrinking body of St Francis Xavier in the great church of Bom Jesu, built in 1594, the toe that a lady bit off preserved in the reliquary, and the silver crucifix on his tomb twisted awry by a Catholic thief a week before and other dubious portions preserved in bottles of spirit, which reminded me of those you see in the windows of Chinese in Kuala Lumpur advertising cures for piles.'

In the latter years of the eighteenth century there were claims that the Jesuits had replaced St Francis's body with that of a dead canon, and in order to scotch the rumours a public exposition was held in 1782. Since then there have been a further fifteen solemn expositions, the most recent in 1994. Father Ubuldo attended an exposition when pilgrims were still allowed to kiss the corpse. 'His hand was very soft,' he mused, 'but his body had begun to disintegrate and his face was just dried skin. Yes, I have been to four expositions.' He seemed to recall them as one would long and interesting journeys. 'And I have been to England, twice,' he continued. 'And to Spain, America, Germany, Italy, yes, I've been all over . . .'

At this point Father Willie d'Silva, a tall, pale-skinned, wavy-haired man of exceptional good looks, came into the room. He was in a hurry as he had a night bus to catch, but he sat down to chat with us for twenty minutes or so. A few days later the principal of the Jesuit college in Mangalore asked me if I had met him. When I told him that I had, he simply said, 'He's a genius, of course.'

Father Willie was a lecturer at Panjim University. He had recently completed the translation of the Bible into Kanarese and he had carried out sociological research on a broad range of issues, including the practice of dowry, expatriate Christian cultures in the Middle East, the status of the untouchables in India and religious conflict. He was a great iconoclast, and his views on the institution of the Church must make the Catholic hierarchy shudder. He estimated that between 10,000 and 15,000 Catholics out of the half million in Goa had deserted the Church to join charismatic groups like the Assembly of God and the New Life Fellowship. I asked him whether he was concerned about this.

'No,' he said cheerfully. 'It doesn't worry me in the least. I see it as a blessing, and not a blessing in disguise. The institutionalization of the Church has led to an accumulation of authority and power. By joining the charismatics, people are reacting against the hierarchical system and all the nonsense that entails.'

Before he rushed off, Father Willie mentioned that there was also a charismatic movement within the Catholic Church and that a group met here, at Jesuit House, on Friday evenings. He suggested I attend one of their meetings. I said I would, but added that I was wary of being drawn into emotional forms of worship.

'I understand that,' he said, nodding. 'I like my own personal space too.'

I asked whether he attended these charismatic meetings.

'No,' he replied, grimacing. 'I don't need to. My room's next door and I hear everything that's going on.'

Father Willie departed and I got up to leave.

'I'm not being inquisitive,' said Father Ubuldo, 'but do you carry much money?'

'No.'

'Are you financially troubled?'

'No. I just leave my money at the hotel.'

'What!' he exclaimed, leaning forward and peering at me as though I were half-crazed. 'How do you know they don't ransack your room when you're out? You'd better stay here with us. I'll only charge you 60 rupees – all in, board and food.'

I thanked him for his kind offer and he invited me to come for dinner after the charismatic meeting on Friday.

~

I would have liked to visit Old Goa, five miles upstream from Panjim, some time between its desertion in the eighteenth century and its recent restitution under the auspices of the Archaeological Survey of India. The Survey's conservation programme has ensured the survival of what remains of Old Goa, but it has robbed the ruined city of its mystery. The creepers and encroaching jungle, the cobwebs and peeling stucco have been cleared away and with them have gone the ghosts which wandered the abandoned streets of a city whose splendour once rivalled that of Rome and Lisbon. When Richard Burton, soldier, explorer and translator of the *Kama Sutra*, visited Old Goa in 1850 he observed that the few people who lived in the deserted city were as 'sepulchral looking as the spectacle around them'. Just over a hundred years later Evelyn Waugh spent Christmas in Goa and attended midnight mass at the cathedral. 'It was a moving occasion,' he wrote in a letter to his family, 'the great building crowded to suffocation with pilgrims from all over India & Ceylon. No mistletoe or holly or yule logs or Teutonic nonsense. Simple oriental fervour instead.' A little later, again on a Christmas visit, Graham Greene was struck by the desolation and silence of Old Goa, although he came across an ill-attended service in the cathedral: 'There was a congregation of perhaps a dozen people sitting in a gloom that the candles could not penetrate, while a choir of old canons sang the mass – elongated, emaciated El Greco figures in dingy scarlet dickies, half starved on 30 rupees a month, and up in the invisible roofs the bats twittered as loudly as their voices. I had a sense that I was attending one of the last ceremonies of Christianity. This might well be St Peter's 300 years hence, if the door on the world is not kept open . . .' (*Illustrated Weekly of India*, March 1964).

Quem viu Goa, excusa de ver Lisboa. He who has seen Goa, went the old Portuguese proverb, need not see Lisbon. By the time St Francis arrived, Old Goa was already a magnificent city, blessed with paved streets, numerous churches, salubrious suburbs, several colleges and a thriving port and commercial centre. By the time his corpse returned, Roma do Oriente, as it was known, had a resident population of around 200,000 and passing travellers were dazzled by its sophistication and splendour. In the bazars, and along the riverside wharfs, they would rub shoulders with German traders, Chinese porcelain-sellers, Portuguese sailors, pearl-dealers from the Arabian Gulf, traders from the neighbouring Vijayanagar empire, priests and nuns of every conceivable religious order, slaves from Africa and courtesans of every colour. Old Goa had the feel and appearance of a city which would last for ever, and yet its greatness was short-lived, even though its death throes were more attenuated than its birth pangs. The Dutch blockaded Old Goa twice in the early seventeenth century; they never conquered the Portuguese enclave, but their aggression weakened it. In 1635, shortly before the second blockade, Old Goa was struck by an epidemic which killed so many of its inhabitants that the Portuguese recruited new settlers from the prisons of Lisbon. Further outbreaks of disease, and especially cholera, reduced the population, which fell from 20,000 in 1695 to under 2,000 by 1775. The seat of government was moved, initially to Margao in south Goa and then to Panjim.

Of the forty-odd churches whose bells rang out to celebrate the arrival of St Francis's corpse, only a handful survive. The Chapel of Our Lady of the Rosary is beautifully sited on Holy Hill, its Manueline façade looking out over the sluggish Mandovi. Behind it, built a year after St Francis's arrival, is the Royal Chapel of St Anthony and, beyond, the ruined tower of St Augustine pokes above the trees like an arthritic finger admonishing the sky. If you walk up to these buildings you will probably have them to yourself, for most visitors spend their time in and around the two great churches which were built at the heart of the city in the latter years of the sixteenth century. There are four reasons for their popularity with pilgrims and tourists. First, St Francis's extravagantly decorated shrine is situated in one of the side chapels of the basilica of Bom Jesu; second, the tearooms and toilets are clustered about the church; third, there is rather a good museum attached to Bom Jesu; fourth, Bom Jesu and See Cathedral are two of the world's great religious buildings. The former's façade is Renaissance baroque; the latter, which is said to be the largest church in Asia, is pure Renaissance.

In the bookstall below the museum you can purchase cartoon pamphlets on the lives of Moses, St Francis and various saints. For sale, too, are posters and cards in which Christ looks like Kevin Costner and hideous lime-green statuettes of St Francis. There are also several serious publications on offer, but most present a sanitized history and say little about the Inquisition, which was established in Old Goa in 1560. To be a dissenting Christian, or even a questioning one, was far more dangerous than belonging to another religion. Certainly, the Hindus of the Old Conquests were shoddily treated, but they were never subjected to the terrors of the Inquisition. Between 1561 and 1774 over 16,000 people were tried in the Palace of the Inquisition, which occupied the ground to the south-east of the cathedral. Here, as in Europe, the Inquisition was an ecclesiastical court founded to weed out heretics, and the Dominicans, the Franciscans and the Jesuits all played a part in its appalling history. Even

St Francis was a supporter. In a letter to the King of Portugal he advocated that the Inquisition be established in India 'to protect the Christian life of those who have been baptized with the Faith'. Those convicted of heresy were subjected to punishments which ranged from the confiscation of property to flagellation and death. In Old Goa the bell would ring to celebrate the *auto-da-fé* – the act of faith – when punishments were read out after mass and those sentenced to death were burned at the stake.

There were still a few priests in Old Goa, and plenty of young nuns at the Mater Dei Institute, but after a few hours I was eager to return to Panjim. By now it was late afternoon and my driver suggested that before returning we should visit a nearby village. Why? I asked. 'One more church,' he replied grimly.

A group of boys were playing football in front of the church at Carambolim and they waved and shouted, 'Welcome,' and 'Hello, sir,' as I climbed up the steps from the road. An elderly man appeared at the door of the low building adjoining the church and waved me towards him. Father Miguel Braganza said in halting English that he would like to show me around. He had a small gold cross pinned to the pocket of his checked shirt and he was wearing grey trousers and sandals. 'I'm an old man,' he said as he shuffled along the gloomy corridors which led from his living quarters to a door at the front of the nave. He apologized for not speaking better English and explained that he had trained at Rachol seminary in Portuguese, in which he was fluent.

He said that the church had been built around 1552. It was dedicated to John the Baptist and a fine gilded baroque altarpiece was illustrated with scenes from his life. One panel depicted the baptism of Jesus in the river Jordan; another showed John's execution. There was also a study of Herod's banquet with John's head on a platter beside a plate of roast chicken legs. Father Miguel crossed himself in front of the altar, then led me to his study.

The Jesuits had come to the village soon after their arrival in

Goa, he explained, and they converted many of the Hindus. The first Goan to be ordained as a priest served here and at one time the parish was rich. Father Miguel said his congregation was small, numbering perhaps 1,200, and that many Christians had reverted to Hinduism around a hundred years ago. Now there were three Hindus to every Christian but the two communities lived peacefully together. Unfortunately, the people were poor and they couldn't contribute much to the church, which was badly run down. Bishop's House did not give much either, and although the Holy See in Rome offered money for the preservation of historic buildings such as this one, some sort of bureaucratic muddle had prevented Carambolim from benefiting. 'We need 100,000 rupees,' said Father Miguel with a despondent shrug. When we walked around the front of the church to inspect the graveyard, the children picked up their football and raced towards the priest shouting, 'Father! Father! Hello, Father!' The priest was clearly delighted by their friendliness. He said they were good boys and they had promised to help him clear the thick grass which choked the laterite steps leading up to the church.

When I first came to India I shared a taxi with a businessman, a Keralite, who claimed that you could always judge the nature of a city or town by studying the character of its taxi-drivers. In Bombay, he said, they were pushy and unpredictable; in Delhi, they were rude and unfriendly. Roughly speaking, I have found this to be true, and in Panjim the taxi-drivers seemed to have much in common with their admirable little town: they were gracious and mild-mannered. No need to hail a taxi on the streets either: simply dial Panjim 228989 and a driver opposite the Hotel Mandovi would answer the phone – it was attached to a wooden shack selling *paan* and cigarettes – and pick you up a few minutes later.

Afternoons in Goa are reserved for siesta and a poor time to visit priests, or for that matter anybody else, so after lunch I often used to hire a taxi and drive around the villages of the Old Conquests. On one memorable afternoon I headed south of Panjim in the company of Robert, a quietly spoken Catholic. As we passed through the village of Bambolim he told me that its priest had recently died; there had been no replacement, and he was unsure whether there would be one. He said that Christians here celebrated Hindu festivals like Diwali as vigorously as they did Christmas, and that the Hindus celebrated the Christian festivals with as much fervour as they did their own. Further south we came to a pretty little village some distance off the main road. There were several old Portuguese villas with beautifully carved wooden windows and ornate verandas, and many smaller houses built of laterite blocks, each with its own fruitful garden. The church was a modest structure by Goa's standards and on its closed doors was pinned a notice which announced an extraordinary general meeting to discuss whether Malaquias Meneses should be allowed to grow cashew trees on an uncultivated plot of land.

The road was no more than the width of a bullock cart and beyond the village it snaked through an exquisite landscape in which every square inch seemed to contribute to the welfare of the country people. In some fields the rice had already been harvested; in others it had yet to ripen and was a brilliant green, like the breast feathers of the bee-eaters which gathered around the telegraph poles, transforming their wires into brilliantly coloured musical scores. The irrigation ditches were seamed with coconut trees and on higher ground there were plantations of areca palm and cashew. Groups of women were winnowing rice, and there were men threshing in the fields and boys urging plodding water buffalo along the country paths. Young children in white shirts and blue shorts were making their way home from school and some shouted and waved as we passed. We skirted around a small lake whose shallows were spiked with lotus and lilies and within the space of no more than a mile we saw four wayside shrines. A simple white cross with a red heart was garlanded with marigolds. A larger shrine, tiled blue like a public convenience, was more profusely decorated with a painting of Jesus, jars of fresh flowers and burned-out candles.

All of a sudden we came upon a monumental baroque church which towered above a broad bowl of paddyland. There was a football pitch in front of the church, a walled graveyard to the side and a huge tree in whose shade we parked. I tried the large wooden door at the front and a smaller one at the side. Both were locked. A metal plaque was hung from a porch spattered with cow dung and bird droppings. Pocked with rust, it had the following words roughly written in yellow paint:

Church of St Anna – 1695
(Founded in 1577).
Declared National Monument
(on 31–3–1931 Portuguese Portaria No. 1360).
Masterpiece of Indian Baroque Architecture.
This cultural inheritance is you.
Revere and Rejoice.

St Anna was slowly rotting away. Lattice screens hung from the windows like bits of driftwood and the great five-storey towers which flanked the façade were crenellated through neglect rather than design. Bushes sprouted from cracks and sills and the once white stucco was crumbling away. At one time, before plague wiped out most of the inhabitants of the district, the church had 19,000 parishioners. Today there were fewer than 300.

The following day I travelled further south to the market town of Margao, then on to the seminary at Rachol, where in 1662 Father Thomas Stevens, an English priest, published the first translation of the Bible in an Asian language, in this case Konkani. At Sancoale I met the sisters of the Holy Family of Nazareth and they gave me a Coca-Cola at a table which was covered with postcards of the Pope, the Virgin Mary and other heroes of the faith. Their garden was beautifully tended and full of red hibiscus and other colourful shrubs, yet their sitting-room, with its high-backed chairs primly arranged around a small table, was decorated with vases of plastic flowers. The sisters had five schools in Goa, including one with 700 pupils in Sancoale itself. Many of the children were Hindus and the school celebrated Holi and Diwali as well as Easter and Christmas. The sisters also worked with prostitutes in the slums of Vasco da Gama, the main port of Goa. The prostitutes, they said, earned more in a day than most women could in a month, yet those who had children still sent them out on the streets to beg. The sisters were looking after ten of the children – they boarded at the school – and intended to find them work once they had finished their studies.

On another afternoon we headed across the Mandovi, then turned west and travelled through a string of somnolent villages. Two young men in frayed jeans were lying in the porch of Our Lady of the Rock of France in Britona. They said the priest was asleep and invited me to join them for a smoke. Outside the baroque church in the next village, Pomburpu, we came across a twig-limbed girl who said she was hoping a bus would come by. It seemed unlikely, so we offered her a lift. She was cheerful and self-possessed, although she was a long way from home: she had been dispatched to Goa from Bihar, on the other side of India, to work as a housemaid. We briefly stopped at a church in the next village: it was closed, like all the others, but there was a drunk in the porch and two old ladies in black were laying flowers beside a fresh grave. We passed through many other villages, and in my memory they all look similar, each with its grand whitewashed church, and beside the church a football pitch and a graveyard, and sometimes a free-standing pulpit and a laterite dais where plays are performed at Christmas. Beyond the church lies a patchwork of paddies and palms, their browns and greens enlivened by splashes of brighter colour: the orange blossom of a flame-of-the-forest tree; a woman in a red sari, her hips swinging as she walks by a hayrick; a kingfisher, a chip of turquoise flashing across a muddy stream. In my imagination, this is what paradise looks like.

Imagining paradise is easy enough. Getting there is an entirely different matter, and in the Christian view it requires the aspirant to do more than turn up at church on Easter day, refrain from adultery and be kind to animals and children. It requires faith, penitence and prayer. All forms of worship involve the latter, which takes a myriad of forms, from the stupendous formality of a sung Eucharist or a requiem mass, involving hundreds or even thousands of people, to the simplicity of one person offering up a few words, perhaps to a wayside shrine or while going about his daily business. St Augustine defined prayer as the 'raising of one's mind and heart to God, or the requesting of good things from God'. This is as good a description of prayer as I have found, but I am also rather taken by St Luke's introduction to the parable of the importunate widow: 'And he spake a parable unto them to this end, that men ought always to pray and not to faint' (18:1). On my last day in Goa I witnessed a religious event where the participants were doing something which appeared to be a good deal closer to fainting than praying. The reason I ended up on Mount Batim was simple: I had been told, at the charismatic meeting at Jesuit House, that the Blessed Virgin Mary would be appearing there between two thirty and three o'clock in the afternoon.

I had gone to the charismatic meeting, which was held in the library at Jesuit House, with some trepidation. I took a seat near the door in case I felt the need to retreat and several people came across to introduce themselves and suggest I join them. A young man, serious and simian in appearance, came in with a suitcase from which he produced the vestments of the priesthood, which he proceeded to don while a woman explained that he had kindly offered to take mass. By the time the priest had prepared himself, and arranged the wine and bread on the table, over fifty people had arrived. There was a disproportionate number of attractive, well-dressed young women, most of whom appeared to be single, but there were also several people who were much older. The service began with three short hymns, which were lustily sung in the gospel style to the music of a guitar. I was somewhat unnerved to find suddenly at my side a strange, fidgety little man who was always accosting me in the street and demanding foreign stamps. Much to my relief, he left before the first bout of talking in tongues. This was initiated by a respectable-looking fellow with a beard and glasses. He began by saying a few prayers such as 'Oh, Holy name of Jesus' and 'Holy Spirit, fill our hearts'. At the end of each prayer or exhortation, the rest of the gathering would shout, 'Amen!' or 'Hallelujah!' Gradually the prayers and responses became more rapid and before long people were ululating incomprehensibly, their eyes closed and their hands raised high above their heads. This lasted no more than two or three minutes and at a signal came to a sudden halt. I noticed that the priest did not join in. Perhaps he was contemplating his sermon, which was easily the most enlightening and thought-provoking I had so far heard in India. The sermon was followed by mass and a few more hymns, during one of which people began to sing in tongues; this sounded even more bizarre than talking in tongues. Finally, a shy woman in a black skirt and silver shirt stood up and delivered her testimony. Apparently she had had a miscarriage the previous year and her husband had left her. Since finding God, however, her husband had returned and she had come first in some exams. Everyone applauded.

As I was leaving the library a man with a carefully groomed beard and suede-brown eyes tapped me on the shoulder and told me that every second Saturday of the month the Virgin Mary appeared on Mount Batim. He gave me directions how to get there and said as a passing comment, 'It's very controversial.'

Someone else came up to me and asked me if it was true that the King of England was head of the Anglican Church.

Much as I had enjoyed the service, and especially the sermon, I felt in need of a stiff drink before joining Father Ubuldo for dinner. I downed a couple of neat vodkas in a nearby bar, then made my way back to Jesuit House, where I was immediately offered a glass of *feni*. Over dinner – soup, fried kingfish, vegetable curry, dahl, rice – we talked about the price of motorcars and the longevity of priests. Father Ubuldo said that in 1962, the year of Goa's independence, you could buy a Mercedes Benz in Panjim for 14,000 rupees, or around £500. He did not drive a car now, but in the garage behind Jesuit House he kept a 500cc BMW motorbike. 'Now I can only see immediately in front of me,' he said. 'I've got tunnel vision, so I don't drive around the countryside. I only drive in town.' He had had one operation for cataracts and another for a spinal problem. He said the hospital was excellent: it cost him 600 rupees for ten days, and this included the price of the operation, a room with attached toilet and three meals a day.

'I'm now seventy-nine and approaching my death,' he said with relish. 'In this house, in twelve years, I have seen five deaths. Three of old age – eighty-seven, eighty-two, seventy-eight. Two by drowning.' Curiously, the two priests who drowned were both German and both young; he said that one of them even had a diploma in swimming.

By now I was quite used to Father Ubuldo's interest in the price of things, but when he said, 'How much is orange peel in your country?' I presumed I'd misheard.

'How much is what?'

'Orange peel,' he repeated. 'I'm a first-class cook. I can get everything here to make a Christmas cake except orange peel. I've got cherries, brandy, wine, liqueurs, almonds, raisins . . . but no good orange peel. Can you send me half a kilo?'

I said I would. 'But what about the customs?'

'Just write on the envelope: "Orange peel. Handle with care. Perishables." '

A couple of months later I sent Father Ubuldo some orange peel. I hope it arrived in time for Christmas. I hope, too, that he is still riding his big motorbike and delighting all who come across him with his idiosyncratic charm.

I ate an early lunch on Saturday and took a taxi to Mount Batim, which lay midway between Pilar seminary and St Anna's church. We were among the first to arrive, so the taxi-driver and I sat and waited in a small tea-shack at the foot of the path which led up to the shrine where the Virgin Mary was said to appear. A group of young girls, their arms charged with garlands of fresh flowers, offered us these and candles; we declined and they returned to the roadside to await the pilgrims. We bought some fizzy drinks from a large, blousy female who ran the tea-shack and she produced an album of photographs, which she held open for our inspection. Most looked like out-of-focus snaps of a swinging light bulb, taken with a very poor camera on a long exposure. What was it? I asked. She said it was the Virgin Mary. She then told me that I ought to go to Potta, a Christian retreat in Kerala about which I had already heard a great deal. Many miracles took place there, she said: cripples were made to walk, cancer victims were cured and so forth. I replied that I intended to spend a day there. 'No,' she said admonishingly, wagging a podgy finger, 'you go for five days. They lock you in, you can't leave before the end.' She added, after eyeing me closely, 'No drinking alcohol. No smoking cigarettes either.'

A small, cylindrical woman in her late fifties or early sixties came to stand in the shade outside the shack. She was dressed in black, she carried a black handbag and her black hair looked as though it had been recently permed and dyed. She asked me, diffidently, where I came from, and then she explained that the Virgin Mary was first seen at Mount Batim on 24 September 1994, and that she communicated every day with a nine-year-old boy from Margao called Martin. He would be arriving soon and she suggested I talk to him. 'Our Lady says the end is very near,' she said. 'That is why terrible things are happening in the world.' She shuffled around in her black court shoes, as though they were too tight, then said: 'Our Lady wants us to say the rosary three times a day. The bishops disapprove of this. They say she doesn't appear here.'

'But you've seen her?' I asked.

'Yes, but not every time. Once I saw her with a crucifix and a horse. Other times just as herself – always in front of the sun.'

'And do you think I'll see her?' I asked.

'She's only seen by people in a state of grace,' she replied firmly.

The girls selling garlands began to babble excitedly and two battered buses ground around the corner and came to a halt. Their occupants remained inside for several minutes and we could hear the muffled sound of prayer. Then they descended and we set out along the footpath. Had we climbed the hill at a brisk pace we would have arrived at our destination in a quarter of an hour. However, we stopped for prayers a dozen times and it took us almost an hour to reach the derelict church on the summit of the hill. When we were some way along the path a man handed me a leaflet suggesting daily prayers for the souls in purgatory. 'The end is coming very soon,' he said in a casual, conversational way, much as he might have commented on the weather or the late arrival of a bus. Shortly before we reached the church the man who had alerted me to this event at Jesuit House – he was a banker from Panjim – appeared at my side, cheery and out of breath. 'I don't know exactly what'll happen,' he said, 'but it might be something incredible. Remember to look up at the sun!'

In front of the church, on a broad expanse of grazed grass, was a wooden cross. When all those with garlands and candles had slung them and lit them, the banker divided the gathering into two groups and instructed each on the manner in which it should respond to the prayers. Throughout the afternoon he stood beside a small boy dressed in black. This was Martin. Beside Martin there was a girl in her early teens, also dressed in black, and a corpulent nun with a frog-like face, dressed in regulation battledress.

The prayers were led by a thin, grey-haired gentleman with a good clear voice. Each of the ten commandments was followed by responses which included Hail Marys, the Lord's Prayer and the Gloria Patri. By the end of the afternoon I knew the Hail Mary by heart, even though I had never heard it before:

Hail, Mary, full of grace,
the Lord is with thee.
Blessed art thou among women,
and blessed is the fruit of thy womb, Jesus.
Holy Mary, mother of God,
pray for us sinners,
now and at the hour of our death.

Endlessly repeated, prayer becomes incantation, robbing the words of meaning but imbuing them with a spell-like quality. After a while many of the pilgrims, and especially the women, were moaning their Hail Marys; one who knelt beside Martin had tears streaming down her cheeks and her voice rose and fell in swoops of ecstasy. After three-quarters of an hour of this, the banker said something to a woman nearby and she began to move among the crowd. 'Look up at the sun at ten to three,' she said in a confidential tone as she passed me. At ten to three the banker shouted: 'Look up at the sun: there is Our Lady arrayed in red and blue.'

I had been told that the Virgin Mary would appear for only a few minutes. It seemed that she stayed for well over an hour, for when I left at four o'clock everyone was still staring up at the sun, moaning, crying, mumbling and speaking in tongues, with the exception of a few people who did not appear to be touched by the experience. During the course of the revelation – if that is what it was – I detached myself from the main body of pilgrims and went over to the church. It was empty, except for two statues of St Simon and St Jude, and it was blissfully cool. My taxi-driver retreated to the shade beside the church and furtively lit a cigarette. I went out to join him, and we in turn were joined by an elderly woman and two young men.

'Have you seen Our Lady?' inquired the woman.

'No,' I replied, 'I haven't.'

'Well, look up at the sun,' she said sharply.

'I already have,' I said. Which was true, although I had done so fleetingly. It struck me as sheer lunacy that there were people here who had been staring at the sun continuously for what must have felt, to their weeping eyes, like an eternity.

'Yes,' continued the woman, squinting at the sun, 'the sun's blue inside, red outside. It's spinning round.'

'You think that's the Virgin Mary?' I asked.

'No,' she replied.

The two young men hadn't seen her either, and they asked me what I thought. I said that the whole thing appeared to be orchestrated by the banker and one or two others, and that I thought we were witnessing mass hysteria. 'If you stare at the sun for long enough,' I suggested, 'then you'll see anything you want.'

I had intended to wait till the end and talk to the boy about his daily meetings with the Virgin Mary, but I found the spectacle increasingly unnerving and the driver and I made our way back down the hill. The five girls who had been selling garlands asked if they could ride to Panjim with us. They were all small and pretty and none of them looked more than fifteen. In fact, two of them were in their early twenties, were married to fishermen and had two children each. One of the older girls spoke good English. This was the first time they had been out here, she said, and they were very satisfied with the business they had done. Next month they would return with more garlands and candles; this was undoubtedly a seller's market.

'Did you see the Virgin?' I asked.

No, she replied, they had stayed down by the road.

'So you don't believe it,' I ventured.

'Yes, I do,' she said.

'But you've never seen her,' I protested.

'No,' she agreed, 'but it is true that she comes.'

I simply could not accept that a good Catholic girl would not bother to walk half a mile to see the Virgin Mary – unless, of course, she thought the whole thing was nonsense. 'Maybe you think it's safer to say that you think she appears,' I said.

She digested this with a furrowed brow before translating what I had said for the benefit of the other girls, who peered hard at me, as though uncertain what to make of my scepticism. Then she shrugged and gave me what I took to be a mischievous smile.

CHAPTER 5

India's Coral Strand

For many years I had wanted to visit Mangalore. I had good Catholic friends whose parents came from there, and they had always spoken highly of it, although they themselves had been brought up in Calcutta. The guidebooks are also kind about Mangalore; they praise its outlook and architecture, its busy port and its venerable history. Six hundred years ago the city conducted a prosperous trade in ginger and pepper with the Persians and the Arabs; it was fought over by the Portuguese and local princes, captured by the British, vigorously and unsuccessfully defended against Tipu Sultan, then retaken towards the end of the eighteenth century. Around a fifth of its half a million inhabitants are Christians, many being descendants of the Catholics who fled the Inquisition in Goa. The refugees were welcomed in Mangalore, as they possessed important skills in the field of growing and processing coconuts. My guidebook, which I perused while I waited for the night bus, described St Aloysius College chapel as the 'Sistine Chapel of south India'; a further claim to fame was that Mangalore produced Ganesh *bidis*, a local type of cigarette. From my vantage point 350 miles north – a noisy bus park in Panjim's outskirts – Mangalore seemed to have an alluring charm and I contemplated the ten-hour journey with rather more enthusiasm than I would have, say, a similar journey to some unprepossessing industrial settlement in Uttar Pradesh.

The bus was only a quarter full when we left Panjim, but by

the time we crossed the state border with Karnataka three hours later all the seats were taken. The journey to the border was a tortuous one: we headed inland a good distance, into the New Conquests where churches were few and Hindu temples many, then curled back to Margao, the largest town in south Goa, before taking the coast road to Mangalore. Soon after we left Panjim I was joined by a Trinidadian student who had a seat at the front of the bus. He explained that he was studying medicine at a college in a small town to the north of Mangalore. Over half his fellow students were foreigners: it was cheaper to come here than to study medicine in Europe, the United States or for that matter in many much poorer countries. The course was satisfactory, but he looked forward to finishing his studies and returning home. I asked him whether he had made many Indian friends. He shrugged. 'Some, yes, but they can be very racist, the Indians.' He added that if he, an Indian and I were to go into a shop together, I would probably be served first, the Indian second and he last. He pointed out that he was far lighter-skinned than most southern Indians and he wondered if I was surprised that he should find himself discriminated against on the grounds of colour. I said I was not; Indians, after all, discriminate against one another on the grounds of colour and to see this you only have to read the matrimonial columns in the newspapers. Take, for example, the advertisements from that day's *Herald*, published in Panjim. 'Alliance invited for Mangalorean RC girl, fair, beautiful' began one. Fair means pale-skinned. Another spinster, described as 'intelligent, fair, beautiful', was seeking a 'smart, tall, handsome, well-qualified/settled Bombay-based bachelor with sober habits and respectable Mangalorean RC family'. Colour, caste and creed are the defining factors of eligibility, among Christians as well as Hindus. The Trinidadian and I chatted on for a while, then he returned to his seat and through the open window I watched the moist, scent-laden world go by. A full moon cast a pale light across the Western Ghats, which reared in jagged humps to our left, while to our right the limpid sea stretched into the distance like a vast sheet of black polythene. Sleep was out of the question: the monsoon rains had left the road rutted and pocked; in places it had been washed away altogether and our progress was reduced to a snail's-pace judder.

We reached Karwar, the most northerly town in Karnataka, around midnight. In the main square several hundred people were watching a play about the goddess Durga under an awning slung with glittering baubles and fairy lights. Our bus pulled up beside three others and we joined their travellers in a cavernous restaurant whose glossy blue-green walls were starkly illuminated by fluorescent lights. Had I not been to Karwar in the daytime on a previous visit, I would have thought, on this night's viewing, that it was no more remarkable, nor any less chaotic, than a thousand other small towns in India which elude the attentions of tourists and guidebooks. In fact, it is a very pleasant little place with broad, tree-lined streets and a fine harbour. It is flanked by magnificent beaches, far more beautiful than most of those in Goa, and untouched by tourist development. This may not last long: the port is being developed as a naval base, a nuclear power plant is being constructed in the hills behind the town, and well before the end of this century it will be linked to Bombay and Goa to the north, and to Mangalore to the south, by the Konkan railway, whose construction was already nearing completion in the states of Karnataka and Maharashtra.

When I returned to the bus I found my seat occupied by a fierce-eyed young man whose parents, when the time comes, will probably describe him in the matrimonial columns as 'Handsome Brahmin Class I Engineer belonging to respectable, well-connected family in Mangalore'. I learned this and other details about his caste and occupation soon after I ejected him from my seat, which he had coveted on the perfectly reasonable grounds that it was more comfortable than his, which was perched on a wheel arch. He had been to visit his father at the Kaiga nuclear power station and was now returning to college in Mangalore. 'You are liking my English, my Indian-style English?' he jabbered as we left Karwar. He advised me to return to Karwar in a few years' time. He said it would be unrecognizable, what with the new naval base and the railway. He had heard about the opposition to the Konkan railway in Goa and he disapproved of it. He insisted on smoking, despite the fact that smoking was prohibited on the bus, and he announced in a confident voice that when he qualified as an engineer he would visit a great many countries.

'You mean, to find work?' I asked.

'No, for eating,' he replied in his rapid English. 'I am always interesting myself in food. I am hoping to eat all the different foods in the world.'

The road in Karnataka was in better repair than it had been in Goa and I eventually fell into a queasy sleep. We arrived in Mangalore as dawn was breaking; I checked into a large businessman's hotel, assassinated three cockroaches in the bathroom and went to bed. It may have been the sound of pneumatic drills in the street outside which woke me a couple of hours later, or perhaps it was the intense humidity. I ate *idli sambar*, a spicy south Indian breakfast, then headed off in search of Bishop's House. It was less than ten minutes' walk from the hotel, but by the time I arrived my silk shirt was streaked black with sweat. I was led into a large office where I was greeted coolly by a young priest in a cassock. He listened while I explained that I wished to meet members of the Catholic community in Mangalore, then inquired how long I intended to stay.

A few days, I replied.

'Are you telling me,' he asked indignantly, 'that you spent ten days in Goa and you only want to spend a few days here? Don't you realize that Mangalore is the "Rome of the East"?'

I didn't, but he left the room before I had time to ask when his city had taken over Old Goa's mantle. He returned shortly and said: 'We can't help you. No one can see you now. You'll learn nothing in just a few days.'

'Well, in that case,' I said petulantly, 'I'll go and see the Jesuits.' I would have shaken hands, but the priest had already turned his back on me and buried himself in the papers on his desk.

As I climbed up the hill to St Aloysius College, I reflected, with diminishing anger, that with the exception of this one awkward encounter I had met with nothing but warmth and kindness on my journey through India. I had spent hours, sometimes days, in the company of priests, nuns, bishops, slum-workers, historians and others; all had been immensely generous with both their time and their knowledge.

After skirting around several playing fields I finally arrived at the Acropolis of Mangalore, as one poet fancifully described the college. It was a lengthy building, in places colonnaded and loosely based on Sir Philip Neri's Oratory in Rome, with a square tower in the centre, the chapel at one end and the Academy Hall at the other. I followed the signs to the college office and asked a secretary if I could arrange to meet a member of staff later in the day. A few minutes later she led me into the study of Father Valerian Prashant Madtha. I had expected the principal of one of India's most prestigious colleges to be in his sixties at least. I doubt whether Father Valerian had even reached fifty. He was handsome in an angular way, with brown eyes and crinkled slicked-back hair, and his looks and manner were suggestive of a profound intelligence tempered by a good sense of humour and a willingness to breach convention.

In 1858 leaders of Mangalore's Catholic community asked the Holy See to hand over the local mission to the Society of Jesus which, they hoped, would establish an educational institution similar to those run by German Jesuits in Bombay, by Belgian Jesuits in Calcutta and by French Jesuits in Trichy. Further petitions followed over the next two decades till finally, in 1878, Pope Leo XIII assigned the Mangalore mission to the Jesuit Province of Venice with the intention that it should open a college. On 31 December 1878 nine Jesuits – five from Italy, four from the Bombay mission – arrived by steamer at Mangalore and just over a year later St Aloysius College opened its doors to 150 students. Today it has over 6,000 students and 120 staff. It is a secular college fulfilling one of the Jesuits' main apostolic missions, the education of young people. Approximately half the students are Christians, most being Catholics, while the rest are predominantly Hindu.

I had heard it said that no Indian government would ever dare tamper with the Jesuit colleges: they were widely perceived to be centres of excellence, and many leading figures within the non-Christian world had passed through the Jesuits' hands. However, I wondered whether a shift of government from the Congress Party to the Hindu BJP – elections were to be held the following year – might possibly constitute a threat to St Aloysius and the other Jesuit colleges.

'The basic philosophy of all the political parties is much the same,' replied Father Valerian in almost accentless English. 'We will be respected as long as we run institutions of higher learning where their sons are educated. Institutions like this do have a good influence. They're one of our great achievements in India. The Christian community is a mouse, but its influence makes it look like an elephant.'

All the same, the elephant's behaviour does not impress everyone. What rankles with many Hindus is not so much the Christian faith as the Christian community's adoption of European mores and manners. Mangalore's Christians, like those of Goa and Bombay, are highly Westernized. When the British were in power the Christians were the élite; they were bestowed with privileges and they gained high positions in the Civil Service. According to Father Valerian, there were many among them who regretted the passing of the Raj. 'Hindus often accuse the Christians – and the Muslims – of not fully belonging to this country,' he said. 'And I think there is some truth in that, certainly as far as the Westernized city-Christians go. The Hindus want us to come more into the mainstream – at least culturally.'

The Catholic Church has attempted to answer the criticism that Christianity has brought about the emotional deracination of converts by a process which it calls acculturation. The use of local languages, local folk customs and Indian modes of dress and eating have been encouraged; in some areas the priests have even urged converts to retain their tribal creation myths, rather than jettison them in favour of the Genesis story. Vatican II may have provided the impetus for change, but the recent attempts to Indianize the Christian religion are nothing new. Some of the early Jesuit leaders, most notably Robert de Nobili, who established a mission in Tamil Nadu in the early 1600s, mimicked the Brahmins, the Hindu priest caste, in all but their faith; they wore the same clothes, performed the same ablutions, followed the same dietary prohibitions and applied to their foreheads a dot of sandalwood paste. These priests were following the evangelizing technique sanctioned by St Paul: 'Unto the Jews, they became Jews, that they might gain the Jews; to them that were without law, as without law. They were all things to all men, that they might by all means save some' (1 Cor. 9: 20–22). The Jesuits had some success, even among the higher castes, who had most to lose by renouncing their faith, and they allowed converts to retain certain practices which were commonly associated with Hinduism. However, the other religious orders in India took exception to the Jesuits' accommodation with alien ideas, accused them of encouraging idolatry and informed the Vatican. Pope Benedict XIV issued a series of papal bulls which forced the Jesuits to preach Catholicism in all its purity, in other words in the Western manner approved by Rome. The Jesuits reluctantly complied and many converts, as they anticipated, returned to their old ways.

Abbé Dubois, a French priest who spent thirty years as a missionary in India around the turn of the eighteenth century, wrote in disgust: 'This event proved the last blow to the interests of the Christian religion. No more conversions were made; apostasy became almost general in several quarters; and Christianity became more and more an object of contempt and aversion, in proportion as the European manners became better known to the Hindoos.' Dubois was deeply gloomy about the possibility of successfully implanting Christianity in India and he claimed that the only Church with the slightest hope of gaining new converts was 'the Catholic form which you Protestants call an idolatry in disguise: it has a *Pooga* or sacrifice; it has processions, images, statues, *tirtan* or holy-water, fasts, *tittys* or feasts, and prayers for the dead, invocation of saints, &c, all which practices being more or less a resemblance to those in use among the Hindoos'.

Numerically the Catholics have been the most successful of the Christian groups to enter India over the past five centuries. In part, their success can be attributed to their early arrival, but they have made much more effort than the Protestants to give their faith an explicitly Indian flavour. This has been especially true in rural areas. Father Valerian was quick to point out that there was a profound difference between the Westernized Christians of Mangalore and those living in the surrounding countryside. From a theological point of view, he had some reservations about rural Christianity, which still echoed with Hindu ideas and customs. 'You know the concept of karma?' he asked. 'Every birth is a rebirth, and one's present situation is a reflection of one's past lives and actions. If I sin this time, I might come back as an animal next time. This is a Hindu belief, but it has influenced Christianity. What's the hurry? Why bother? There are more lives to come.' He reflected on this for a few moments, then asked, in a more animated tone of voice, 'Why doesn't this country prosper? That is why!'

Father Valerian went on to talk about the lack of outstanding Christian leaders in India, and about the growth of evangelical groups, one of whose attractions stemmed from the fact that they represented a revolt of the lower strata of society against the higher strata. This led us to the subject of caste. Many Hindus had converted to Christianity precisely because they saw it as a way of escaping the caste system, yet the baggage of caste has been handed down through the generations, like an heirloom that no one dares reject. 'It always come to light at weddings,' said Father Valerian. 'Seventy per cent of Christian marriages are arranged marriages still, and people nearly always marry within the caste they originally came from.' To corrupt George Orwell's famous aphorism: all Christians are equal, but some are more equal than others, which is why in south India the Christian of Brahmin origin will almost always seek a partner of similar background, rather than marry a Christian with low-caste ancestry. The Jesuits had led the fight against caste within the Christian community, but Father Valerian thought its eradication would be a slow and lengthy process.

I wondered aloud what other significant changes he anticipated for India's Christians over the coming years. He answered, obliquely, by saying there were two different concepts of the role of the Church. 'On the one hand,' he said, 'you have the traditionalists. Their preoccupation was how to bring more people into the Church. This was the Vatican's aim. Their theology claimed that there was no salvation outside the Church. Their views prevailed in the past, and the Indian Christians imbibed Western Christianity, took on Western names and so on. The traditionalists still think like this, but many of the recent generation of clergy don't accept their view. They look at the wider concept of the Kingdom of God. Jesus didn't come to start a Church. He inaugurated the Kingdom of God – it's about equality, dignity, working with the oppressed. What religion or denomination people are is a peripheral issue.'

There was no need to ask Father Valerian where his sympathies lay, nor any time, as he had to go to a meeting. His views, I am sure, were in keeping with the 'Aloysian ideal', which was outlined in the handbook he gave me. The college was a minority institution run primarily for the education of Catholic youth, but everyone was welcome, without distinction of caste and creed, 'in a fellowship of people of all faiths'. The college stressed the importance of academic and creative excellence and placed a strong emphasis on helping its students, whatever their faith, to further their spiritual development: 'Ultimately a person is what his spiritual and moral values are, and the aspect of your education that you will carry with you all your life will be this one . . . The time in College is the period when you have to build up your value system; honesty, justice, co-operation, fellowship and concern for others, belief in and filial devotion to God and a universal love that embraces all people cutting across barriers of religion or caste or nationality.'

I did not see Mangalore's Sistine Chapel; the man with the keys was absent. Instead I was shown around the college museum, a marvellously odd monument to the eclectic interests of half a dozen generations of Jesuit priests. There were the usual things which you would expect to find in any small-town museum in India: cabinets of fossils, rocks and seashells; tribal arrows; snakes in bottles of formalin; skeletons of crocodiles, leopards and other mammals, including the bones of a whale washed up on a Kerala beach in 1926. Nor was there anything particularly unexpected about the collection of keys, or the Bakelite telephone, or even the De Dion car, imported from Paris in 1906 and the first to appear on the streets of Mangalore. Rather, it was the disparate objects that bore little or no relation to one another which lifted the museum out of the realms of the mundane. There was a letter from Sir Winston Churchill thanking the college for sending its felicitations on his ninetieth birthday; there was a flute which had belonged to a shepherd in Bethlehem, a piece of the Berlin Wall, and – the most bizarre of all – an Air India mannequin beside statues of Gandhi, Nehru and St Ignatius Loyola. The curator, Mr Gilbert Sequera, said that when he took on the museum it was little more than a junk room and it had taken him over a thousand hours to sort it out. I told him that I had enjoyed my visit to his museum more than to any other in India, including the famous ones in the big cities. I don't think that he believed me, but it was true, and I made my way back down to the centre of town feeling much refreshed by my brief encounter with Mangalore's Jesuits.

Among the objects in the museum was one of Tipu Sultan's cannons, salvaged from his camp in Tellicherry, a picturesque fishing village to the south of Mangalore. Tipu Sultan was the Muslim ruler of the state of Mysore and both he and his father were a constant nuisance to the British during the latter decades of the eighteenth century. Tipu wanted to rid his state of the British, but he also sought to eradicate Christianity. He fought two wars against the British, who eventually killed him in 1799, and conducted sundry campaigns against the coastal Christians. Over 10,000 were killed when he invaded what is now Kerala in 1789; it is said that in one settlement he had the Christians hanged from trees around their churches. According to Abbé Dubois, more than 60,000 Christians were captured on another occasion and taken to Tipu's capital at Seringapatam. There the men were circumcised and forced to convert to Islam. 'Oh, shame! – Oh, scandal!' wrote Dubois. 'Will it be believed in the Christian world? – no one, not a single individual among so many thousands, had courage enough to confess his faith under this trying circumstance, and become a martyr to his religion.' Soon after Tipu's defeat Dubois was sent to Mysore to help rehabilitate these apostates, who told him that they had always kept Christ in their hearts, even if they had not risked their lives for him. Around 20,000 returned to Mangalore and rebuilt their churches. 'God preserve them all from being exposed in future to the same trials,' wrote Dubois sourly; 'for should this happen, I have every reason to apprehend the same sad results, that is to say, a tame submission, and a general apostasy.'

Dubois's contention that only the Catholics could entertain any hope of converting significant numbers of Hindus was based on what he saw. There were a few Lutheran congregations, but they had had 'no sensible success' over a period of a century. When he heard that the Lutherans kept a native catechist in one particular place he decided to pay him a visit. He supposed his flock to be numerous, but when he arrived he found that the congregation consisted of three individuals, a drummer, a cook and a horse-keeper. He noted that in the early eighteenth century the Moravians had taken one look at India, decided there was no possibility of evangelizing the Hindus, attempted without success 'to convert the savage of the Nicobar Islands' and eventually established a small mission at the Danish enclave of Tranquebar. The latter lasted no more than sixty years; in 1793 the priests were called back to Germany and the mission closed.

In his intemperate and entertaining critique of Christian failure, Dubois fails to mention that when he arrived in India, in 1792, Protestant missionary activity was in its infancy. The English Baptists were founded as a mission society in 1792; the London Missionary Society in 1795; the Church Missionary Society in 1799. Men and women from these and many other societies were dispatched, in the words of a famous hymn, to Greenland's icy mountains, India's coral strand, Afric's sunny fountains and wherever else they could find 'the heathen in his blindness'. However, they were not granted immediate access to all of India; prior to 1813, when its charter was renewed by Act of Parliament, the East India Company opposed the entry of new missionaries within its sphere of influence. After 1813 Protestant missions from Britain began to move into India in significant numbers, but it was only in 1833, when the Company's charter was further revised, that non-British missionaries were allowed to enter British India. Among the first to arrive was the Basel Mission, a Lutheran organization based in Switzerland. The mission began work in and around Mangalore in 1834. One of its first missionaries, Samuel Hebich, proved to be a great success with the British officers stationed in the area, despite his poor command of the English language, of which he knew a mere 550 words. One British regiment even became known as Hebich's Own. However, the Basel Mission is better remembered for its business acumen: Christians, they believed, needed fodder as well as faith, and they established a variety of industrial enterprises manufacturing such articles as Basel Mission tiles and Basel Mission textiles.

I had intended to seek out the living fruits of the Basel Mission's labours – its enterprises passed into the hands of the Commonwealth Trust during the First World War – but by mid-afternoon I was thoroughly disenchanted with Mangalore. Why, I am not sure, although the enervating humidity and the traffic-choked streets may have had something to do with it. Or perhaps, less tangibly, Mangalore and I simply disagreed with one another, much as some people do with oysters or port. Whatever the reason, I determined to leave at the earliest opportunity and after a poor dinner and a few hours' troubled sleep, I made my way on foot through the quiet streets to the railway station, where I hoped to catch the 0415 train to Cochin. A couple of bedraggled-haired *sadhus* with yellow trident streaks on their dark foreheads sat near the ticket office, knees hunched to chin; they gazed about with a look of admirable disinterest while a steady stream of travellers, many carrying heavy cardboard boxes and rope-trussed suitcases, stepped around the sleeping bodies which were scattered about the foyer like wizened parsnips.

'How much is a second-class ticket to Cochin?' I asked the ticket clerk.

'Five hundred kilometres.' He yawned expansively to reveal a perfect set of teeth bedded into gums discoloured a livid purple from years of betel-chewing.

'No. How much?'

'Oh, sorry! 372 rupees.'

I said I would have a ticket.

'No,' he replied. 'Full. Go first-class.'

I agreed, paid 503 rupees and went in search of my seat. The first-class and second-class air-conditioned carriages were next to one another. The former might have been built in the days of the Raj. The arm-rests were mostly broken, the stuffing in the seats had hardened into jagged slabs, the windows were covered with a grime so thick that the brightly lit platform was barely visible, the fans were broken and the WC was malodorous and cracked. The second-class carriage, in contrast, had clean windows, efficient fans in addition to the air-con and reclining seats with blue upholstery. I hovered about till the train was due to depart, then occupied one of the many untaken seats in the second-class carriage. I intended to make up for lost sleep – something which would have been difficult in first-class – but no sooner had I drifted into oblivion than the conductor woke me up, inspected my ticket and ordered me to go to the first-class carriage. I had anticipated something of the sort and had formulated two lines of argument, both of which I now deployed. I explained, first of all, that the quality of service should be reflected in the pricing structure; the more one pays, the better the service; the less, the poorer.

'This is not second-class ticket,' replied the conductor, unmoved. 'This is first-class ticket. You must be going first-class.'

I then asked if he would mind if I took a seat in second-class (ordinary), which is how Indian railways describe the overcrowded and extraordinarily cheap third-class carriages which make up the bulk of most trains. I think he was about to say that he wouldn't mind, but he checked himself, smiled smugly and repeated his request that I decamp to first-class.

This altercation had caught the attention of a young man in a seat across the aisle from where I sat. He asked to look at my ticket, went to inspect the first-class carriage and returned to remonstrate on my behalf with the conductor. He was a lawyer and he put on a very fine performance indeed: I was eventually allowed to stay. When we reached Tellicherry, soon after dawn, I was joined by a squat character who introduced himself as

Alfonso. He announced, *à propos* of nothing I had said, that there were 150 million Christians in India and that he came from one of the Catholic fishing communities at Cape Comorin, at the southernmost tip of India. 'We were Christians long before St Francis Xavier came here,' he said. 'My people have very strong faith, but very poor.' He himself was a naval architect, and relatively prosperous; he could probably have afforded to travel first-class, but he had had the sense not to.

CHAPTER 6

In the Wake of the Jews

I dislike watching rats while I eat, so in the evenings, when they scavenged across the floating beds of water-hyacinth which glided past the Sea Gull Hotel's restaurant, I would take a table a little way back from the railings. If I arrived early, and the sun had recently set, I could still watch the lazy flight of the bulbous-eyed fruit-bats as they made their way across the narrow channel of water to feed on Vypin Island; and later, when a damp darkness had enveloped the coast, I could observe the endless procession of trawlers as they passed by the tip of Fort Cochin, haphazardly illuminated like exotic constellations.

'Good evening, sah,' said a tall, handsome waiter in white shirt and black bow-tie as I took my seat one evening. 'You eat breakfast tonight, sah?' The service was erratic and charming but never obsequious. I ordered rice and fish, and while I waited I studied the other diners. Facing me was a young man I took to be European; he had pale skin, gingery hair, a moustache of similar colour and a powerful nose and jaw. He was devouring a rice dish as though he was determined to finish it before the cigarette smouldering in his ashtray burned itself out. The only others in the restaurant were two middle-aged men, businessmen I imagined, who sat at a table overlooking the water. From time to time they would throw peanuts through the railings, presumably for the rats, and they talked in Malayalam, the language of Kerala, in a manner which suggested that they were perennially ill-tempered. They were drinking large quantities of local whisky and sweating like wrestlers. Soon after my food arrived, and while they were ordering yet another drink, they began to argue with the waiter. At first he answered whatever their complaint was in a conciliatory manner, but then he too began to shout and gesticulate. I noticed that the other diner, who by now had finished his food and returned to his cigarettes, was listening attentively. Eventually, the waiter stormed out; his protagonists slapped some money on the table and left. When the waiter returned to clear away the empty whisky glasses, he made a comment in Malayalam, then turned to me and said, with a grin, 'They call me bloody bastard!'

'Did you understand all that?' I asked the man with ginger hair.

'Of course,' he replied. 'I come from here.' He asked whether he could join me and he came across with his beer and his cigarettes. He introduced himself as Len and explained that he was one of Cochin's last surviving Jews.

Races which have been persecuted always have the longest and most complex memories of their past. This is not to say that Len exhibited any signs of resentment or self-pity; he simply had a profound sense of his people's history. He said that there was probably a Jewish colony living in Cranganore, a port a little distance to the north of Cochin, when St Thomas arrived in AD 52. Later, when I visited him at Cochin's synagogue, he gave me a booklet which claimed that the first Jews arrived in King Solomon's merchant fleet. Whatever the truth of this, there is known to have been a large Jewish colony in Cranganore, with its own prince, from the fifth to the sixteenth centuries. In 1524 a Moorish army laid waste Cranganore's Jewish quarter on the grounds that the Jews were interfering with the pepper trade, and most fled to Cochin. Len's family arrived from Spain, some 450 years ago, as Jew Town was beginning to take shape.

At one time there were over 50,000 Jews in India and at least 4,000 in Kerala. Now there were just twenty left in Cochin; the youngest, said Len, was one of his cousins, who was twenty-three. He had an intense love for Cochin and India, but he thought he too would have to leave soon. He would go to Israel, where he would be able to find a wife and raise a family. Kerala's Jews, he explained, were orthodox in their beliefs. They had remained racially pure – the few who had bred outside the community had been ostracized – and they were strict in their observance of religious festivals. This was one of the reasons why many of Cochin's Jews had left since the founding of the state of Israel: those who were in government employment were expected to work on Saturday, the Jewish sabbath, and school examinations frequently coincided with the Passover and other Jewish holidays.

When Marco Polo visited India in the latter years of the thirteenth century he found the people of the Malabar coast – 'Idolaters, though there are some Christians and Jews among them' – living in a landscape of great fertility. 'Everything there is different from what it is with us and excels both in size and beauty,' he wrote. 'They have no fruit the same as ours, no beast, no bird. This is a consequence of the extreme heat.' What they had was a profusion of spices – spices which had long been traded by Jews and Arabs and which were later to attract the attentions of Europe's greatest powers, and whose cultivation still dominates life in the countryside. If you walk south from the Sea Gull Hotel and follow the road which leads towards the synagogue, you will pass scores of warehouses and shops which appear much as they must have done many centuries ago, when *dhows* would sail in on an easterly wind and barter their ballast of brass and cargo of cloth and other commodities for pepper, ginger, cardamom, nutmeg, cloves, turmeric and other spices. These and many other rural products – rubber, coir, cashew – you will see laid out along Bazar Street, awaiting the inspection of housewives and retailers.

When I arrived at the synagogue I was greeted by Len, who proudly explained that it was the oldest in the British Commonwealth. It was an exquisite building, bathed in light and suffused with opulent colours. A raised pulpit in the centre of the synagogue – this was the only place in the world which had such a feature, according to Len – was lit by a magnificent crystal chandelier, the walls were hung with silk screens and the floor was laid with more than a thousand blue-and-white Cantonese tiles, each with its own design.

The Jews were among the few foreign communities who came to settle in India without imperialistic intentions. The same was true of the Parsis who, like many Jews, were fleeing persecution in their homeland, the Armenians of Calcutta and Madras and two small African communities whose ancestors were brought to Gujarat as slaves for a maharaja. Both the Parsis and the Jews did well under the British, who elevated them to what would now be termed middle management in the Civil Service, but the Jews were roughly treated by the Portuguese, who not only destroyed the remnants of their colony at Cranganore but also sacked Cochin's Jew Town in the 1550s. When the Dutch arrived in 1661 the Jews openly supported them; unfortunately, the Portuguese briefly won Cochin back and destroyed the synagogue. The Dutch remained in power for over a century, but they were eventually ousted by the British in 1795. Each invader partially erased the creations of the vanquished: the Dutch destroyed the entire Portuguese quarter and all the Catholic churches except St Francis church and the cathedral, which the British destroyed, along with the fort itself, when they took over. All the same, buildings and streets of all eras did survive, and with them the mongrel character which reflects to this day the religious preferences and architectural talents of the Portuguese, the Dutch, the British and, of course, the Jews and the Indians.

~

On the west coast of India the Roman Catholic Church exudes confidence. As soon as I stepped into Bishop's House, in Cochin as in Goa and Mangalore, I felt that I was in the presence of a well-organized institution of considerable power. The Catholics seemed to have a sense of importance about their mission, and a sense of rightness about their presence, which I had failed to discern in my encounters with most of the Protestants in the north. When I think of the Catholics now, I see a world of brilliant colours and elaborate rituals; when I think of the traditional Protestant Churches, I see a drabber, sepia-toned world, at the level of the laity less devout than the Catholics and certainly less enslaved by dogma and ritual. This is not meant as a criticism of either; it is, in any case, a caricature, but theologies, like places, generate their own peculiar atmosphere. Abbé Dubois understood this, and his assertion that Hindus would more readily become Catholics than Protestants was based on the feel, on the atmosphere, of the Catholic faith, rather than on any theological merits it might possess.

Bishop's House was built in 1506 as the residence for the Portuguese Governor. The Dutch took it over after the conquest of 1663, then when the British came it passed into the hands of a private family. In 1888 it was purchased by the twenty-seventh Bishop of Cochin, and it has undergone modifications and enlargements on four occasions since then. Surrounded by beautiful gardens, it is a fine, low-slung building whose Gothic entrance leads into a succession of cool, spacious rooms, beyond which is a courtyard with an aviary. The thirty-third bishop of Cochin, Joseph Kureethara, was taking tea with three nuns when I arrived. His study was full of good statuary, gilded furniture, chairs and settees upholstered in the same purple as his cassock and some fine light fittings: the sort of room that Balzac would have given a bourgeois Parisian. I had heard that there was a museum in Bishop's House and asked whether this was it.

'Yes and no,' replied the bishop, a small, bespectacled man with grey hair and an affable manner. 'I am a museum piece, but the real museum is next door.'

The bishop was eager to talk about England. He had travelled to Warrington, Preston and other industrial towns in the north. He recalled that he had prayed for one childless couple to have a baby; eventually they did, and they had invited him over to stay. He was only the third Indian to be a bishop of Cochin during the diocese's 439 years of history – the first thirty had been Portuguese – and he suggested that I study the town's past from the mural in the main hall.

The mural had been designed by the bishop and painted, with considerable competence, by Captain Ludvic Kurisumkul. It took up the entire wall around a Gothic arch at one end of the hall and depicted, in thirty-six panels, events both great and small in Kerala's and Cochin's past. It showed St Thomas's arrival in AD 52, the arrival of Thomas of Cana and a band of Middle Eastern Christians in AD 345, the missionary endeavours of St Francis Xavier and the subsequent invasions of various European armies. It illustrated the outlawing, by the Portuguese in 1599, of the practice of killing female, deformed or unwanted babies and the outlawing, by the British in 1829, of *suttee*, the Hindu practice of burning widows on the funeral pyres of their husbands. The mural looked at the world through Catholic eyes, yet it acknowledged some of the Church's blacker deeds: the burning of books belonging to Kerala's Syrian Christians in 1599 and the Catholic insistence that they acknowledge the Pope as head of their Church.

Another wall was taken up with statistical information for the year 1985. It gave details of the religious persuasion of people in Cochin diocese, Kerala, India and the world. Christians made up 26 per cent of the population of Cochin diocese and 20 per cent of that of the whole of Kerala. The league tables suggested that 96 per cent of Cochin's Christians were Catholics, which was probably true, but the figures for Kerala were more questionable. One table suggested that there are – or were in 1985 – 5,230,000 Christians in Kerala. Another claimed that there are – or were – 4,271,600 Catholics and 2,982,868 Orthodox Christians; this would bring the figure for Christians up to 7,254,468, and then there is the matter of a million or so Protestants, whom none of the tables mentioned. I was reminded of the man on the train from Mangalore who inflated the number of Christians in India by a factor of five or more; perhaps he used the same accountant as Cochin diocese.

When I returned to the Sea Gull from Bishop's House I was immediately subjected to an interrogation by a man who was eating lunch. What was my name? What was I doing in Cochin? Was I staying here? Where did I come from? London? Yes, but which part of London?

'Near me,' he replied with satisfaction when I told him. 'Sit down. I'm from Surbiton.'

His name was Joseph Xavier and he explained, waving across the water, that he had been brought up here and lived for many years on Vypin Island. He was involved in the import–export business, and he and his wife were spending a month in Kerala – they were staying in a hotel in Ernakulam, the busy city on the other side of the harbour – investigating the possibility of doing trade with his native state. Among other things, he was looking at the ground spices which were being produced and packaged by Aroma, an organization established by the Cochin Social Services Society. The society was run by an old friend of his, a priest called Father Xavier Palackal. 'You want to meet him?' asked Joseph. 'We'll meet him together,' he said before I had time to reply.

We would have met him the following day had it not been for the strike. The governing of Kerala oscillates between the Congress Party and the Communist Party of India; at present the former was in power, and the Communists were quick to side with the trade unions in political disputes. There had been trouble at a Hindu ashram in southern Kerala – what this had to do with party politics I never did understand – and the unions and the Communist Party had called for a general strike. Early in the morning Father Xavier rang to say that the strike would affect everything, including the work of his society, and we arranged to meet a day later. Shops, offices, schools and factories were closed, taxis and rickshaws were off the street and the ferries which connected Fort Cochin to Ernakulam and Vypin Island lay idle, so I spent a languid day reading while the fishing vessels chugged back and forth past the Sea Gull, oblivious to the strike.

I took to Father Xavier the instant I met him. He was practical, energetic and quite obviously much loved by the dozens of individuals whom we saw during the course of a day. Wherever we went – a mechanics' garage, an electronics workshop, a room of trainee seamstresses – he would introduce each person in turn with the same respect and cordiality regardless of their age, status or skills.

We began the day – Joseph, his wife and one other in attendance – in Father Xavier's office, where he described the operations of the Cochin Social Services Society. Established by the Catholic Church in 1966, it was by far the largest institution helping the poor and a model of bureaucratic efficiency. Father Xavier, who had been chosen as director and secretary by the bishop, had three associate directors, all priests, and under each of these there were five diocesan coordinators; the coordinators oversaw the work of twenty or so chief animators, each of whom watched over the activities of a further fifteen to twenty animators. Each animator looked after seven churches, each of which had an elected seven-woman committee. 'You see,' explained Father Xavier, 'it's the women we are concentrating on. We are helping them to be self-sufficient.' Over 14,000 women were receiving some form of assistance from the society.

The Church, like many other voluntary organizations, had discovered that unconditional charity is frequently abused or wasted. 'For the first twenty years we spoiled people,' recalled Father Xavier. 'We gave them everything for free, but they never appreciated it. Now it's very different – it's mostly their money, not ours, that's helping them, and they appreciate the fact that they participate in all the decisions that affect them.'

Seven years ago the society helped establish credit unions in every parish; at the time of my visit these held over 4.4 million rupees (or around £88,000) in various bank accounts. This money was collected each week in dribs and drabs from the 14,000 or so beneficiaries by the animators, whose small wages came out of the interest on deposited funds. 'It's very well organized,' said Father Xavier with pride. 'It's working very nicely.' He explained that the women in the scheme could take out loans from the credit-union funds, and these were generally used to finance small business ventures. Some had used them to buy milking goats, others to set up grocery stalls and market gardens. The loans were provided at an annual interest rate of 12 per cent – the commercial rate was 60 per cent – and they had to be repaid in three years. So far hardly anyone had defaulted on loan repayments.

In addition to its work with the credit unions, the society had recently built 150 houses for poor people – these were funded by loans, which the homeowners had to repay, and by subsidies – and the society also gave financial assistance to 400 poor children, to over 500 women who had lost their husbands and to 170 disabled people. The society was expecting to build, with government help, a further 1,000 homes for the poor in the near future, and it had already set up loan schemes to help replace coconut-leaf roofs, which leak, with tiled roofs, which don't.

I asked if it was only the Catholics of Cochin who were benefiting from the society's work. No, replied Father Xavier emphatically, it was not. Of the women who were covered by the credit-union schemes, 20 per cent were Hindus and 8 per cent were Muslims. 'In one place,' said Father Xavier, 'the Christians felt that they should be the only ones to benefit; they didn't want us to help the Muslims. We said, "Nothing doing." The Muslims really appreciate the social leadership we give. In the Muslim community even coming out from the family is taboo for the women. But because of our work, they do now. Their women are very enthusiastic. In fact, that's one of our best groups.' He added that the society never had any intention of bringing non-Christians into the Church. Although the people were often poor, they were relatively well educated. This was borne out by figures for literacy: 87 per cent of women in Kerala could read and write compared with 14 per cent in Uttar Pradesh and 28 per cent in Madhya Pradesh. 'We have religious harmony here,' said Father Xavier. 'When people are educated, they can appreciate other religions.' Hindus attended Christian festivals, and even helped pay for saints' days feasts, and Christians took part in Hindu celebrations. This was not to say that the society was shy of its Christian ethics. 'Automatically, our concern for the poor is being witnessed,' said Father Xavier. 'We show our love for the poor. People notice that.'

Father Xavier's office was situated in the society's Industrial Training Centre, and once we had taken mid-morning tea he led us around. Since 1966, he explained, over 3,000 young people had been trained as fitters, welders, turners, mechanics, plumbers and computer operators. Many had found lucrative work in the Gulf, traditionally an important destination for Keralites, and others had set up their own enterprises in Cochin. The students paid fees for their training, varying from 120 rupees a month for some courses to 300 rupees for others, but these fees were much lower than those charged by similar government institutions. Over eighty staff were employed at the centre, which was funded partially by its commercial operations: the police, for example, had all their vehicle repairs done here. The society's other centre at Cheriakadaru, a picturesque site overlooking the backwaters, combined training with business. One building was occupied by young women making high-quality embroidered saris, another by women manufacturing electrical goods such as current stabilizers and the ground floor of the latter by Aroma, the spice packagers. There were eighty-five people employed full-time here, and all profits were channelled into the society's charitable works. 'This is a poor diocese,' said Father Xavier, 'but this business makes money. The other great thing about it is the way it changes the outlook of the women. In India women tend to do what their husbands tell them, but this is making women think for themselves. They are earning their own living and they are making their own decisions.'

When Evelyn Waugh visited south India in 1953 he was impressed, as every traveller before and since, by the beauty of the women. 'The women here are all charmingly dressed and so feminine they made all European women seem Lesbian,' he wrote boldly in a letter to his wife. He added, less irrefutably: 'The men are nearly all quite grotesque. The only dignified people are the servants.' Most of the women at the embroidery and spice workshops were dressed in shimmering saris, and many of the younger ones had racemes of scented jasmine woven into their shiny dark hair. However, the most eye-catching was one of the oldest, with a heavily lined face and grey hair tied in a bun. She wore a *chattu* and *mundu*, a white blouse and a white ankle-length, wrap-around skirt, not unlike a man's *dhoti* but with a fan of pleats, like a bird's tail, at the rear. She also wore heavy gold earrings which were hooked over the top of her ears. This was the traditional way of dressing for Catholic women, explained Father Xavier, but the custom was dying out now, especially among the young in urban areas.

We talked of these and other matters in Father Xavier's jeep as he drove us at unnerving speed to the Sea Gull Hotel. We discussed politics – Father Xavier said that he, like half of the town's Catholics, always voted for the Communists – and the evangelical movement, which he mistrusted, not least because it lured the poor into its fold with offers of money. I told him about my experience on Mount Batim, and he said that he had witnessed a similar gathering – in Yugoslavia, I think – where people claimed to see the Virgin Mary. 'Mass hysteria,' he said curtly, 'and very dangerous.'

We took a table beside the water at the Sea Gull and ordered beer – 'Good for the digestion,' suggested Father Xavier – fried fish and 'meals', which is Indian-style English for the set lunch, in this case an admirable feast of half a dozen vegetarian dishes, served in little aluminium bowls, together with rice, chutney, yoghurt, dahl and papads. During the course of the meal I asked Father Xavier about the caste divisions which were still said to exist among the Catholics of central Kerala.

'You understand the old custom of dividing people on the basis of work?' he asked. 'You know, the *brahmins* offer sacrifices and look after the temples; the *kshatryas* are the warriors and look after law and order; the *vaisayas* are the traders; then there are the *sudras*, the workers and the servant castes.' He took another mouthful of food, chewed it pensively, then said: 'This system is five thousand years old. It's been here so long that it's in the atmosphere. You can't get rid of it overnight.'

When Portuguese missionaries arrived in Kerala in the sixteenth century they worked among both the fishing communities along the coast and the trading and farming communities inland. The fishing communities had their own traditions and culture, and they married among themselves. Likewise the inland communities had their own culture and manner of doing things, and they too married among themselves. When these Keralites converted to Christianity they remained quite separate, and the caste divisions between the Anjootty community, which makes a living from fishing, and the Ezhunootty community, which does not, have persisted to this day. They have even determined the shape of the local dioceses.

In 1952, explained Father Xavier, Cochin diocese was divided in two. The southern portion was given over to a new diocese centred on, and named after, the port of Alleppey. The majority of villages in the northern portion, still called Cochin diocese, were occupied by non-fishing Ezhunootty, most in the new Alleppey diocese by the fishing Anjootty. However, there were four Anjootty parishes in Cochin diocese, and these chose to be administered by Alleppey diocese, with which they felt greater kinship; and there were four Ezhunootty parishes in Alleppey diocese which insisted, for the same reasons, on belonging to Cochin diocese. 'Their priests would happily change matters,' said Father Xavier, 'and belong to the diocese where they find themselves. But the people simply aren't willing.' The fishing community has traditionally been looked down upon by the inland traders – as *sudras* are by *vaisayas* among Hindus – and at one time Anjootty were not even allowed to become priests for fear of upsetting the more influential Ezhunootty. 'Up to fifty years ago, when the division was still acute,' said Father Xavier with a look of distaste, 'a priest from the fishing community couldn't even enter a church of one of the non-fishing communities. It's tragic, really.'

Gradually, thought the priest, the old enmities were beginning to fade. Now that fishing in central Kerala had become highly mechanized, people from the inland Ezhunootty community were finding jobs in the industry, and there was some inter-marriage, albeit on a modest scale. The Catholic Church was continuing to do what it could to break down the caste barrier, and Father Xavier pointed out that the Catholics had been the first to help the lower castes. 'They were never allowed into schools or temples before,' he said. 'But we encouraged them to enter the church, to come into our schools. This was when they began to realize their human dignity.'

As we rose to leave after lunch he motioned across to Vypin Island. 'If you go over there, you'll find three Catholic churches. One for the fishers, the Anjootty; one for the non-fishers, the Ezhunootty; and one for the Anglo-Indians. They don't mix.'

~

'In the old days,' explained Rev. Korula, the vicar of St Francis church, 'this place was only for British people. Indian Anglicans had to go to St Andrew's.' When the British left the Indians took over St Francis, and St Andrew's, a modest building not far from the Catholic Bishop's House, became a village hall.

In fact, St Francis church had served four separate communities since it was built in the early 1500s. Under the Portuguese it was a Catholic church, and the remarkable collection of tombstones which line the walls date from that period. One lies over what is reputed to be the burial place of Vasco da Gama, who died in Cochin on Christmas Day 1524. When the Dutch ousted the Portuguese they immediately ordered all the Catholic priests to leave Fort Cochin, and St Francis church – in those days it was dedicated to St Bartholomew – was given to the Lutherans. When the British came the Dutch clergy voluntarily gave the church to the Anglicans, and it remained in their hands till 1947, when the Church of South India, an amalgam of denominations similar to its northern counterpart, came into being.

There were two services on Sunday morning: one at eight o'clock in English, another at nine thirty in Malayalam. I attended the first of these, along with twenty-two others, including the vicar. After the service, as we left the courtyard and turned into a broad street shaded by magnificent epiphyte-encrusted trees, a tall gentleman with silver hair, a toothbrush moustache and a safari suit – I presume he was Anglo-Indian – came across to pass the time of day. He spoke clipped English of the Sandhurst variety and asked me where I came from.

'Ah, you're from good old London,' he said, nodding his head sagaciously. He waved towards the grand villas which surrounded the playing fields beside the church. 'This was where your British chaps used to live,' he said, then proceeded to rattle off the names of those he had known in the days before Independence. One of the villas which he pointed to had been a club: 'No Indians allowed in, of course.'

I said I always felt embarrassed when I heard such stories.

He flapped a hand dismissively. 'You lived too late,' he said without a trace of irony, as though I might have wished to have lived the grand life of the British ruling classes.

There are certain parts of the world – I am thinking, in particular, of Africa – where many people prefer to attribute their present woes to the colonial past rather than to the incompetence of their own governments; where the modern traveller from a former colonial power is expected to shoulder some of the guilt for the activities of his ancestors. When people in India choose to discuss the colonial days I am always astonished by their fairness; indeed, sometimes they appear to be prejudicially in favour of the old rulers. They tend not to mention the snobberies of the Raj – exemplified by the segregation of the Christian communities – or Mountbatten's clumsy partition of the subcontinent, or the massacres at Amritsar and elsewhere. Rather, they will tell you about the benefits their country derived from the British presence: the unifying influence of the English language, the creation of the rail system, the introduction of cricket and a Civil Service which was once honest and competent and, at the higher levels, still is.

Throughout their history, it seems, most Indians have been remarkably tolerant of other people's customs and ideas. Take, at a parochial level, the Hindu rajas of Cochin. In the sixteenth century the raja gave trading rights to the Portuguese, in return for which the newcomers built Mattancherry Palace, a grand edifice near the synagogue, and St Francis church still possesses the palm leaf on which were etched its title deeds, granted by the raja. The Portuguese were less tolerant: Albuquerque, conqueror of Old Goa, wrote to his king requesting permission to exterminate all the Castilian and Portuguese Jews who had fled persecution in Europe and come to live in Kerala. The raja, in contrast, gave the fleeing Jews of Cranganore a site next to his palace where they could build homes and a synagogue; he even drafted some of them into his army, and Portuguese writers called him 'King of the Jews'.

On a broader canvas, India's tolerance can be seen in the

assimilatory nature of Hinduism. 'Tolerance,' wrote one Hindu scholar, 'is a duty, not a mere concession. In pursuance of this duty Hinduism has accepted within its fold almost all varieties of belief and doctrine and accepted them as authentic expressions of the spiritual endeavour.' Hinduism, unlike Christianity, is not based on an exclusive doctrine; there are many paths to salvation. Hindus often have icons of Christ in their home, alongside Krishna, Ganesh and their own gods. I even heard of Hindu villagers in Bihar who worship a statue of Queen Victoria, though this strikes me as stretching the principle of tolerance a little too far.

Most Indians – and most Hindus – are appalled by the xenophobic views of people like Ms Rithambara: she stigmatizes foreigners and blames the nation's ills on their activities, much as Hitler blamed the Jews for Germany's economic problems in the 1930s. 'Abroad is unutterably bloody and foreigners are fiends,' as Uncle Matthew says in Nancy Mitford's *The Pursuit of Love*. It would make a good motto for the RSS, and it is a sentiment which some Indian politicians now openly pander to. At its most prosaic, the prejudice against foreign influences is seen in the jettisoning of the old names of cities and streets: Bombay is now officially known as Mumbai, and Delhi's Connaught Place has been given a name I can neither pronounce nor remember. The persecution of minorities represents a more sinister strand of xenophobia. A former RSS leader criticized India's Christians and Muslims not for their faiths but for their ostensible lack of patriotism: 'Together with the change in their faith,' wrote Guru Golwalkar in his *Bunch of Thoughts*, 'gone is the spirit of love and devotion to the nation. They have also developed a feeling of identification with the enemies of this land.' It is this belief which inspired Bal Thackeray, leader of Shiv Sena, the ruling party in Bombay, to promise that everybody would one day to have take *diksha*, initiation, in the Hindu religion; it is beliefs such as this that fuelled the fury of the mob who destroyed the mosque at Ayodhya, and it is this gut-felt intolerance – in political as well as religious thought – that led to the bizarre persecution, while I was on my travels, of Kentucky Fried Chicken. The branch in Delhi was closed down when the authorities claimed that they had discovered flies and harmful bacteria in the kitchen. If they were to be consistent, they would have to close down virtually every eating establishment in India. A few months later angry farmers broke through a police cordon and smashed up the Bangalore branch. The farmers belonged to a nationalist organization and they wanted Kentucky Fried Chicken to leave the country on the grounds that its food was 'un-Indian and unhealthy'. Which is probably true, though that is beside the point.

I am not sure what to make of such strange acts of violence. It would be easy to ridicule them as one might the tantrums of a child, but they can also be seen as an expression, admittedly extreme in nature, of a broader unease, now felt by many, about India's relationship with the outside world and about its perceived inability to assimilate Western ideas, and to cope with Western-style consumerism, without corrupting or destroying those aspects of Indian culture which give the country its peculiar flavour and historical identity.

I don't know what Bangalore's rioting farmers would have thought of the Europeans I had met on my travels so far. Not much, I imagine. With the exception of an Australian social worker, met in the YMCA's swimming-pool in Delhi, and half a dozen dedicated British girls working in Pune's slums with Deep Griha, virtually all the Europeans I had encountered were rude, ignorant or arrogant and, quite often, all three. There was the retired Danish soldier, tattooed from neck to ankle, who wandered around the bars in Panjim scattering racist insults like confetti; there was the middle-aged English engineer, in India on business, whom I heard swearing at a ticket clerk in Pune; and in Cochin, on my arrival, I was forced to sleep in a room next to two Americans, pseudo-sophisticates both, who played loud music late into the night and behaved as though the Sea Gull was their own private fiefdom. I was beginning to despair of finding pleasant European company, but the Americans left two days after I arrived and their rooms were taken over by a succession of warm and thoughtful travellers: a Dutch couple who later accompanied me on the journey to Kottayam; an American Jew and his Japanese fiancée; a French couple who spoke not a word of English. I was glad to have some non-ecclesiastical companions to chat with at breakfast and wander about town with in the evenings.

One of Fort Cochin's great blessings is its partial isolation: most of those who go to work in Ernakulam take the half-hourly ferry which crosses the harbour; few rely on buses or cars, which must make a circuitous journey many miles to the south of Cochin before crossing by bridge to the mainland. Consequently, Cochin's streets are among the quietest in India, and you can stroll at a leisurely pace wherever you wish without fear of being run over or even hooted at. Early in the mornings, when the placid water and hazy sky were the palest of blues, and late in the afternoon, when the sun dropped into the ocean like a globe of molten iron, I would saunter, sometimes alone, sometimes in company, along the stone promenade which ran from the customs jetty to the Dutch cemetery. The promenade was lined by a score of cantilevered Chinese fishing nets, identical, it is said, to the ones introduced by courtiers of Kublai Khan some eight centuries ago. At rest their roughly hewn timbers looked like the mandibles of some prehistoric mantids, but as soon as a five- or six-man team set them in motion they were transformed into things of grace and beauty, their nets dripping spray like sparks from a welder's torch. And if the nets were not being used, then there were always the boats to watch: trawlers with names like *God's Country* and *St Thomas*; a cruiser called *Tippu Sultan*; container ships from Africa, the Gulf and China; naval frigates and patrol boats; 30-foot canoes with outboard motors and high prows like pharaonic funerary boats; and all manner of smaller craft ranging from launches to paddle canoes, some oddly rigged with patchwork sails. When the sun had finally set, the crowds would drift away, back to their homes or into town, and I would visit the fly-infested fish stalls where I would buy a couple of fresh pomfret, or a kilo of king prawns, and have them cooked, for a few rupees, over a charcoal brazier in a nearby café.

After supper, on the evening before I left Cochin, I walked from the seafront down to what passes for Fort Cochin's town centre, a crossroads illuminated by some weak street lamps and the garish signs of a few modern shops. When I reached there a Flying Squad jeep was making a slow perambulation of the streets and a uniformed policeman was delivering a message in Malayalam through a megaphone.

'A hooch tragedy,' said a man who had stopped outside the fax office to watch the jeep's progress. The policeman, he explained for my benefit, was delivering an urgent message for anyone who had been drinking adulterated liquor in Mattancherry, a settlement to the south of Fort Cochin. 'So far eight people dead,' said my interpreter. 'What the police are saying is, if you have been drinking the liquor, go to hospital.'

I made a telephone call in the fax office and set off for the Sea Gull, passing on my way the General Hospital. An agitated crowd had gathered outside the gates and an autorickshaw came hurtling by, presumably with another victim. Back at the hotel the staff decided to close the iron gates. They said it would be tense in the streets tonight and they advised the guests not to venture out too far.

A few days before the hooch tragedy, Father Xavier had introduced me to some of the female animators employed by Cochin Social Services Society. Like everyone who works with India's poor, they had witnessed the violence and misery caused by alcoholism. It was the men who drank and the women and children who suffered. There was nothing they could do to stop people drinking, but they had had some success in closing down liquor stores which were illegally sited less than 400 metres from schools and places of worship. They had organized groups of women to picket the shops and discourage people from entering; on one occasion they had kept up a picket for three months until the shop owner had eventually been forced to give up business. All the same, said the women, the police were easily bribed to turn a blind eye to shops flouting the distance laws or, worse, to shops which sold spirits adulterated with methyl alcohol.

The morning after the tragedy there was still a large crowd milling around the hospital and the *Indian Express* described the scene in Mattancherry in typically lurid terms: 'Cameos of grief, silhouettes of sorrow, with wails and cries as background, come into sharp relief as in rewind . . . Neighbours flock out of pity, curiosity or courtesy as women and children huddle over postmortemed bodies in abject sorrow. The *dénouement* of a life enslaved to highs.' Accompanying the text were photographs of women wailing over a body below Christ on the cross, of the illegal liquor store, which had been ransacked by a mob, of a boy who had been beaten up by the police for telling them where the liquor had been hidden and, most gruesome of all, of six contorted bodies lying on the dirty floor of the morgue. Over the next few days there was much indignation, melodramatically expressed in the newspapers, about police collusion in the illegal liquor business. According to the *Indian Express* the area in Mattancherry where the tragedy had happened had 'obviously remained cocooned in anarchy, poverty and crime, a scenario that was capitalized upon by the corrupt police and excise staff'. The paper pointed out that nine liquor stores flourished in the vicinity of two churches, a mosque, a high school and a college: all were breaking the 400-metre distance law. The papers had also gathered testimony about the effects of the illicit liquor from survivors. One said: 'We continued to drink it because it did something to our heads,' and another, 'I know it is spirit [methyl alcohol] but I get a stronger kick at lesser cost. I have been drinking illicit hooch for the last thirty years. This hooch destroys taste buds but gives a good kick.' Good enough, in fact, to kill over a thousand people a year. Which is more than can be said for Kentucky Fried Chicken.

CHAPTER 7

The Syrian Christians

Six months before I embarked on this journey I travelled the length of the Kerala coast in the company of an erudite civil servant who was greatly intrigued to meet a European who believed in God and the life hereafter. Most of the Westerners he had met were atheists, or at least showed little interest in spiritual matters. It took us the best part of a week to travel from the state capital of Trivandrum, or Tiruvanantapuram as it is called in Malayalam (a language which my companion described as 'like driving very fast over a bumpy road'), to the ancient town of Calicut, where Vasco da Gama arrived by sea in 1498. During the course of the journey we visited a great many prawn farms – I was writing about an aquaculture project – and, when time allowed, the odd church and site of historical interest. Most intriguing of these was Cranganore, or Kodangullur, a port to the north of Cochin whose prominence in maritime trade during classical times led Pliny to describe it as the *primum emporium Indiae.* King Solomon's fleet acquired ivory, gold and cloth from the merchants of Cranganore, the Hindus were alleged – by Christian historians – to have learned the art of writing from Phoenicians who came this way and it was here, less than twenty years after Christ's death, that St Thomas is thought to have introduced the gospel to India.

Cranganore is now but the merest shadow of its former self. Admittedly, we arrived in the dark, around nine o'clock in the evening, but I think that we saw most of what there was to see: a scattering of fishermen's huts, a few civic buildings, a mosque and the Marthoma Pontifical Shrine, which looked as though it had been modelled on St Peter's in Rome. The shrine was a strangely tacky affair consisting of a small classical basilica and a semicircular colonnade surmounted by two dozen inferior statues – of disciples and saints, presumably, although we couldn't tell in the dark. We studied a raised relief which depicted St Thomas's arrival, then went in search of the priest. He was having a bath, explained a young boy who was looking after a stall of booklets and icons. Eventually the priest appeared from his living quarters and led us into the church. He looked like an ascetic version of Karl Marx with his rectangular beard, white hair and long, thin fingers. In rapid English he told us that St Thomas had landed here in AD 52, converted a great many Hindus and Jews and founded seven churches in Kerala, which the priest named one by one, counting them off with the bony forefinger of his right hand. It was a speech he had obviously delivered hundreds of times and on its conclusion he fished a key out of his white cassock, approached a contraption on the altar which looked like a gold-plated microwave, sank to his knees, offered up a prayer, then unlocked two doors of what turned out to be a reliquary containing a bit of bone. It was part of one of St Thomas's wrist bones, explained the priest, and it came from the arm which poked a doubt-dispelling finger into the gash on the risen Christ's side. It was the only relic of the apostle outside Italy. He offered up another prayer, locked the doors of the reliquary and led us out into the hot night. We thanked him for his kindness and I bought two tattered books from the boy who had alerted the priest to our presence.

One of the books began with the claim that Cranganore was known as the Rome of India in the fifteenth century, an appellation, it went on to say, which had as much to do with its famous trading harbour, now silted up, as its importance in the Christian world. The other book provided a charmingly odd survey of the bewildering array of Christian denominations – twenty-one in all – to be found in Kerala. On the subject of what it called 'Jehoas Withnesses', it had this to say: 'Very recently they have made Kottayam their Headquarters and a few young men and women are rigorously working with financial assistance from somewhere.' The Brethren Church was now 'controlled by a Registered Company'; the Pentecostals had learned to speak in tongues 'by incessant prayer and tarrying for the Holy Ghost'; and, most delightful of all, the Metropolitan in charge of the Mar Thoma Church had 'initiated and completed a number of social schemes aimed at improving the poor asses'.

When the Portuguese missionaries arrived with Vasco da Gama and in the larger fleets which followed they were pleased to find the coast of Kerala studded with churches. After all, they had been sent here to convert the heathen, and their job, it seemed, had already been partly done. The Portuguese and Indian Christians were initially on very friendly terms, but the more they got to know about one another the less they liked what they saw. The Portuguese were Roman Catholics: the Pope was Christ's Vicar on Earth and theirs was the only true Church, outside which there could be no salvation. The St Thomas Christians, on the other hand, recognized as head of their Church the Patriarch of the East, who consecrated their bishops and dispatched them to India from his headquarters in Mesopotamia. The bishops were all Syrians and the liturgy was an Eastern rite conducted in Syriac, which is why all Keralites descended from the Christian communities which predated the arrival of the Portuguese still call themselves Syrians, regardless of which Church they belong to now.

Besides the issue of leadership, there were other obvious differences between the Catholics and the Syrians. These related to the use of sacraments, the nature of the eucharist, the celibacy or otherwise of the clergy, the doctrine of purgatory and the use of images. As the years slipped by the Catholic missionaries determined to reform the Syrians. In 1541 the Franciscans opened a boys' school in Cranganore; a few years later it was turned into a seminary, one of whose purposes was to Romanize the students. Other less subtle attempts were made against the Syrian Christians, and by the end of the sixteenth century they had been forced to accept the authority of the Pope. A group within the Church successfully revolted against Rome half a century later, but even today the coast of Kerala remains firmly in the grasp of the Catholics – revealingly, the shrine containing St Thomas's relic is Catholic, not Syrian – and the resurgent Syrians were forced to establish new headquarters inland, in and around the town of Kottayam.

Christians and spices are what Vasco da Gama came to India for, and Christians, spices and rubber are what you get in Kottayam, a small town two hours' drive from Cochin and pleasantly situated where the backwaters meet the foothills of the Western Ghats. I arrived around midday, checked into a hotel on KK Road and went in search of a priest whose name I had been given by Father Xavier Palackal. One end of KK Road was dominated by goldsmiths' shops where a modest necklace cost more than many would earn in six months, the other by two towering churches, both Catholic and remarkable as much for their ugliness as for their size. A chaotic procession of lorries and rickshaws travelled from the churches down to the gold shops, this being a one-way street. Their luxuriantly painted tailgates and door lintels were decorated with slogans which might have been written by the priests to admonish the merchants: 'Prayer is Power', 'Praise the Lord', 'Time and Tide Wait for No One'. The public buses bore names rather than slogans: Jesus, St Jude, St Sebastian, the Virgin Mary, St George, Ganesh, Krishna. Christian saints outnumbered Hindu and other gods by a factor of two to one, which accurately reflected Kottayam's status as Kerala's most important Christian town. Two-thirds of its people are Christians.

I asked my rickshaw-driver to take me to the Catholics' Bishop's House, where I hoped to find Father Xavier's friend, Father Sebastian. We eventually reached there, but not before we had called in on two other Bishop's Houses – Syrian Orthodox and Syro-Malabar – and visited several churches. A nun at the Syro-Malabar Bishop's House said, quaintly, that it was so many furlongs to the Catholics' Bishop's House or 5 rupees by rickshaw. When I did eventually find Father Sebastian he was addressing an audience of animators who worked for the Social Services Society. He suggested I return another day and one of his colleagues invited me to look round the modern cathedral. He explained that although we were in Kottayam diocese as far as the Catholic Knaniya Christians were concerned, we were in the Vijayapum diocese of the Latin Catholics and the Changanacheri diocese of another Syrian Catholic group. He then went on to explain that there were two main factions within the unreformed Syrian Church and he suggested I also call on the reformed Syrians, or the Mar Thoma Church, which was in communion with the Protestant Church of South India. 'You'll find it most confusing,' he said cheerfully.

'What's your programme?' asked Father John Thomas after the Sunday morning service at Cheriapally, an ancient church surrounded by trees and fields on the outskirts of town.

I replied that I did not have one.

'Come. Have breakfast with me.'

Father John had already removed the splendid robes in which he had taken the service and donned a black cassock and black pill-box hat. A handsome man with a broad face, he had wide-set brown eyes, close-cropped hair and a well-controlled beard. He led me around the side of the church to a small room which was simply furnished with a table, a bed and a few chairs, and a church warden produced a breakfast of egg curry, *appam*, *idli* and tea. Father John asked what I had made of Holy Qurbana, which is what the Syrians call their eucharist. I said that I had found it fascinating, and sombre despite the flamboyance of the ritual, but as I had never been to an Eastern-rite service before and spoke no Malayalam, I had understood little of it, although I had recognized the *Kyrie eleison* and the significance of some of the rituals.

I had been among the first to reach the church, a little before seven o'clock in the morning, and I had watched the congregation arrive from the lawn outside. Although the priest and his assistants began chanting and praying at seven most people came half an hour later, the men filing in through the door at the side of the nave, the women through a long pantiled narthex which partially obscured a beautiful baroque façade. I had been in two minds whether to enter the church for fear that the presence of an outsider might not be to everyone's taste, but a succession of men suggested I follow them in and I eventually took my place at the rear. The men stood – there were no pews – on the left-hand side of the nave, while the women, all of whom had half-saris pulled over their heads, occupied the right. Between them, suspended from the ceiling, was a brass lamp. The walls of the nave were white and unadorned and a flight of shallow steps climbed up to the barrel-vaulted *madbaha*, the holy of holies, which contained the altar.

At times I felt I was watching an elaborate and highly ritualistic play. There was much genuflecting, on the part of both the priest and the crowded congregation, in addition to which there was no end of signing the cross and incensing of the altar. I was reminded of a dismissive aside in Abbé Dubois' *Letters on the State of Christianity in India*: 'Their waste of frankincense is very considerable, as they perform no religious ceremonies in their churches, and at home, without being surrounded by clouds of smoke of incense.' From time to time the curtain which separated the nave from the *madbaha* was drawn while the priest performed certain tasks, one being the blessing of the sacrament, away from the gaze of the congregation. Towards the end of the service he gave a brief sermon, during which everyone sat on the floor, and finally, after some two hours, the congregation received the Qurbana and went on its way.

I asked Father John, as we began our breakfast, why he had received one woman on her own before the main body of the congregation had surged forward for the Qurbana. 'She wanted to make her confession,' he replied. 'So that's what I did.'

'And what did you say?' I asked before I could prevent myself.

He smiled pleasantly and said: 'I told her to read Psalm 51, to contemplate it as a sort of punishment.'

He was obviously an intelligent and well-educated man – his English was perfect – and the story of how he came into the Church was an intriguing one. As a boy he wanted to be a priest, but he was the eldest son in his family and he felt that he should make a living to help support the others. He took a job at Grindlay's Bank in Bangalore and worked there for some time. 'Then one day,' he explained, 'a Hindu I knew told me that money wasn't everything. No Christian ever told me that.' He then began to think seriously about entering the priesthood. While on business in the Gulf he set up an ecumenical church group, then moved to the United States, where he studied at the Reformed Church and Ukrainian Orthodox seminaries. He was ordained in 1984 and he was presently the secretary of the Orthodox Christian Student Movement (OCSM). He added that a third of the twenty or so Orthodox bishops in Kerala had also been secretaries of the OCSM.

'You are Syrian Orthodox, aren't you?' I asked tentatively, aware from my encounter the previous day that there was the possibility of confusion.

'No,' replied Father John, grinning, 'we are Orthodox Syrian. The head of our Church is the Catholicos, here in Kottayam. The head of the other Church – the Syrian Orthodox Church – is the Patriarch in Antioch.'

He thought there were around 2 million Orthodox Syrian Christians in Kerala and 600,000 Syrian Orthodox Christians, who were also known as Jacobites. To confuse matters further, his Church, the Orthodox Syrian Church, was sometimes called the Malankara Church. The two Churches held the same theology and followed precisely the same liturgy; their disagreement revolved around the question of authority and who had the power to appoint bishops. Unfortunately, the dispute had led to bitter legal battles over the ownership of property. No doubt I had read about them in the newspapers, said Father John, who evidently had no wish to elaborate further.

However, he was eager to talk about the relationship of his Church, and indeed of the Syrians in general, with the non-Christians of Kerala. The Syrian Christians, he said, were on far better terms with Hindus and Muslims than were the Catholics and Protestants. A Hindu raja had given the Syrians permission to build Cheriapally and the neighbouring church of Valiapally, which was now occupied by Jacobites; the raja had even supplied some of the materials to build the churches, and a similar story could be told for many other Syrian churches in Kerala. The two communities had been living amicably together for well over a thousand years when the Portuguese arrived, and they remained on excellent terms today. 'When I was a child,' recalled Father John, 'we lived near a Hindu temple. The Hindus would come and collect money from us for their festivals and dramas. You see, we Syrians are part of the local culture.'

After breakfast Father John said he would take me to the Old Seminary, which was close to his home, and he asked if I wanted to see the paintings inside the *madbaha* before we left.

I said I had been told that only priests could enter the Holy of Holies.

'Yes,' replied Father John with a shrug. 'But it's all in a good cause, isn't it?'

The vegetable-dye frescos which lined the walls of the *madbaha* were said to have been painted at the time the church was built, around 1550. They were naïve in style and amateurish in execution. The crucifixion was watched over by a large number of soldiers and clerics who looked more Portuguese than Roman, and there was a dreamy depiction of Adam and Eve at the Tree of Knowledge, fringed by an abstract floral design which looked thoroughly Moghul in character. Father John said he knew little about the frescos, but he thought that they had been painted over by the British, then later restored.

We climbed on to Father John's scooter and headed towards his home down a narrow lane which was lined with rubber plantations and spice trees. I had spent so much time with Catholic priests over the past few weeks that I had come to assume that all priests were celibate, and I was taken aback when Father John led me into his house and introduced me to his wife, who was watching television. 'We have married priests as well as celibate ones,' he said when he saw my surprise. The latter, he added, were the only ones who could become bishops. He gave me a nutmeg from a tree in the garden and we walked to the Old Seminary, where he introduced me to Father K. M. George, the acting principal, before going on his way. Father George was in the middle of a meeting with a group of oppressively gloomy German Christians, and he suggested I return to see him the following day. In the meantime, he asked a man with the admirable name of Jacob Zachariah to show me around the seminary, a pleasant collection of buildings, some dating back to the early years of the last century, scattered across low-lying ground beside a backwater canal. Mr Zachariah was very knowledgeable about rubber – he worked for a company which made rubber slippers – and as he was transporting me back to Cheriapally on his motorbike he said: 'I've got two acres of rubber, some paddyland, a wife and two children.' This struck me as an admirable state of affairs. Why did I want to return to the church, he inquired? Was I going to the wedding? No, I replied, but I was meeting one of the wedding guests, a gentleman who had approached me after the morning service and who wished to tell me about the Joint Christian Temperance Movement, of which he was secretary.

Mr P. J. Kuriakose, a neatly built man of late middle age with heavy-rimmed spectacles, a small moustache and an earnest manner, detached himself from the colourful crowd when we arrived and led me into the room where the priest and I had taken breakfast. He spoke in an exceptionally loud voice, as though he was competing with the wedding ceremony, which got under way as soon as we sat down. Roman Catholics, Orthodox Syrians, Mar Thoma Syrians, the Church of South India and the Jacobites were all involved in the temperance movement, he said. The organization had been set up in 1955 and a Catholic bishop had been made president in 1961. The bishop toured Kerala preaching temperance, and priests were also encouraged to tell their congregations that drink was a sin.

'You mean, drinking heavily?' I asked.

'St Paul said drunk will never get into Kingdom of Heaven,' replied Mr Kuriakose emphatically. 'Drinking itself is not a sin – but leads to sin. Drunks kill for money. They have wife-beating and incest after drinking. They cause accidents. These things don't always come to limelight.' He said that people continued to abuse alcohol, despite all the warnings from priests and others: 'In the rich classes a sophisticated way of drinking is there. The rich have copied the European planters, who were drunkards.' While the rich drank imported scotch and expensive brands of liquor, the poor became addicted to arak and toddy.

The temperance society had set up an educational programme and Mr Kuriakose and his colleagues gave talks on the subject in schools and colleges. 'Good children listen well,' he said, 'but there are perverts among children too.' They also went into the slums, where the problem of alcoholism and drug addiction was at its most acute. In addition to this they helped the professional staff in various treatment centres in Kerala, one of which he offered to show me after lunch.

I did not wish to keep Mr Kuriakose from the wedding any longer, so I arranged to meet him later. While we searched for a vehicle to take me into town he said that his organization was also campaigning for prohibition in Kerala. I mentioned that I had shared a couple of bottles of beer with a Catholic priest earlier in the week; surely drinking in moderation was not to be discouraged? 'It will lead to drunkenness,' he replied severely.

The idea that drunkenness is the cause of much evil is as old as the art of distilling, and King James I was speaking for puritans of all ages when he described it as 'the root of all sins'. By nature I am intemperately anti-puritan, but it would be perverse to deny that alcoholism has had a profoundly unpleasant impact on certain sectors of Indian society. As I had seen in the slums of Delhi and Pune, it lay behind much of the cruelty meted out to women and children by their menfolk, and at the Asha clinic in Kottayam I was told a similar story by a full-figured counsellor called Sindhu Mary Jacob. She said that one study suggested that 38 per cent of alcoholic men sexually abused their daughters; she knew, for sure, that at least a quarter did. They also tended to beat their wives, most of whom suffered from depression.

Some of the clinics run by TRADA – Total Response to Alcohol and Drug Addiction – were government-financed and did not charge for their services; others, such as this one, were supported by fees, which were paid either by wealthy patients or by employers, one regular client being the local newspaper. 'Journalists are expensive to train,' explained Sindhu, who then proceeded to describe the course of treatment in considerable detail. The clinics were successful, she thought: over 60 per cent of those treated stayed off the drink, and this particular clinic treated over 1,000 people a year.

The following morning I read the *Hindu* at breakfast and came upon a short paragraph, tucked away in the inside pages, under the headline 'Twenty-two killed in hooch tragedy'. As usual, the victims of the spurious liquor consumption were slum-dwellers, in this instance in Sattur, a town on the other side of the Western Ghats. Prohibition or no prohibition, hooch tragedies will continue to happen wherever there is poverty in India and wherever large numbers of people are gathered together in miserable slums. As a sign declared on the side of a lorry I passed on my way to the Old Seminary after breakfast, 'God Help the Poor.'

~

When Father Willie d'Silva told me, during our brief encounter at Jesuit House in Panjim, that the rise of the evangelical Churches was to be welcomed as they represented an attack on the institution of the established Church, I wondered whether he was being outspoken – Jesuitical, so to speak – simply for the fun of it. When I reached Kottayam I began to understand more clearly his aversion to institutions, with their tendency to accumulate authority and power and, at times, to abuse it. The way the Roman Catholic Church behaved towards the St Thomas, or Syrian, Christians in the fifteenth and sixteenth centuries was shameful by any standards, and their despotic actions are resented to this day. Every Orthodox Christian will tell you about the Synod of Diamper in 1599 – 'a fateful date and one of the darkest in the history of relations between Latins and Orientals', as a Catholic historian, E. Tisserant, recently acknowledged – and it is stamped on their collective memory like a hallmark that can never be erased. I knew, as I sat down in Father George's large, ill-lit office at the Old Seminary, that it was a topic that would soon be raised. We began, however, by discussing whether or not St Thomas really did bring Christianity to India.

'From the angle of Western historiography, there's no proof that he came,' said Father George, who looked nothing like the portly, bushy-bearded and generally bespectacled metropolitans whose portraits were hung around the walls. His appearance – he wore a spotless white cassock and black pill-box hat – was matched by his speech, which suggested a precise and confident mind. Western historiography, continued Father George, failed to take community traditions into account: 'I do believe that

St Thomas came here. The coast of Kerala was well known by Arabs, by Jews and by Romans long before Christ was born. When they built the Temple of Jerusalem, they used ivory from here, and there are words which we find in Greek and Hebrew that came from this coast.' The Hebrew words for peacock and monkey, he explained, were derived from a south Indian language, as was the Greek word for rice. 'For me,' continued Father George, 'there's no doubt that a Palestinian Jew could easily have come to Kerala and that St Thomas would have arrived at Cranganore with a group of merchants.' He added that he probably introduced himself to the local rajas as an architect.

We moved, inexorably, on to the Catholic persecutions of the Syrian Christians; these Father George described with a hint of distaste, much as an aggrieved wife might recall the infidelities of an erring husband when citing the reasons for divorce. The persecutions, he explained, began midway through the sixteenth century. By then Goa was an archbishopric, with suffragen sees in Malacca and Cochin. The archbishop was effectively the highest authority of the Western Church in Asia and there was a belief among the Catholics that the Syrians should be brought into the fold. Some of the Syrian bishops were accused of heresy – one, Mar Joseph, was twice arrested by the Portuguese and dispatched for trial in Lisbon – and matters eventually came to a head with the arrival in Goa, in 1595, of a young and highly autocratic archbishop, Aleixo da Menezes. In January 1599, he descended on Cochin with a large army, induced the Syrian archdeacon to sign an acknowledgement of the Pope's supremacy, ordained a hundred or more priests and convened a synod at Udiamperur, or Diamper to give its anglicized name. The synod was held on 20 June 1599 and attended by 660 lay people, 153 priests, the majority of whom had been recently ordained by Menezes himself, and twenty deacons. Six days later everyone present, including Syrian priests who understood little or no Portuguese, the language in which the synod was conducted, signed the decree which brought to an end the independence of their Church. Menezes sealed his triumph by burning most of the books at Angamali, the seat of the Syrian bishops. This is one reason why the historical records about the early Christians are so scanty.

For a little over half a century all Syrian Christians remained within the Roman Church, but many disliked both the Jesuits and the Portuguese and they became increasingly disenchanted with the Church's denial of the privileges granted them at the Synod of Diamper. Eventually, their patience ran out. In 1653 a large crowd of Syrians gathered at Koonan Cross in a churchyard at Mattancherry, scene of the recent hooch tragedy, and took an oath to expel the Jesuits and accept no authority other than that of their own archdeacon until they received a new bishop from the Eastern Church.

The first bishop to be sent by Antioch was Mar Attala, who was captured on his arrival by the Portuguese, sent to Goa, tried by the Inquisition and burned as a heretic in 1654. However, three years after the revolt a Syrian bishop successfully made the journey from Antioch to Kerala. The fact that he belonged to an Eastern Church whose Christology – understanding of the nature of Christ – was diametrically opposed to that of the bishops who had previously served the Indian Syrians made not the slightest difference: they were thankful to be free of the papist yoke. 'Most of the Syrian Christians broke away from the Catholics after Koonan Cross,' explained Father George, 'but the Catholics made great efforts to get them back.' During the following decades, large numbers of Spanish and Italian missionaries descended on the Kerala coast and many of the parishes between Cochin and Kottayam were won back by the Roman Church.

When the Portuguese arrived in south India there were around 100,000 Syrian Christians. They probably numbered the same or thereabouts when Abbé Dubois visited the area in the early years of the nineteenth century. He wrote in his *Letters* that many of the Syrians subscribed to the Nestorian heresy, which is to say that they believed there to be two separate persons in the incarnate Christ, one divine and one human. In this he was wrong: they were actually Jacobites. They believed, in line with the Nicene Creed, that Christ was a single person, simultaneously God and man. However, Dubois' confusion about the Syrians' Christology was probably a reflection of the Syrians' own uncertainty: 'The disturbances which have arisen among themselves during these last two centuries have rendered them so unsettled in their religious tenets that you will scarcely find the most intelligent among them agreeing in the exposition of their faith.' He concluded his brief account with the observation that Protestant missionaries had recently prevailed upon many of the priests, who were formerly celibate, to marry. That, he remarked with characteristic sourness, was the only success they could boast of, which was by no means the case.

The Old Seminary, explained Father George, owed its existence to Colonel Munro, the British resident in Travancore in the early years of the nineteenth century. He took a great interest in the Syrian Christians, partly because he wished to help their Church, but also because he felt they could be useful allies for the Raj, which was busy exploiting the forests in the hills and setting up rubber, spice and coffee plantations. Munro gave financial help towards the building of the Old Seminary, whose construction was completed in 1813. Two years later it opened for classes and in 1816 Munro suggested to the Church Missionary Society (CMS) in London that it should send some of its missionaries to help in the education of the Syrian priests. This it did, and Benjamin Bailey, Joseph Fenn and Henry Barker duly arrived in Kottayam. Bailey translated the Bible into Malayalam and established a printing press which is still standing, near the Asha clinic for alcoholics; Fenn became principal of the seminary; and Barker set up several schools for Syrian Christian children. 'For some years,' explained Father George, 'the collaboration with the missionaries was very smooth. They were high-church and they had come on the understanding that they wouldn't interfere with our beliefs.' This amicable partnership between Anglicans and Syrians prevailed until a new batch of low-church missionaries was sent out from London to replace Bailey, Fenn and Barker, who returned to England between 1826 and 1833. 'They were shocked to discover that we prayed for the departed, invoked saints, mentioned the Virgin Mary in the liturgy and so on,' said Father George. 'They thought this was all superstition and they said that the liturgy should be reformed.' The missionaries introduced the Anglican *Book of Common Prayer* and became progressively more outspoken in their opposition to Syrian beliefs. A falling out became inevitable and eventually the metropolitan banned the missionaries from preaching in Syrian churches and asked them to leave the seminary. The Old Seminary remained in the possession of the Syrians and the CMS established what is still known as the New Seminary. Protestant agitation among the Syrians continued and it eventually led to the founding of the Mar Thoma Church, whose headquarters I intended to visit later.

It was the issue of power, rather than belief, continued Father George, that lay behind the Orthodox Church's recent travails. For the greater part of the past century – much to the sadness and disgust of most Syrian Christians – the Church had been divided into two factions, the Orthodox Syrian or Malankara Church and the Syrian Orthodox or Jacobite wing. The former considered themselves to be autocephalous, with a Catholicos in Kottayam as spiritual and temporal head of the Church; the Patriarch of Antioch exercised his power only as the supreme head of the Syrian Church with the approval of the Catholicos. The Jacobites, in contrast, considered the Patriarch to be the head of their Church and bishops chosen by him were the highest authorities in India. 'The whole business has led to a terrible waste of time and money,' said Father George. 'It's also affected the spiritual life of the Church.'

As Father George led me out into the sun towards the study of another priest, I asked him what he thought would become of the Church in India.

'My feeling is that we were all one Church in India till the sixteenth century,' he said, choosing his words carefully, 'and we should aim for that again. We're anti-missionary – not anti-mission – because of the divisions created by the Protestants. We're anti-Rome because of the Portuguese onslaught on our Church. I tell everyone – Catholics, Protestants, whoever – that we should be one again: an Indian Church, not a Church which looks to Rome, or Antioch, or Canterbury.'

Father George left me in the company of Father Gabriel, who told me about the workings of the seminary, which had over 130 students studying the four-year Bachelor of Divinity course. The daily routine had a monastic ring to it: meditation and prayers at five a.m., noon and from six p.m. to seven p.m.; compline at nine thirty, then bed. Staff and students observed the three fixed lents of the Orthodox Church and the two moveable ones, the longer of which, the Great Lent, lasts for fifty days. During the lents they abstained from eating and drinking all animal products. They also fasted till three p.m. every Friday. At weekends the students were sent out into the parishes, where they preached, visited the sick, counselled people with family problems and did some charitable work among the poor.

We also discussed the issue of caste, about which Father Gabriel was surprisingly candid. The Syrian Christians, he said, believed themselves to be the descendants of converts from high-caste Hinduism, and until recently they treated low-caste Hindus in precisely the same superior manner as their forebears had before their conversion to Christianity. He said that the Syrian Christians had never been looked down upon by high-caste Hindus and Muslims, as had more recent converts, who were still seen as low-caste and a product of foreign colonization, and were resented on both counts. Those Syrians who converted to Anglicanism in the last century, and who now belonged to the Church of South

India, seldom married the low-caste Protestants who formed the backbone of that Church. They were far more likely to marry Syrian Christians from the Orthodox Churches. The Syrian Christians, concluded Father Gabriel, formed a powerful group in Kerala: they were well educated and generally well off.

This had been strikingly apparent at the Sunday service at Cheriapally. Besides the obvious indications of wealth and worldliness in their apparel and demeanour, I was particularly struck by the nature of the worshippers' feet: they were neat, well-manicured feet of the sort which clearly spent most of their time – outside church and the home – in shoes, and decent shoes at that, doctors' feet, lawyers' feet, bankers' feet, a different species altogether from the splayed, callused feet which you will see in the Catholic churches on the coast, and which tell of the hard labouring life led by fishermen, coolies, rickshaw-wallahs and the like.

While on the subject of people's appearance, I recall an afternoon when I found myself in the company of a delightful character who, like me, was hoping to have an audience with a Syrian bishop. Neither of us, as it happens, was immediately successful – the bishop was at a wedding – and we whiled away the time by discussing, among other things, the photographs and portraits in the bishop's study. One wall was hung with portraits of the past dozen or so leaders of this particular church; all sported long grey beards and wore spectacles. The other wall was hung with portraits of the bishops still serving; all sported beards and all but three wore spectacles.

'Have you noticed how nearly all bishops and priests wear spectacles?' I asked idly.

'Yes,' replied my companion, giggling. 'You'll also notice that the bishops have large bellies.' He attributed the poor eyesight of the clergy to endless hours reading the Bible in gloomy studies and seminaries, and the bishops' corpulence to their frequent attendance at wedding banquets. 'Eating a lot, not enough exercise,' he said, again with a high-pitched giggle which reminded me of the demented police chief in the *Pink Panther* films. He looked at his watch. 'Maybe the bishop is still eating,' he said with relish.

'There's another thing that perhaps you're not noticing,' he announced a little later. 'The bishops are nearly all diabetic.' He thought this was probably a consequence of their celibacy. Diabetes was more of an affliction among the Syrian bishops than among Catholic priests, many of whom, he confided, were 'going beyond the limit – sexually speaking'.

Once we had exhausted this subject, we moved on to more serious matters and he told me about life at the ashram where he lived. There was far more to it than contemplation and prayer; he, his wife and several other families ran a home for orphaned boys. Members of the ashram came from many Christian denominations – Orthodox Syrians, Mar Thomites, Catholics, Protestants – and he said that they, like most Christians, were saddened by the divisions within their community. 'These disputes are a great scandal for Gentiles,' he added.

As Kottayam was primarily a centre of importance for the Orthodox Churches, I made no great effort to meet Catholics or Protestants – nor even the 'Jehoas Withnesses' – but I did call on Father Jacob Kollaparambil, a noted historian in the Syro-Malabar Church. This is a Uniat Church with its own hierarchy; its early members were Syrian Catholics who either declined to join the Koonan Cross revolt or returned to Roman obedience soon after.

Father Jacob had made lengthy studies of a group of Keralite Christians known as Southists, of whom he thought there were around 200,000. Unlike the 4 million-strong Northist population, who considered themselves to be descendants of those people who were converted by St Thomas, the Southists dated their presence in India to the arrival in Cranganore in AD 345 of seventy-two Mesopotamian families that had allegedly been dispatched by an Eastern patriarch to help revive the ailing Church. Their leader was Thomas Kinayi, or Thomas Cana as Western historians call him, and the Southists often refer to themselves, through a corruption of his name, as Knaniya Christians. Father Jacob had studied the ancient folklore and sayings of the Southists, visited Mesopotamia and concluded that they were indeed descendants of the families that arrived with Thomas Kinayi, who came from a town on the left bank of the river Tigris. He said that they had preserved their ethnic identity by the strict practice of endogamy, of marrying among themselves, just as India's Jews had. He estimated that around two-thirds of the Southists were Catholics, while the remainder belonged mainly to the Orthodox Churches.

Kottayam is an important centre for the Southists and one of the churches in their possession is even older than Cheriapally, which was built beside it. On my first visit to Valiapally – the big church – I was shown around by a young man of strange and excitable disposition. He appeared with a large bunch of keys while I was studying the noticeboard outside the locked gate of the churchyard. The board declared that this was St Mary's (Knaniya) church. 'Jacobite! Jacobite!' shouted the young man as he searched for the right key. In plain English this meant that members of the congregation were descendants of the families which arrived in Cranganore in AD 345, were party to the revolt against the Roman Catholics at Koonan Cross and now acknowledged the Patriarch in Antioch, rather than the Catholicos in Kottayam, as head of their Church. The young man looked like a south Indian, not a Mesopotamian, as did all the other Southists I met, which suggests either that they were not as endogamous as they would like to think or that they were subject to the same sort of evolutionary processes which have led certain animals to assume the camouflaging colours of their environment. I spent little time in the church, not least because I found my guide's behaviour unnerving. 'Persian cross! Persian cross!' he kept shouting, and when he wasn't shouting, he was banging his hands on the old visitors' book. The Persian cross was a beautiful object carved in stone and it formed the centrepiece of a small shrine on the left-hand side of the nave. Mythology claims that this is one of the seven crosses carved by St Thomas for the seven churches he founded in India. It actually dates from the seventh century, but is still one of the oldest Christian artefacts in the country. 'Visitor book! Visitor book!' screamed my guide as soon as he was satisfied that I had seen enough of the Persian cross. I quickly flipped through the early pages of the book and was intrigued to see that Lord Irwin, the British Viceroy in India, had sent a donation of 50 rupees and asked for a written receipt.

When I returned to Valiapally later in the week, in the hope of a more restful inspection, I was greeted outside the churchyard by a man who was dressed only in a *dhoti*. He was very knowledgeable about both the Southists' history and Valiapally. As we climbed the steps to the church he explained that he lived in New Jersey, but he originally came from this corner of Kottayam and he was now building a house in anticipation of his eventual return. I was glad to have time to study the interior of the church in greater detail, and especially the colourful altar with a dark-skinned St George slaying a dragon. The twelve disciples, whose portraits were carved around the arch which divided the nave from the chancel, looked like Orthodox patriarchs; the surrounds to the Persian cross, and its imitation in stone on the other side of the nave, were also influenced by the iconography of the Eastern Churches. I browsed through the visitors' book once again and came across a cutting which reported that 'the church has attracted many European and native gentlemen of high position'. According to plaques at the entrance, the church had also been graced by visits from one of the patriarchs of Antioch and by Emperor Haile Selassie of Ethiopia. Ethiopians like to claim that their ruling dynasty was founded by a union between King Solomon and the Queen of Sheba, and that Christianity took root in their country shortly after Christ's death. The truth is almost as appealing as the myth: Christianity was introduced into Ethiopia in AD 341 by two Syrian Christians who were shipwrecked in the Red Sea when on their way to India.

~

Diwali, the Hindu festival of lights, is celebrated in most parts of India with joyful exuberance: candles and lamps are lit in the temples and floated down the holy rivers; firecrackers are hurled about, much to the terror of dogs and children, late into the night. Kottayam, being predominantly Christian, seemed to be ignoring Diwali; the local newspapers were more preoccupied with the total eclipse of the sun, which was due to occur the following day, and KK Road looked exactly as it did on any other weekday morning: lorries and rickshaws weaved erratically down the hill from the Catholic churches, night-watchmen wearily awaited the arrival of the day shift outside the gold shops, and on the pavements nuns, businessmen and bureaucrats jostled for position in lengthy bus queues. When I reached the Jerusalem Mar Thoma church, which occupied a spacious enclosure five minutes' walk from my hotel, a passer-by asked whether I wanted to see the pastor, then directed me down a steep alley to the parsonage. I knocked at the door and a youngish-looking man with a thick beard and close-cropped hair appeared. He introduced himself as Father Thomas Philip. 'I'm a bit busy with the cooking and cleaning,' he said. 'Why don't you come back later? Say ten o'clock.'

When I returned I found Father Thomas, dressed now in a smart white cassock and black pill-box hat, sitting in his office at the side of the church. If I wanted to learn about the Mar Thoma Church, he suggested, I should really go to Tiruvella and meet the metropolitan, Alexander Mar Thoma. Tiruvella was the headquarters of the Church; even if I failed to meet the metropolitan, I would be able to see other key figures in the administration. In the meantime, he said, he was happy to tell me about the Mar Thomites, who in his opinion had taken the best of the Orthodox tradition and blended it with the best of the Anglican.

The key figure in the nineteenth-century reformation of the Orthodox Church was Abraham Malpan. A professor of Syriac in the Old Seminary, Abraham Malpan – *malpan* means teacher – was greatly influenced by the CMS missionaries, whose critique of the Orthodox Church he largely accepted. The present metropolitan has suggested that the Orthodox Church in the early nineteenth century needed to realize – as the missionaries urged its believers – that salvation was by the grace of God, not through the observance of arcane rituals. 'The pre-reformation Church,' he wrote in his portrait of the Mar Thomites, 'was satisfied with the observance of certain rites and ceremonies. It was believed that by praying to the saints and celebrating special festivals connected with them, benefits could be derived and evil could be avoided. This was very much like the festivals observed by the non-Christian community around them. They just formed another social group observing Christian ceremonies but having no special message for the world.'

After the Orthodox Church severed links with the CMS and ejected its missionaries from the Old Seminary, Abraham Malpan and twelve priests under his leadership submitted a memorandum – a Trumpet Call of Reformation – to the British resident. This had no perceptible impact, so Abraham Malpan proceeded to introduce reforms at the church of Maramon, where he officiated. He began to celebrate the Holy Qurbana in Malayalam, which was intelligible to all Keralites, rather than in Syriac, which wasn't, and he made significant changes to the liturgy. He omitted prayers for the dead and all invocations to saints and the Virgin Mary. He also did away with prayers that suggested the idea of transubstantiation. 'Unlike the Orthodox Church,' explained Father Thomas, 'we give the bread and the wine separately, like the Anglicans. We don't believe in transubstantiation. A transformation takes place within us – not, as the Orthodox and Catholic Churches maintain, after consecration.' Under the reforms the use of incense was no longer seen as a ritual which helped reconcile man with God, and the word 'mystery' was omitted wherever it might be construed as implying that magic was at work during the giving and receiving of the eucharist. The reformers also laid much greater emphasis on the Scriptures and on the preaching of the gospel than their traditionalist counterparts. All the same, Abraham Malpan made only changes which he considered to be theologically enlightened and necessary. The form of the service remained substantially the same; priests continued to wear Orthodox vestments and the sexes to worship apart: 'Ladies to one side, gents to the other,' as Father Thomas put it.

Abraham Malpan wished to reform the Orthodox Church, not to create a new denomination. In this he failed, though the split came long after his death: the Mar Thoma Church eventually came into being as a separate entity late in the nineteenth century. This being Kerala, and these being Syrian Christians, the divorce was fractious and messy. The warring factions took their grievances to the courts, which decided that with the exception of the churches at Maramon and Kozhencherry, all properties should remain under the control of the unreformed Malankara Church. Perhaps this was a blessing in disguise: disputes over property, and over its ownership and disposal, have done immense damage to the Churches of North and South India, whose trustees and administrators frequently behave in a corrupt and thoroughly un-Christian manner, and at times it seems that the Orthodox Churches expend as much energy in the courts, fighting one another over property, as they do at the altar.

The Mar Thoma Church embarked on its journey into the twentieth century with a keen sense of mission – its evangelistic association, established in 1888, was the first indigenous self-supporting missionary organization in India – and with precious little in the way of material assets. It now has ten bishops, over 1,000 pastors and close to 1 million members. 'You must come back in February,' suggested Father Thomas before I left for Tiruvella. The Mar Thoma's Maramon Convention, he explained, attracted over 100,000 people each year to a dried-up riverbed near the church where Abraham Malpan began the reformist movement. Father Thomas also suggested I visit one of the Mar Thoma mission stations outside Kerala, which I did the following month. The Church was evangelical, but its eagerness to 'win India for Christ' – this being the motto of its evangelistic association – was complemented by its belief that faith had to be backed up by action. 'I'd say we give far more importance to social work than any other Church,' said Father Thomas bluntly. He recounted how he and his church, which he described as democratic and relatively wealthy, were about to establish a hospital guidance centre in Kottayam similar to one which already existed in Trivandrum. 'When the villagers come for hospital treatment,' he explained, 'they're exploited by the middle men who find them accommodation. We're building dormitory accommodation for thirty men and thirty women, so villagers will be able to stay at very low cost while they or their relatives are having hospital treatment.' The Mar Thoma Church was also setting up a rehabilitation centre for drug addicts in Kottayam.

I arrived at Tiruvella soon after midday, had lunch at a restaurant called Whynot and introduced myself to the general secretary of the Mar Thoma Church, Rev. A. C. Kurien. A man of great charm and good looks, he spent the early afternoon describing the polity of his Church. Like the Anglican Church, the Mar Thoma Church is episcopalian in the sense that it has a hierarchy of metropolitan and bishops, but it is far more democratic. All decisions affecting the administration and the faith of the Church are taken by the Sabha Prathinidhi Mandalam, two-thirds of whose members are elected by the parishes, the remainder comprising pastors and bishops. To ensure that the larger parishes do not dominate the proceedings, the Church has devised a system whereby a parish with 100 or fewer baptized members elects one person, a parish with between 100 and 2,000 members elects two, and a parish with 2,000 to 5,000 members elects three. The Mar Thoma Church also promotes women into positions of influence, and if a parish has a right to elect two members to the Mandalam one must be female. 'And we're thinking about ordaining women priests,' added Rev. Kurien, 'although there is some reluctance among the members about that.'

On several occasions I heard Syrian Christians being roundly condemned for their élitism and contempt for *dalit* Christians, who make up the majority of communicants in the Protestant and Roman Catholic Churches in south India. However, Rev. Kurien was quick to point out that the Mar Thoma Church was actively assisting disadvantaged groups. 'We've got 15,000 *dalit* members,' he said, 'and we're doing everything we can to help them. We're trying to assimilate them into the mainstream of the Church, but that's not easy because the *dalits* actually want to remain as a separate group. I understand that. When they come here' – he waved outside the open window to the church nearby – 'they feel inferior. If they have their own church they can run it themselves and they prefer that.' Although *dalits* represented less than 2 per cent of the Church's membership, a quarter of the jobs within the Church were reserved for them.

A few days later I called on Joseph Mar Irenaeus, the Mar Thomite bishop of Trivandrum diocese and at the time of my visit chairman of the National Council of Indian Churches, an organization which was pressing the government to give Christian *dalits* the same privileges, in terms of job reservations and legal safeguards against persecution, as were currently enjoyed by Hindu, Sikh and Buddhist *dalits*. We talked about three things: the struggle to help Christian *dalits*, the social programmes run by the Church and salvation. As far as the last was concerned, he recalled the words of Dr Stanley Jones, an evangelist who regularly used to preach at the Maramon Convention: 'If Gandhi's not there in heaven, heaven will be a desert.' There is no denying that the vast majority of Mar Thomite Christians are well off, well educated and, in terms of their genealogy, high-caste, yet at first glance this reformed branch of India's most ancient Church struck me as being compassionate and egalitarian.

CHAPTER 8

An Ancient Dominion

I woke up at three o'clock in the morning and realized, with a feeling which approached euphoria, that I was experiencing the very thing which I had missed most on my journey from one end of the country to the other: silence, and if not total silence, then something free of the sounds of human endeavour and discord. I lay awake for a long time, gazing through the open window at the palms silhouetted against the indigo of the distant sky, listening to the rustle of frond against frond and the wet slap of waves against the sand on the beach below and, between the rustles and the slaps, to the silences themselves. I tried to recall when I had last experienced such natural peace. In Shimla, on the walk down to Kaylog cemetery? There was the sound of wind in the boughs of the deodars, and of songbirds too, but couldn't I hear, however hard I tried not to, the distant grinding of lorries as they climbed up towards the bazar? In Delhi, Bombay and Pune there was never any peace, even in the middle of the night, and by the end of each day I felt as though my head had been spun through an antiquated noise machine. There were moments of great tranquillity in Goa – at St Anna's church, for example, and in some of the villages to the east of Mapsa – but in the distance there was always the buzz of a tractor or the whine of a plane coming in to land at the airport. When I arrived at the Sea Gull Hotel at Cochin I anticipated quiet nights, but had reckoned without the constant traffic of trawlers heading out to the fishing grounds or back to the harbour with their catch.

Eventually, I fell into a calm, restful sleep, as though the murmurings and silences of the world outside were a much needed balm, and woke again a little after dawn, not to the sounds of rickshaws backfiring, or taxis hooting, or men expectorating and shouting, but to an Indian cuckoo calling and the less mellifluous sound of crows squabbling in the coconut palm outside my window. I was about to drift back to sleep again when the chanting began. It was some distance away but clear enough, and its tone and vigour implied hard, rhythmic work. I climbed into some clothes, splashed water on my face and headed along a jagged footpath to a small bay where forty men and boys were hauling in a fishing net.

I walked down to the beach, then climbed on to the purple rocks behind the fishermen. It was a lustrous day and the greens and oranges, vermilions and turquoises of the fishermen's *dhotis* looked preternaturally bright against the soft ochres of the sand and the frothy blue of the sea where it met the shore. The men were dark-skinned and sinewy; some wore lengths of cotton wrapped around their heads, others were bare-headed, and few wore shirts. They were split into two groups, some fifty yards apart, and each group pulled one end of a thick coconut-fibre rope whose middle portion, half a mile or more out to sea, was slung with the net. Each man held a segment of rope in a vice-like grip and walked backwards up the shore, balls of the feet digging deep into the sand; he released the rope when he reached the top of the shore, then jogged back to the water's edge to take it up again. It took over three-quarters of an hour to pull the net in and the nearer it came to the shore, the easier was the fishermen's task and the more animated their chanting. When it was no more than fifty yards out – wooden and plastic buoys signalled its position – half a dozen of the younger men dived into the sea and began slapping the water to drive the fish into the back of the net.

Finally it was hauled on to the shore; the chanting gave way to a hubbub of shouting and then to recriminations. There were scarcely enough fish to fill a couple of baskets, and most were anchovies, a species of relatively little value.

Half an hour later two large canoes took the nets and paddled them out to sea again. The men onshore sat and smoked, and in some cases argued, and waited for the canoes to return with the rope-ends. From start to finish the next bout of man-powered purse-seineing took over half an hour half. The catch this time was more substantial, perhaps 15 kilos of assorted fish, and the fishermen seemed less disconsolate, although the proceeds would have been minuscule when shared among those present. The men then returned to the village of Vizhinjam, on the other side of a long promontory decorated with a mosque which glistened an opaque nacre-white in the morning sun, and I returned to a very different world, the tourist resort of Kovalam Beach.

The first time I witnessed this laborious method of extracting fish from the sea, on a visit to Kerala's coast in 1991, I felt like a voyeur watching an unusually cruel game where even the highest gains were so meagre that they seemed to mock the participants; it looked more like an aversion therapy for Gamblers Anonymous than a sensible way of making a living. I had come to Trivandrum and the fringing coast neither for relaxation, which I hoped for now, nor for Christians, but to study the state of the fishing industry. I talked to people attached to a Catholic agency which was working with the fishing communities, to members of a fishermen's trade union, to marine biologists and to some of the fishermen themselves. Kerala's 30 million inhabitants may be among the best-educated, least fecund, healthiest and politically most sophisticated people in India, but the coastal fishing communities in the south are as impoverished, disease-ridden and malnourished as any you will find. The Communists in the state say that they are the victims of naked capitalism, and they are probably not far wrong. It is a complicated story, but it can be briefly told.

Before the 1960s there were no motor-driven fishing boats in Kerala. Around Alleppey the fishermen favoured fifteen-man canoes, or *thanguralloms*, while those further south used small mango-log *kattumarams*. Whatever type of boat they used, they were interested mainly in fish; when they caught prawns they were as likely to use them to fertilize their coconut groves as sell them for food. However, with the arrival of bulk refrigeration in the late 1960s local merchants discovered there was a good market for shellfish abroad. While fresh fish might sell locally for 150–200 rupees a tonne, the prawns could fetch 4,000 rupees in the States and double that in Japan. Thus began the rush for Kerala's 'pink gold'. Businessmen moved in on the industry and hired groups of fishermen to run their new trawler fleets. In 1971 the total fish and prawn catch in Kerala was 445,000 tonnes, about 90 per cent of which was taken by the artisanal or peasant fishermen. Four years later the catch was down to 420,000 tonnes, by which time the mechanized fleet of trawlers accounted for 43 per cent of the fish taken. By 1980 the catch had slumped to 280,000 tonnes and the peasant fishermen took just over half. This meant that 100,000 or more peasant fishermen had seen their catch decline from 398,000 tonnes to 144,000 tonnes in ten years. As far as prawns were concerned, the catch had risen from 30,000 tonnes in 1970 to 83,000 in 1974, but it had fallen back to 30,000 tonnes again by the end of the decade. In 1970 the entire prawn catch was taken by peasant fishermen; in 1980 all but a fifth was taken by the trawlers.

The peasant fishermen had reacted to the mechanized competition in various ways: violently, by burning trawlers and attacking their crews; more constructively, by sticking outboard motors on their canoes in the hope that these would enable them to get to the fishing grounds faster and catch more fish. Now half the traditional craft are motorized, but in their quest to compete with the trawlers many fishermen have fallen into debt to the money-lenders. The consequence of all this, explained the woman I met at the Catholic agency, was an increase in poverty. Alcoholism and wife-beating were rife and the children of the fisherfolk were ill-fed, illiterate and ill-kempt. I asked her if she would take me to one of the villages, but she declined. So I went with a marine biologist, who was an Englishman, and one of the villages we chose to visit was Vizhinjam.

Despite its proximity to Kovalam Beach, Vizhinjam was rarely visited by foreigners and when we walked down to the beachside slums we were greeted with a mixture of curiosity and suspicion. The beach looked like a lumber yard, and what little sand was visible between the *kattumarams* was soiled by human excrement. The biologist explained that about an hour before dawn all the women of the palm-leaf shacks – and there were several thousand here – came down to the beach to do their business, which they buried beneath the sand; a little later the men would follow and do the same. There were no latrines in the fishermen's quarters, nor was there any piped water, which explained the lengthy queues at the standpipes in the street behind. The Muslim fishing families occupied the northern portion of the beach, adjacent to their spectacular mosque. Christians occupied the southern portion; they had an old church near their shacks and a modern one, an edifice of grand proportions, on the hill behind. The biologist said that he was disgusted by the Catholic Church. Its priests lived in splendour, leeching the fishermen of their hard-earned rupees to build vast churches, but they did nothing practical to help the poor. At the time I had no idea whether he was right or wrong, although the fact that he was a convinced atheist presumably did not predispose him to be sympathetic to religious institutions.

After we had visited a few smaller fishing villages we dropped into Kovalam Beach for lunch. I seem to remember we ate spaghetti, or perhaps it was a pizza – anyway, something un-Indian and unhealthy – and during the course of the meal the biologist said that the state government was happy to provide electricity, piped water, paved roads and so forth for Kovalam Beach, as tourists brought in much needed foreign currency, but it did nothing to help the fishing people of Vizhinjam. There was, he thought, something obscene about Western tourists being provided with facilities which, in a just society, would be given to the impoverished locals in the neighbouring bay. I accepted his point, and silently vowed that if I ever visited this part of India again I would stay in Trivandrum.

Over the years I remained true to my vow and I probably know Trivandrum's middle-range hotels as well as anybody. The best, incidentally, although it is noisy, is the Pankaj, whose rooftop restaurant provides fine views of the neo-classical secretariat, outside which the government has kindly provided space and shade for demonstrators and hunger-strikers, the latter being a perennial feature of Kerala's turbulent political life. Trivandrum itself is one of the pleasanter small towns in India, scattered around a cluster of low hills and well supplied with public parks and attractive buildings with tiled pagoda-style roofs. Such virtues, however, were not enough to deter me from staying at Kovalam Beach on this particular occasion. There were two reasons why I decided to forsake my old vow. First, and most compellingly, I wished to spend some time by the sea, as far away as possible from the frenetic activity of city life. Second, I had come to the conclusion that my aversion to Kovalam Beach and the pleasures it afforded was vaguely ridiculous. When I first visited this coast I had been scarcely a week in India, and like many first-time visitors I was disgusted by the unfairness and inequities which I saw. I still am, though I am more used to them now, but I have come to realize that first impressions are often misleading. The poverty of Vizhinjam was not, I knew now, a direct consequence of the government favouring Kovalam Beach; nor, as I was to discover, were its Catholic inhabitants coerced into funding the institutions of the Church.

Kovalam Beach consists of four sandy bays divided from one another by rocky headlands and fringed by steep hills covered with palms and scrub. At one time it was the preserve solely of fishermen and Western travellers, a peaceful retreat on the long road around the subcontinent, fully equipped with cheap accommodation and restaurants which served European food and rock music. Over the years it has gone upmarket and there is now a smattering of classier hotels, many of which attract package tourists during the European winter season. All the same, it has yet to suffer the crass overdevelopment which is marring many of Goa's beaches and it does have the languid charm that the glossy pictures in tourist brochures hope to project. It is also a beguilingly entertaining place, as I discovered on my first evening.

I had arrived in mid-afternoon, having taken the morning train from Kottayam and lunched at the Pankaj, and I found a small hotel behind the red-and-white-striped lighthouse. It had half a dozen rooms, good views over the sea and no restaurant or bar. I went down to the beach around five o'clock, swam in magnificent surfing waves and took a bamboo seat in one of the many outdoor cafés overlooking the bay. The package-tour season had yet to begin and there were probably no more than a hundred people messing about on the beach, swimming or sitting in the cafés watching the sun gradually turn from yellow to blood-orange as it sank towards the horizon. A group of six young Indian tourists had covered themselves with black sand; greatly delighted by their African appearance, they asked a passing tourist to take a photograph. There were several Indian families who had come from Trivandrum or elsewhere to take the evening air. One consisted of a husband who was dressed in a suit, a wife with a figure like Queen Victoria and two glamorous teenage daughters, both in expensive Punjabi pyjamas. The whole family waded into the sea up to their thighs. The father had rolled his trousers up to his knees but his womenfolk made no effort to keep their lower garments dry. Such propriety struck me as all the more admirable when I caught sight of two Oriental men – Koreans, I guessed – who sauntered past the café wearing skimpy G-strings. A dreadlocked, well-muscled European of Latin appearance jogged up and down the beach – he was a resident artist, I learned later – and an unreconstructed hippy, kitted out with a penny whistle, a bunch of coloured balloons and clothing which might have been snatched from a fairy in *A Midsummer Night's Dream*, attracted an excitable group of naked children, the progeny of two bejewelled tribal women who ran a stall selling garments between two of the cafés.

The sun set and I ordered a second bottle of Kingfisher beer and barracuda and chips. While I ate I gazed at the alluring scene: the sky above was spangled with stars; away to my left the beam of the lighthouse periodically skimmed across sea and surf, and to my right the curve of the bay was sprinkled with flickering lights and candles. This was an India I had never known before, although I was soon brought back to a more familiar reality by the waiter, who came to talk to me before I had finished eating. He said he had an engineering degree, as had many other waiters here, but he was unable to find work in his profession. I had no reason to disbelieve him: I had read somewhere that many bus drivers in Kerala had Ph.Ds, although their academic achievements had done little for their sense of prudence, Kerala having one of the worst road records in India. The waiter then said: 'Two days ago I experienced a great tragedy.' He shuffled around for a bit with his head bowed and a big toe scraping patterns in the sand. 'On Wednesday my wife was burned to death.' He explained that he was a Christian and that he had married a young Hindu girl in secret. When her family found out they doused her with kerosene and set her on fire.

In Delhi and other parts of north India the practice of bride-burning is not uncommon; well over a thousand women die this way each year. Nearly all these deaths are related to the dissatisfaction of the groom and the groom's family with the size of dowry given by the bride's family. If the latter fails to come up with sufficient cows, televisions, Sumeet mixers, rupees or whatever, retribution is simple: the bride is immolated, often within a few months of the marriage, by her husband or his relatives. However, I was under the impression that bride-burning seldom happened in the south, and there was something about the waiter's story which didn't ring true. I mentioned it the following morning to the young man who ran my hotel. He said he would have heard if such a thing had happened and he suspected that the waiter was a fantasist. He added that the only violent deaths that he had heard of recently had happened in Vizhinjam, although they were nothing to do with brides or dowries.

Vizhinjam looked much as I had remembered it, although I was surprised to see so many policemen on the street which led down to the beach. There must have been well over sixty, some standing around on street corners twiddling their weapons, others sitting with bored expressions in the riot-proof buses parked half-way down the hill. My rickshaw sped past the fishermen's shacks, across a canalized river where women and girls were washing clothes, then up towards the church through an area of palms and more salubrious housing. When we arrived the rickshaw-driver went in search of the priest. He returned with a middle-aged man, Mr Fernandes Pereira, who told me in halting English that the priest had gone to see his mother in hospital; however, he said, he would be happy to show me the new church tower.

Our Lady of Good Voyage had been built in the late 1970s with contributions from the Catholic fishing community. It was a large structure with a high ceiling, a tall nave without pews and little in the way of architectural embellishment apart from the tower, which was still in the process of being built. Mr Pereira led me to the base of the tower and we began the long ascent to the top, up reinforced-concrete steps which seemed to become progressively more sheer the further we went. He announced proudly that the tower was 146 feet high with a 13-foot statue of the Virgin at the top. It was the fishing people, he explained, not the priest, who had decided to build the tower and they were paying for its construction themselves. When we reached the summit we sat on our haunches and admired the view. The sun was low in the sky, falling towards the domes and minarets of the mosque, and the palm-leaf roofs of the fishermen's shacks glinted like chips of mica in a slab of granite.

Mr Pereira was willing to talk about the recent deaths, but his meagre stock of English meant that I heard the most rudimentary account. On 14 May two Muslims had been killed by Christians, and on 10 July four Christians had been killed by Muslims. He added that on the small strip of beach laid out before us there were 12,000 Catholics and 12,000 Muslims. Poverty and over-crowding may not have been the actual cause of the murders, but they were contributory factors. As soon as we descended from the tower Mr Pereira led me behind the church to see the grave of the four Christians. It was a huge marble affair with four black-and-white photographs of the victims: tough, solid-looking characters with moustaches and serious expressions befitting their unfortunate fate.

I returned to Vizhinjam on two other occasions, but I never did meet the priest. In Trivandrum and elsewhere I heard more about Vizhinjam's problems, but nobody, including the authorities at Bishop's House, appeared to understand precisely what had happened. It seems that the trouble had been sparked off by a boat crash – between Muslims and Christians, presumably – but there was some suspicion that 'external agencies' had had a hand in the murders. Apparently the Muslims had been killed with a home-made bomb of the sort used for dynamiting fish and the Christians had been beaten and buried alive. One priest I spoke to pointed out that immediately after the July killings the state government announced a massive port development plan for Vizhinjam, and indeed a new pier was already under construction: the murders, he implied, might have been arranged by the business community, or by local politicians, as a means of attracting capital investment to the area. I have no idea whether this is credible, but everyone seemed to agree that poverty rather than theology lay behind the communal violence. The population along the beach had doubled over the past four years and the people were poorer than ever. The local priest and the diocesan authorities had opposed the construction of the new church tower, as they felt that the money could be better spent on alleviating poverty. However, the Catholic fishing community was determined to have the tower. 'Put on the full armour provided by God, so that you may be able to stand firm against the stratagems of the devil,' wrote St Paul in his letter to the Ephesians (6:11). He was speaking metaphorically, of course, but the literal interpretation would have suited the fishermen. The tower, I imagine, was their 'shield of faith', an expression of their collective identity, and they intended the world to know it.

The village of Puthiathura, half an hour's drive further down the coast from Vizhinjam, was constructing communal toilets rather than church towers, and these were the source of some pride to the priest, Father Stephen Josemethachery, whom I awoke from his afternoon siesta. He appeared from his living quarters, bleary-eyed but welcoming, in a white vest and green *dhoti* and led me into a small office. His sexton went out to make tea and while we waited the priest told me about the toilets and the village. Puthiathura was smaller than Vizhinjam, with a population of around 7,000, all of whom were Catholics who dated their conversion back to the days of St Francis Xavier. The people were for the most part traditional fishermen who worked the inshore waters and they lived in small shacks on a narrow strip of beach less than a mile long. Many of the men were addicted to arak, and drunkenness led to much trouble within and between families. The overcrowding was so acute that during the dry months the menfolk often slept on the shore. Hardly any of the families had their own toilets, the exceptions being the few who had worked in the Gulf and built up some savings. The parish was divided for administrative purposes into three sections, and with the help of Trivandrum Social Services Society they had built a communal toilet for the women of two sections. The priest hoped that another toilet would be built for the remaining section soon.

Father Stephen had been brought up in Cochin, but he had worked in Trivandrum diocese for the last two decades. He had found there to be considerable differences in the standard of living and attitudes between the fishing communities in and around Cochin and the ones here. 'In Cochin the people are better educated, more cultured,' he said in his slow, little practised English. 'In the south, the fishermen are very rough and rebellious, and they trouble us for everything. In this village, they're not so rebellious, but they're very poor, very uneducated.'

I asked Father Stephen whether this meant that fishermen's wives had many children, high fertility rates often being a reflection as much of ignorance as of poverty. No, he said, most couples now limited themselves to two or three children; although the Vatican was explicitly opposed to artificial methods of birth control, few priests here preached against family planning, and in fact the government of Kerala had made great efforts, largely unopposed by the Catholic Church, to promote smaller families. Nearly all the priests whom I had spoken to about family planning had said the same: they would tell newly married couples about the Vatican's views, then add something along the lines of 'Make sure you don't have any more children than you can feed and educate.' The only members of the Catholic Church in India who flatly denied that priests took this liberal stance on birth control were the bishops and archbishops I met; but then they had more to lose by speaking out against the established order.

The fishing communities had such low levels of educational achievement, explained Father Stephen, that they were unable to provide sufficient priests for the coast, which was why he and others from northern Kerala had been drafted into the area.

Even so, India's second largest Catholic diocese was still severely understaffed, with 120 priests looking after 400,000 people. The lack of education also helped to perpetuate practices which the Church wished to stamp out. One of these was the dowry system. The parents of a bride had to supply goods and chattels for the groom's family and many were deep in debt as a result. The Church at Puthiathura was tackling the dowry system by arranging what the priest termed 'community marriages'. Eleven couples in the village were about to be given 10,000 rupees each from a fund to which the fishing people themselves had contributed; Father Stephen hoped that this would lessen the demands for dowry from the grooms' families. However, these measures were unlikely to affect the age at which girls married. Indian civil law decrees that girls should not marry until they are eighteen years old. 'But poor people want to get rid of the girls as soon as possible,' said Father Stephen, 'and in this village many are married at fourteen or fifteen.'

I am not sure where the tea came from, but it eventually appeared in a plastic Thermos flask with some delicate cups of pink floral design. All of a sudden the office was plunged into near darkness and a tremendous storm made conversation impossible. By the time the rain had abated we had finished our tea and Father Stephen said he would take me to see the Salesian sisters who lived nearby. He returned to his living quarters and reappeared a few minutes later in a white cassock. He was a big man, very impressive to look at, especially in his working clothes, and he walked slowly in the way big men do, like a heavyweight boxer or a night-club bouncer. The sisters' house lay among palms on the other side of offices which were occupied on a part-time basis by the Society of St Vincent de Paul, an organization of Catholic lay people which works among the poor.

Some of the sisters were away on business, but the four who remained gathered to discuss their work in the little hall behind the front door. It was a spartan room and the hard-backed chairs in which we sat had to be fetched from elsewhere in the house. The only decoration I can recall was a painting of Dom Bosco, the founder of the Society of St Francis de Sales. The sisters were of various ages and all wore wimples and had large wooden crosses on their chests. The Salesian sisters, explained one, had come to the village to support the poor, and especially the women and children. Their mission was partly educational: they helped the more backward children with their work outside school hours, they ran literacy programmes for women and they assisted in the religious education of children preparing for their first communion. Father Stephen added that the fishing people were so ill educated that until recently very few knew what he described as 'even the preliminary lessons of the Catholic Church'. The sisters also spent a good portion of their time working in the slums on the beach. 'There are so many drunken husbands,' said one. 'That's the big problem.' They conducted group prayers in the evenings and these were well attended by the women and children, although the men were less enthusiastic. Did they ever experience any aggression? I asked. 'No,' replied the youngest and prettiest, 'they like having us here.'

On the way down to the beach the priest showed me one of the communal toilets. There were four cubicles, all spotlessly clean; it was, said Father Stephen, a wonderful thing for the women to be able to do their daily business here instead of on the beach. Unfortunately, there was a problem with the water supply at present, so they were having to flush the toilet manually. By the time we arrived on the beach we had gathered a crowd of inquisitive children and they followed us across a bumpy football pitch, past one of the fourteen concrete stations of the cross and down to the water's edge. The beach was strewn with *kattumarams* and larger canoes, and groups of men were lying about, mending nets and working on their boats. Behind the shore were the palm-leaf shacks where they lived and beyond I could see the white tower of the church poking through the green canopy of coconut palms. With the bruised clouds rolling in off the sea, pierced some way to the west by a bright shaft of sunlight, the scene had all the ingredients of the picturesque. However, I found it oppressive and disturbing. Many of the children were malnourished and some looked withdrawn and traumatized. Though gracious in their movements, the women were aged beyond their years and most of the men appeared surly and watchful.

I had intended to ask the priest to show me inside some of the fishing people's shacks, but I decided it would be an unwarranted intrusion. As he led me back to my taxi he said that he came down to the beach every afternoon. Some days a fisherman would ask him to bless a new boat, on other days to bless a new shack. I reflected, as I left him, that he had a difficult job, though he never said as much himself and he never once complained about the fact that he had been sent to look after such an impoverished and awkward parish. By the time I arrived in mid-afternoon he had already conducted two masses, a wedding and a funeral; now he was going to bless a new shack.

The Catholic Church may be doing its utmost now to help the fishing people on the Kerala coast, in particular through the work of the diocesan Social Services Societies, but it is hard to think of any other Christian community in India which has been so persistently ignored by its own religious authorities. Most accounts of missionary activity concentrate on the Tamil-speaking Paravas of India's south-east Fisher Coast, rather than on the mixed Parava and Mukkavar communities which are found between Trivandrum and Cape Comorin, but their history has been much the same. When the Portuguese arrived in the sixteenth century the fishermen and their families saw Christianity as a potentially liberating force. Ten thousand or more Paravas on the Fisher Coast were baptized *en masse* in 1536, in return for which the Portuguese offered them protection against the Muslim forces that habitually raided their villages. However, they were left to their own devices, spiritually speaking, and it was six years before they saw another priest. Luckily for them, it was St Francis Xavier, whose diligent evangelizing is remembered with gratitude still. 'He arrived to find an untutored mob,' writes the historian Stephen Neill; 'he left behind a church in being.' By the end of the sixteenth century each Parava village on the Fisher Coast had its own resident priest, and the Jesuits also moved among the fishing villages on the south-west coast and made many more converts.

Early accounts of the Paravas and Mukkavars speak of crushing poverty, widespread alcoholism and universal illiteracy. The visitor today is struck not so much by the changes to their condition as by their lack of material and educational advancement, despite over four centuries of supposedly enlightened Christian influence. 'My people have very strong faith, but very poor,' as the naval architect, a Mukkavar, had told me on the train to Cochin.

The Jesuits who followed in the steps of St Francis evidently introduced a sense of Christian discipline into the villages – no fishing on Sundays, a tax on the fish catch to help support the Church – but they did little for the education of their new converts. However, the expulsion of the Jesuits after over two hundred years of continuous presence still came as a serious blow. In 1773 Pope Clement XIV reacted to Portuguese, French and Spanish agitation against the powerful Jesuits, who were accused of sedition, by ordering the dissolution of their society, the sequestration of all the society's property and the withdrawal of all its missionaries. Abbé Dubois' organization, the Paris Society, took over some of the Jesuits' activities in southern India, but the Fisher Coast received in return for the expelled Jesuits just a handful of Goan priests whose lackadaisical and immoral behaviour scandalized the more pious locals. 'Everywhere,' writes Neill, 'there was the same feeling of desertion, desolation and almost despair.'

The Jesuits returned to India half a century later – Pope Clement's order that they never be called into being again was overturned – and they found a new force in place. Prior to the departure of the Jesuits, Protestants were confined to small enclaves, most notably in Tranquebar, where Danish Lutherans had established a mission in the early years of the eighteenth century, but when they returned to south India they found many more Protestant denominations vying for the souls that their own Church coveted. The Protestant missions wanted people to read the Bible for themselves, rather than rely for their Christian knowledge on the expurgated snippets delivered from the pulpit. An Anglican missionary, Samuel Mateer, noted in his study of south Kerala, *The Land of Charity*, that the vast majority of Catholics possessed little religious knowledge and that four centuries after St Francis Xavier's mission 'no portion of the Holy Scriptures has been translated into Malayalam by the Roman Catholic missionaries'. The Paravas – or at least the few who could read – were marginally more fortunate: by the mid-nineteenth century Catholic priests had made available Tamil translations of the Gospels and the Acts of the Apostles. Many of the Jesuits in India steeped themselves in the Tamil language – Father Robert de Nobili wrote a five-volume theological work, *Gnanopadesam*, and Father Constant Joseph Beschi wrote an epic poem that became a Tamil classic – yet none devoted their intellectual energies to the most obvious of tasks: translating the Bible into the vernacular.

The Danish Lutherans had arrived in Tranquebar in 1706. Within five years the leader of the mission, Bartholomew Ziegenbalg, had completed his translation of the New Testament into Tamil. Little wonder, then, that the Protestants used to berate the Roman Catholic Church for its paternalistic attitude towards its flock, whom it seemed happy to keep in a state of ignorant obedience. Indian Catholics will often tell you that they, rather than the Protestants, have been leaders of the field of education. They generally fail to mention that it was the activities of the Protestant missionaries in the nineteenth century – they sought to provide education for all Christian converts, rather than for a chosen few – that forced the Catholics to become less élitist. And they seldom mention that the offspring of wealthy high-caste Hindus frequently receive an excellent education at the Jesuit colleges, whereas the children of fishermen and low-caste Christians seldom, if ever, do.

When I was wandering about the coastal villages I tried to imagine how the ancestors of these fishing people reacted to the gospel when they heard it for the first time. Did the missionaries tell them about the parables and explain their meaning? Did they give an honest account of the disciples and their background? If they did, then the fishermen must surely have felt that there was a commonality of experience which linked them to the first-century Palestinians who followed Christ or, indeed, who ignored or reviled him. I read St Matthew's Gospel while I was in Kerala and what struck me now, as I attempted to see its story through the eyes of these coastal converts, was the wealth of imagery that related to peasant life, to a life dominated by sowing and reaping, to casting nets and living off the fruits of the sea. And when the fishermen were first told the story of creation by the Portuguese missionaries, of how man was to have 'dominion over the fish of the sea, and over the fowl of the air, and over the cattle, and over all the earth and over every creeping thing that creepeth upon the earth' (Genesis 1:26), would they not have felt a certain sense of pride? Were they not, after all, fulfilling one of the first tasks which God assigned to man?

Clearly the Christian converts from the higher castes did not interpret the Bible in these terms, and for them the coastal fishing communities remained an object of scorn, as Abbé Dubois discovered when he gave a sermon in Tamil at a place called Carricaul:

> I several times repeated that the Christian religion had for its founder a *peasant of Galilee, the son of a humble carpenter*, who took for his assistants twelve low-born men, twelve ignorant and illiterate *fishermen*. These words *the son of a carpenter! twelve fishermen!*,

> many times repeated, gave offence to my audience, which was entirely composed of native Christians; and the sermon was no sooner finished than three or four of the principal among them came and informed me that the whole congregation had been highly scandalized by hearing me apply to Christ the appellation of *the son of a carpenter*, and to his apostles that of *fishermen*; that I could not be ignorant that the castes both of carpenters and of fishermen were two of the lowest and vilest in the country; that it was highly improper to attribute to Christ and his disciples so low and abject an origin; that if pagans, who sometimes come through motives of curiosity to their religious assemblies, heard such objectionable accounts of our religion, their contempt and hatred of it would be considerably increased, &c. &c. Finally, they advised me, if in future I had occasion to mention in my sermons the origin of Christ or his apostles, not to fail to say that both were born in the noble tribe of *kshatryas* or rajahs, and never to mention their low profession.

When I was in Trivandrum earlier in the year I went along to a Church of South India service at the London Missionary Society (LMS) compound. On my way there I passed another church, a smaller and more attractive building, which also came under the Church of South India and had Malayalam and English services at precisely the same times. I arrived at the LMS compound while the Malayalam service was still in progress and fell into conversation with a retired civil servant. I asked him why he came to this particular CSI church rather than the one I had passed on my way.

'They're Syrian converts,' he replied.

'Why don't you worship together?'

'Oh, they won't even mix with us,' he said. 'They think they're far too superior.' In fact the Syrians considered themselves so superior that they refused to belong to the local diocese, most of whose 540,000 members came from the low-caste Nadar and the *dalit* communities. The Syrians had chosen to belong to the Central Kerala diocese of the CSI, whose headquarters was in distant Kottayam and where there were other Syrian CSI congregations.

It is easy to berate the church authorities for failing to eradicate what one bishop described to me as the curse of casteism, but the fault lies not so much with the authorities as with the minority of Christians who consider themselves to be high-caste. In any case, one should remember that the Christians, and especially the Protestants, were in the forefront of the movement to better the lot of the poor and outcast communities during the last two centuries. Samuel Mateer called his account of south Kerala *The Land of Charity* because that was what the Brahmins called it. They were referring not to any largesse on their part but to the generosity of Travancore's rulers, who did much to support the Brahmin priests and the Hindu religion. Between the highest Brahmin and the lowest slaves there were over eighty separate castes, and those at the top showed precious little charity – in either sense of the word – to those at the bottom. The ones who suffered most grievously were the Pallars, the Pariahs and the Pullayars, the slave castes who in Mateer's day, the mid-nineteenth century, were four times more numerous than the Brahmins. They were subject to 'horrid and aggravated cruelty' from their masters – Syrian Christians being as culpable as high-caste Hindus – and lived in conditions comparable with those in which the poorest fishermen now find themselves. At one time the deed of transfer for slaves contained the clause 'You may sell him or kill him.' The etymology of the slave castes says much about the way in which they were viewed by the higher castes. 'Pariah' has become a synonym for the outcast and the word 'Pulayar' was derived from *pula* or funeral pollution. The Pulayar could never use the word 'I' in speech to the higher castes – instead he said, 'Your slave'; he had to keep a hand over his mouth while speaking lest he pollute the person he addressed, and he referred to his children as monkeys or calves.

It was pressure from the Christian community which led to the emancipation of government slaves in the 1850s, and Christians were also prominent in the famous upper-cloth or bosom controversy. Until 1865 Pulayar women and the women of certain other slave castes were forbidden by Hindu law to wear any form of clothing which covered their breasts. Nor were they allowed to wear any ornaments more valuable than brass or beads, or any shoes, or even to use an umbrella to protect themselves from the sun or rain. At certain times of the year many Pulayar families would travel from south Kerala to the province of Tirunelveli, a great centre of Protestant activity in what is now Tamil Nadu, in search of work. There the women were able to cover their breasts and they evidently took a liking to doing so. On their return to their home villages in Kerala some of them continued to wear an upper cloth and this caused a great scandal, especially among the Hindu *sudras*. In 1858, wrote Mateer, a Christian woman had her top torn off in a public market. Later the *sudras* claimed that the government had issued an order to strip the offending women of their tops. The controversy rumbled on for several years and low-caste women, many of whom had converted to Christianity, continued to suffer persecution by the *sudras*. In one instance a mob of 200 attacked Christians at Talakudi, stripping the women and beating them. On another occasion 500 *sudras* went on the attack. Eventually, the government reacted to protests from the Church and others by issuing a proclamation which recognized the right of all women to dress themselves with due modesty.

I spent a week at Kovalam Beach, and besides my sorties into the fishing villages I made several visits to Trivandrum. I spent some time at the Catholic Bishop's House, where a young priest who looked like Omar Sharif told me about the diocese's attempt to give the laity, and especially women, more say in the running of church affairs. The Catholic Church was becoming more democratic. This was a message I heard again when I visited the secretary of the Trivandrum Social Services Society. There had been a great deal of soul-searching in recent years and the society had transformed itself from a paternalistic charity dispensing alms to the poor into a modern development agency. The Church of South India, whose headquarters I visited in the LMS compound, was also engaged in a range of development programmes, as was the Salvation Army, whose military rhetoric seemed strangely at odds with the gentle and self-effacing manners of the officers I met.

I was alerted to the Army's presence by a poster which was gummed on to the gate post at the LMS compound. It read:

Salvation Army Youth Club Central Corps
presents the band IX.H.R.S.
'Rockin on all night long
to turn ur brains into mashed rice.'

When I entered the Army's territorial headquarters and passed its crest with the motto 'Blood and Fire', I braced myself for a heavy dose of fundamentalism. Instead, I found myself in the company of the mild and wryly amusing territorial commander, Jillapegu Israel, who began our conversation by praising India's long tradition of religious tolerance. 'Some think – like the Israelites – that God is exclusively for us,' he said. 'But we respect other faiths; we cannot think exclusively like that. India is a tolerant country, but tolerance does not mean we have to sacrifice our faith.' He added that at the Army's primary schools, and at its high school next door, they always had morning prayers, but these were never explicitly Christian. 'We just pray to God,' he said simply.

The Salvation Army has around 150,000 members in India, approximately a fifth of whom live in Kerala, and the vast majority are *dalits*, although its first convert in Kerala, made in 1896, was a Brahmin called Yesudhasan. When the Army began work in

India, explained Captain John, who ran the editorial department, it tried to convert the higher castes, but it didn't have much success. So it changed its policy and preached the gospel to the lower castes and the untouchables: 'This was a grand success,' said the captain. 'The untouchables couldn't believe that a big man would come and live with them, eat their food, touch them. It was heaven on earth for them and that's why they joined the Salvation Army.' Unfortunately, Christianity was bad for one's job prospects. While Hindu *dalits* could take advantage of the government's policy of positive discrimination in the job market, the Christian *dalits* could not. 'If they were Hindus, they'd get jobs,' said Captain John. 'Many Christians have reverted to Hinduism in order to take advantage of the job reservations.' He added that some had simply changed their names to make it seem that they were Hindus: 'In their hearts they remain Christian,' he added with satisfaction.

CHAPTER 9

Pride and Prejudice

I found George Gregorian, or Geo. E. Gregory as he signed himself, hunched over a large wooden desk in what used to be the Armenian church's mortuary. He looked up as I entered the open door and exclaimed: 'Good heavens, my dear! How tall are you? You must be at least seven foot!' He slowly rose to his feet, extended a bony hand, gripped mine, then ushered me towards a seat on the other side of the desk, among whose stacks of papers I noticed a recent statement from the branch of Lloyd's Bank in Curzon Street, London. Mr Gregorian settled himself in his chair, gazed at me with liquescent blue eyes, then explained that he was both busy and tired, having been up half the night with toothache. Nevertheless, he said he was delighted to see an Englishman.

'Have you looked at our church?' he asked.

Not yet, I replied.

'First we'll talk a little. Then you can spend as long as you like. But I can't talk too much, my dear – it's my teeth, you see.'

Mr Gregorian's sharp features, wide-set eyes and goatee beard reminded me of Lenin, or at least of what Lenin might have looked like had he reached his mid-eighties. His skin was pale and sprinkled with age spots, and his grey hair had thinned to wispy streaks on either side of a bald crown. He had arthritis, which contorted his hands and made him stoop; he was hard of hearing, which meant that he shouted; and his thin legs were covered with a filigree of varicose veins. Yet the moment he began to talk about his life, and about the Armenian Church of the Holy Virgin Mary, which he had saved from ruin, I realized that I was in the company of one of those rare people whose enthusiasm and vitality would never be dimmed by the infirmities of old age.

Mr Gregorian was born in Persia in 1913, but left soon after the First World War began. His parents took him to Bombay, travelling for much of the journey on camelback. Between the two world wars Mr Gregorian lived in Calcutta, where he worked as a government servant for the British. During the Second World War he joined the Red Cross, then after Independence he spent six years in London, where he worked in the Dorchester Hotel's wine cellar, before returning to India, this time to Madras. 'And so you see, my dear, I found the church in ruins. We have restored it, rebuilt it, looked after it . . .' Mr Gregorian was the last Armenian in Madras – at one time there were several hundred – and he lived with his Anglo-Indian wife in what used to be the priest's library. Soon, he said, he would be handing over the running of the church to a young Armenian who was going to move down to Madras from Calcutta. 'Now look around the church, look at whatever you want, then come back and see me.'

The church compound was sheltered from the bustle of the streets outside by a row of old houses and stores on one side and by high walls on the other. An arched passage from Armenian Street led into a cobbled courtyard whose flowering shrubs and pots of herbaceous flowers put me in mind of an Islamic paradise. Immediately to the left was the sexton's office, the old one-room mortuary; ahead and to the right, just a few paces away, was the church itself and a detached bell-tower. Consecrated in 1772, the heavy-walled church consisted of a plain nave with a simple altar with Orthodox icons and a burning lamp. The bell-tower was particularly fine: a three-tiered structure, painted yellow and pastel blue, classical in design with a beautiful dome surmounted by a small cupola. A flight of wooden stairs led to the belfry, which contained six large bells. One came from a foundry in Armenia and was dated 1754; another was stamped Thomas Mears, London, 1837.

Before I returned to see Mr Gregorian I spent a little time in an alcove on the outside of the church. Hung on the walls were several newspaper cuttings about the church's history and photographs of the bicentennial celebrations; among those present was a Syrian metropolitan from Kerala, an Armenian bishop, the chief of police and other important figures in south India's religious and political life. A watchman who had been observing my perambulations summoned me across the courtyard and pointed to a dozen or so large pencil sketches on the walls of a covered arcade. 'Mr Gregorian,' he explained. And indeed they were all signed by the sexton, and very competent they were too. There were several of Christ in his Kevin Costner incarnation and many more of famous figures in the Armenian Church, bearded patriarchs not dissimilar to the metropolitans whose portraits I had seen in Kottayam. There was also a portrait of the Rev. Shamavorian, who had the misfortune to lose two sons in one week, came to Madras in the 1780s, served as vicar of the church for four decades and earned the sobriquet 'Venerable Father of Armenians Journalism', according to a little booklet which Mr Gregorian gave me. Rev. Shamavorian set up a printing press and published books in classical Armenian as well as the world's first Armenian journal. Not only did he fashion the type himself, he also made the paper from cotton pulp.

'So you're an artist,' I said when I returned to Mr Gregorian's office.

'No.' He smiled. 'Just a copycat.'

If Mr Gregorian was saddened by the disappearance of Madras's Armenians – they had arrived more than three hundred years ago – he didn't show it, and he said he had no intention of moving to Calcutta to join an Armenian community which still had its own church, schools, old people's homes and so forth. 'Madras is dirty and overcrowded,' he mused. 'There's more production in the homes than in the factories, but it's not rotten like Calcutta. I'll never go there again.'

It was approaching midday and Mr Gregorian said he had a few more papers to attend to before his siesta. As usual he had risen at three o'clock in the morning, taken over from the night-watchman and been here ever since. He would sleep for an hour or so after lunch, then be back at his desk by two thirty. When he accompanied me out to the courtyard I asked him whether he knew the name of the exquisitely fragrant trees which had cast their fleshy white flowers on to the shaded cobbles. He said he did not, although he had planted them himself some thirty years ago. He told me to return whenever I wished, gave me a bear hug and waved me on my way. When I reached the street outside I felt as though I had come out of a memorable play – a play about a great sweep of history seen through the eyes of one of its more quixotic participants. Even if Madras were the most hellish place on earth, I would have been predisposed to like it now.

Abbé Dubois mentioned the Armenians of Madras in so far as he wrote: 'I have made no mention . . . of the Armenian clergy in Madras because they at no time attempted to make proselytes among the Hindoos, and their only business has always been to attend the Armenian congregation settled at that place.' They were Orthodox Christians, he added, whose beliefs differed little from those of the Catholics, in common with whom they admitted the seven sacraments. However, they did not recognize the authority of the Pope and their liturgy was in Armenian.

When the first Armenian merchants arrived in the 1660s they worshipped in the Catholic chapel of the Capuchin fathers in the Fort, but it was not long before they acquired their own place of worship: in 1688 the East India Company extended to their growing community the same rights and privileges as it did to the British and offered to build them a church. Thus began a cordial relationship with the British, to whom they remained loyal when the French took Madras in 1746 and seized all their property.

Today the Christian population of Madras is divided fairly evenly between Roman Catholics and Protestants, the Catholics and the Church of South India having some eighty churches each. There is also a rapidly expanding Pentecostal movement. It is the Catholics, however, who are in possession of the great pilgrimage sites associated with St Thomas, and I decided to visit these after I left the Armenian church.

Before I found a rickshaw to transport me to San Thome Cathedral in the southern suburbs I ate a *dosa* in a vegetarian café and dropped in to the Catholic co-cathedral on Armenian Street, where I sat for a few minutes digesting lunch and studying a map of the city. The church was ugly and popular, and a constant stream of devotees, office workers mostly, came in to say a quick prayer or, in some cases, to light candles below images of saints and the Virgin Mary. Most of the images looked as though they had been sculpted out of Plasticine by a low-grade pre-Raphaelite artist. The oddest of all was a statue of a man dressed like a maître d' with a black suit, a white shirt and black bow-tie. In one hand he held a book on which was written 'Sin is worse than death', which is debatable, like much else I heard and read during my afternoon pilgrimage.

In most Indian cities you can convince a rickshaw-driver to use his meter, especially if you are giving him plenty of business. In Madras you would have to threaten to shoot him to get a reasonable deal. I eventually hired a driver near the high court and was happy to meet his exorbitant demand – a taxi would have cost little more – as he was an engaging fellow with a good knowledge of the city and its pilgrimage sites. Shortly before we reached San Thome Cathedral he veered off the main road and sped the wrong way down a one-way street to Luz church. He explained that it was the oldest in Madras and indeed there was an inscription on the walls dated 1516. It was a handsome building, whitewashed with orange beading like a two-tone wedding cake. I tried the door, but it was locked, and I spoke briefly to two self-consciously pretty students who sat in the shade of a buttress, revising for their exams, and to an elderly couple who were having a picnic lunch on the church steps. They were Protestants from Madurai and they had come to Madras for a brief sightseeing holiday. 'I was very much astonished when we arrived,' said the husband, who looked Anglo-Indian. 'When we last came here thirty years ago, all this area round the church was jungle. Just look at it now!' It was surrounded by suburban housing and it must have been a pleasant place to live. In Tamil the church is still known as Kattu Kovil, which means 'jungle temple'.

San Thome Cathedral was situated within sight and sniffing distance of the sea in the old city of Mylapore, some four miles south of the Fort and now part of suburban Madras. Like many Catholic churches built during the past century – it was exactly a hundred years old – it was marginally more attractive when seen from a distance than it was close up. Spiky Gothic, with a profusion of pinnacles and spires, it looked like a Cubist porcupine that had clambered through a tin of white paint. The monsoon rains had streaked the walls grey and black, and in places below the guttering the paint had begun to peel away. The interior, by contrast, was in immaculate condition and the furnishings seemed restrained when compared with the showiness of the exterior. I picked up a leaflet on my way in and sat in one of the solid wooden pews to read it. There was a fair number of statistics – nave 112 feet, transept 104 feet, spire 155 feet and so on – but most of the text was devoted to the story of St Thomas's tomb, which was situated in a crypt in the middle of the transept and currently occupied by a family who were recording their visit on video. The tomb, explained the leaflet, had been opened for the third time on 2 July 1523, when the Portuguese unearthed skull bones, a bit of spine and a spearhead. I waited for the family to vacate the crypt, made a brief inspection myself, then followed them to the seaward end of the transept, where they were busy filming themselves in front of a statue of the Virgin Mary. According to a plaque in front of the statue, 'This altar of Our Lady of Mylapore stands where formerly was the parish house in which St Francis Xavier resided for four months in 1545.'

When I came out of the cathedral I was mobbed by a gang of children who had just been released from the primary school inside the grounds. They followed me across the courtyard, shrieking their demands for rupees and Biros, to a modern museum where I bought some postcards and booklets from a Franciscan nun. The nun showed me a splinter of bone implanted in a silver cross and a spearhead. The bone had belonged to St Thomas, she said emphatically, and the spearhead was the one that killed him. She suggested that I go to St Thomas Mount, the site of his martyrdom, and there I would see a cross carved by the apostle himself and a painting of the Virgin Mary which he had brought from the Middle East to India when he came in AD 52. The painting, she added, was by St Luke.

'Are you sure?' I asked.

'Yes, we know for sure it is by St Luke,' she replied with the confidence of the credulous.

Half an hour later my rickshaw stuttered to a halt at the foot of St Thomas Mount and I made the long ascent to Our Lady of Expectation. It was very quiet here; the sun had gone and the scrubby land on either side of the stone stairway was enveloped by a grey drizzle, reminding me of the Yorkshire Pennines on a humid summer's day: the distant city might have been Leeds or Bradford rather than Madras. There were Friesian cows and buffaloes grazing in the fields and I savoured the smell of fresh dung and fresh grass. I passed an unattended flock of goats on the way up and the first people I met were two old beggars who sat at the top of the steps, waiting for alms with outstretched hands. There were three policemen in a building behind the chapel, and in the chapel itself a man and a woman knelt before the altar.

In 1711 a Jesuit priest wrote that the little barrel-vaulted chapel, built by the Portuguese in the sixteenth century, was 'the monument most celebrated, most authorized, and most frequented by the Christians of the Indies, especially by those who are called St Thomas Christians'. Then, as now, pilgrims came to see the cross above the altar. 'There is a general belief among the Indians, both Christians and pagans,' wrote the priest, 'that this cross was made by St Thomas . . . and that it was at the foot of this same cross that he died, pierced by the lance of a Gentile Brahmin. If anyone thought otherwise of the mission and death of the great Apostle, he would expose himself to the indignation and resentment of the Christians of all India. This tradition is so certain that [it] would be dangerous to rise against it.'

The famous artefact was a close relative of the Persian cross which I had seen in Veriapally church in Kottayam; hewn out of granite, the cross was surmounted by an open-winged dove and enclosed by an arch and pillars. The inscription above the arch was in Pahlavi. According to *The Penguin Guide to the Monuments of India*, it reads: 'Ever pure is in favour with Him who bore the cross.' According to the wooden board beside the altar it reads: 'Through the cross – suffering. The Messiah (Christ) brought salvation to the world.' The wooden board was also inscribed with the following information:

> You are standing on a sacred spot. It was here that St Thomas the Apostle was pierced with a lance and killed. There is now evidence that the stone cross on the altar was made by St Thomas himself and it is considered 'miraculous'. There is recorded evidence that it sweated blood several times between the years AD 1551 and AD 1704.
>
> The picture of Our Lady seen on the main altar was brought by St Thomas to India when he came here.

There is absolutely no evidence that the cross was fashioned by St Thomas. According to modern palaeographic study, it dates from the seventh or the eighth century. As far as the painting of the Virgin and Child is concerned, one can only remark that if it really had been painted by St Luke it would be in the Vatican, or perhaps the Getty Museum, by now; instead it is propped against the altar, garlanded and unguarded and poorly illuminated by red electric lightbulbs. One of the booklets which I had bought from the Franciscan nun began with the clarion observation: 'A historian who is biased will not find St Thomas in India, but he will not find him in any other part of the world either.' Well, the same could be said for the unbiased historian too. St Thomas may have come to India; he may even have been martyred on St Thomas Mount; but the more the Catholic Church decks the bones of the legend with fanciful flesh, the less credible it seems.

The bishop might just be able to spare a few minutes, said his secretary uncertainly over the phone, and he suggested I present myself at the Church of South India's Bishop's House around four o'clock that afternoon. I arrived as Bishop Azariah was coming out of his house. He shook my hand enthusiastically, led me across the garden into a bizarrely decorated office, then proceeded to entertain me for the next two hours. Shortly before the conclusion of our meeting his eyes fell on a scrap of paper. 'Look here,' he said, shaking his head and laughing, 'here's a note to say that you are coming to see me this afternoon!' It was a measure of his warm and open nature that he had so readily invited someone of whom he had no previous knowledge into his office. It was a measure too of another side of his character: he was a great self-publicist, a man who spoke the lyrical language of the rhetorician and was keen for the world to hear his message. He was dazzlingly handsome, with the dark skin of a Tamil, a thick mass of black hair with a becoming sprinkling of grey, a fine set of flashing white teeth and wonderfully expressive hands.

For the first hour or so he talked about the fate of *dalit* Christians. The bishop was a *dalit* and he evidently saw himself as their cheer-leader and spokesman. 'You see these three people here,' he said, a sweep of his hand indicating the gentlemen who sat beside me, facing the bishop. 'These people are all *dalits*, and they've all experienced the stigma which goes with it.' They were unusual in that they had risen above the poverty and ignorance which shackled most of their people: one was a priest, another was a doctor of philosophy. 'None of these men you see here could have married a non-*dalit* Christian woman,' continued the bishop. 'The stigma is always there.' He added that the battle against racism, or casteism, within the Church was more important than the struggle to win job reservations for *dalit* Christians through changes in legislation.

Over three-quarters of the Church of South India Christians within Madras diocese were *dalits* and the proportion of *dalits* and non-*dalits* was roughly the same for both Protestants and Catholics throughout Tamil Nadu. They were oppressed, poor and ill-fed; the bishop estimated that only 3 per cent received a decent education. The Church of South India had done more to help the *dalits* than the Catholics, according to the bishop, and as evidence he cited the proportion of *dalit* bishops. In the Church of South India eight of the twenty-one bishops were *dalits*; in the Catholic Church only six out of more than 120 bishops were *dalits*. And what about the Syrian Christians? I asked. 'Two thousand years after Christ,' said Bishop Azariah with an imperious look of disdain, 'those people in Kottayam haven't changed. And the Mar Thoma Church is as bad as the Orthodox Churches in the way it treats *dalits*.'

The bishop briefly described the caste system, reeling off the four *varnas* – *brahmins*, *kshatryas*, *vaisayas*, *sudras* – on the fingers of one hand, before raising his thumb, a symbolically stunted digit, to represent the *dalits*. 'In all,' he said, 'there are 250 million *dalits* in India – scheduled caste people, scheduled tribes. But there are divisions there too. We *dalits* are between the devil and the deep blue sea' – the devil being caste Hindus, the deep blue sea the scheduled tribes, who consider themselves to be superior to the scheduled castes.

Outsiders are easily confused by the lively and at times divisive *dalit* debate in India, not least because the language of discrimination is so complex. In the old days Hindu outcasts – those who did not belong to the four *varnas* – were called untouchables. The term related to the abstract notion of pollution which underlies the working of the caste system. At one extreme are the *brahmins*, who in habit and diet keep themselves as far away as possible from polluting events like meat-eating, midden-cleaning, death; at the other are the outcasts who are engaged in servile tasks such as sweeping and butchery. A strict code of practice ensures that the higher castes are protected from pollution by the lower castes; in practical terms this means that the outcasts cannot cook for higher castes, allow their shadows to fall across them, cut their hair, enter their homes, drink water from the same wells, use the same footpaths and so on. The term 'untouchable' is seldom used today except in a pejorative sense or out of ignorance. It was replaced in 1932 first by the expression 'depressed classes'; this was soon usurped by 'scheduled castes'. This term was invented not by the two great champions of the downtrodden, Dr B. R. Ambedkar and Mahatma Gandhi, who failed to agree on the matter when consulted by the British rulers, but by the British Prime Minister Ramsay MacDonald. The term has stuck, although till recently the untouchables were more likely to be referred to as *harijans*, or 'children of God', the name which Gandhi gave them. The scheduled castes are listed in detail by the Indian Constitution, and the 1950 Scheduled Castes Order determined who should benefit from positive discrimination, especially in college and government job reservations. It was amended in 1956 to include Hindu converts to Sikhism and in 1990 to include Buddhist converts. As Sikhs and Buddhists are defined as Hindus in the Constitution, this was a relatively simple matter. Converts to Christianity and Islam were excluded from the Scheduled

Previous page: Chinese fishing nets at Fort Cochin. These ingenious devices are said to have been introduced to the Malabar coast by courtiers of Kublai Khan.

Top: The Mar Thomite bishop of Trivandrum, Joseph Mar Irenaeus. The Mar Thoma church blends the rituals and traditions of the Orthodox Church, from which it departed last century, with the theological outlook of Western Protestantism.

Bottom: Over 14,000 women – Christians, Muslims and Hindus – are receiving help of some sort from the Cochin Social Services Society, which is run by the Catholic Church. Women are involved in the manufacture of electronic goods, clothes and spices.

Above left: A Catholic church near Ernakulam.

Above right: Palms and spires dominate Kerala's backwaters.

Below: Fishermen from Vizhinjam at Kovalam Beach. Although Kerala's 30 million inhabitants are among the best-educated and healthiest in India, many coastal fishing communities – which are predominantly Christian and Muslim – suffer extreme poverty.

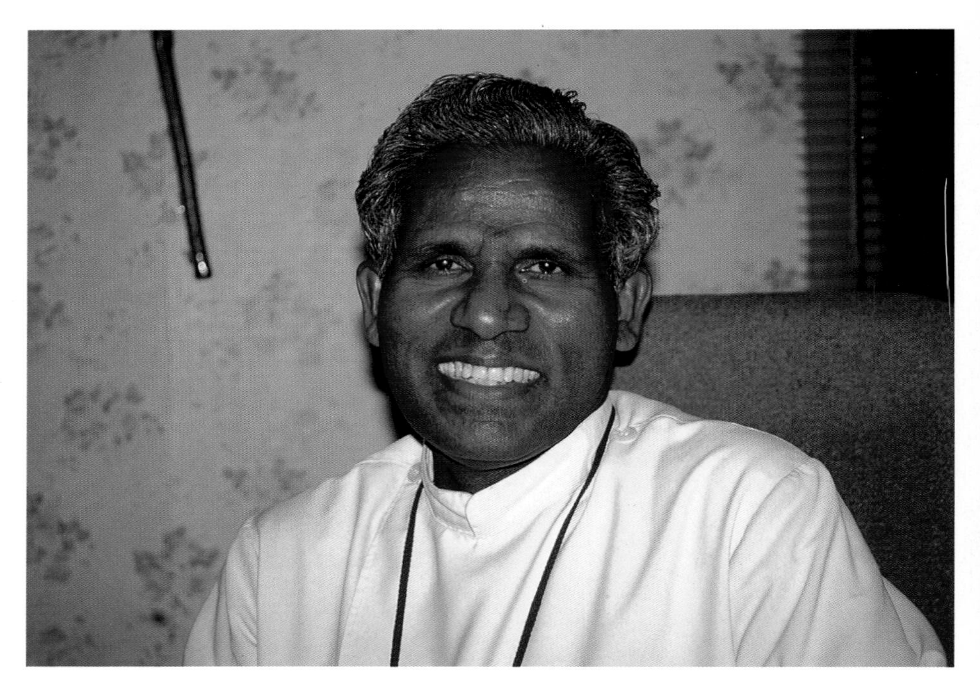

Above: The Right Reverend M. Azariah, the Church of South India bishop of Madras. The bishop is a *dalit* and an outspoken and tireless champion of India's downtrodden.

Below left: All the houses at Balaramapuram leper colony, near Madras, have a shrine tacked on their gables. Christians favour the Virgin Mary.

Below right: Mr A. Prakasam, president of the Balaramapuram Leprosy Rehabilitation Society, and himself a sufferer. Balaramapuram is a beautifully planned village, established by the Catholic Church and now home to 110 families, two-thirds of whom are Hindu.

Above: Children playing cricket at South Park Street cemetery, Calcutta, which was opened in 1767 to serve the large British community in the 'City of Palaces'.

Below: George Gregorian in his office, which was once the mortuary of the Armenian Church of the Holy Virgin Mary, Madras. Mr Gregorian is one of the last Armenians in a city that was once home to many.

Top: A soup kitchen in Calcutta's South Park Street, run by the Assembly of God, which also runs a high school and hospital.

Bottom: Children being taught to read by Calcutta's Cathedral Relief Service, which was established in 1971 to help victims of the Bangladeshi war. Today it is involved in a wide range of development activities and provides health care and education in seventeen slums. These children are from the Muslim-dominated slum of Tiljala.

Above: The first church and cemetery established by the Welsh missionaries who arrived in Cherrapunji in 1841. Today around half the 700,000 Christians in the Khasi Hills are Presbyterians.

Below: All Saints, Shillong, is one of the smallest cathedrals in India, and arguably the loveliest. The original was flattened by the great earthquake of 1897.

Overleaf: Wayside shrine, Goa.

Castes Order. However, many come from the same outcast background and together they are part of the wider family of *dalits*. Depressed classes, *harijans*, scheduled castes, backward classes, Pariahs – these were among the names given to the outcasts by the higher castes; *dalit* is the name they have given themselves. It means 'oppressed', or 'broken', but it is used by people like Bishop Azariah with a sense of pride and hope rather than shame and fatalism.

The bishop was unimpressed by Mahatma Gandhi's reputation as a defender of the poor. 'He gave us a label we could have done without,' he said dismissively. The very nature of untouchability belonged to what he called 'that Hindu nonsense'. He talked with greater respect about Dr Ambedkar, an untouchable Hindu who converted to Buddhism and led 3 million others in the same direction, and who helped to draft the Indian Constitution. And then, his eyes twinkling, he asked if I had heard of Swami Chinmayananda.

I said I hadn't.

'He was the first president of the VHP,' explained the bishop. Like the BJP and the RSS, the Vishnu Hindu Parishad wished to turn India into a Hindu state. 'I was on a plane with him one day. Just imagine, me an untouchable fellow sitting next to a Brahmin! So I turned to him and said, "*Namaste*, Swamiji," and I told him I was a great admirer. I had attended one of his lectures on the *Bhagavad-gitā*, and it was very fine, very witty. I told him that I was a Christian pastor, that I had read a lot of his stuff and written a monograph in Tamil on modern religious movements.'

The bishop paused for dramatic effect and I noticed that the three gentlemen beside me were gazing at him with a mixture of devotion and awe. They had probably heard the story before, but they were enjoying its retelling.

'And do you know what he said?' continued the bishop. 'He said, "There are only two types of people in India. Those who were Hindus and those who are Hindus." I said, "Nonsense!" If you could have seen the horror on the face of his acolytes! This big Brahmin being spoken to like that! I said to him, "I've never been a Hindu, nor were my parents, nor my grandparents. But we are still treated as untouchables, as polluted, by you caste Hindus. We were here before you Hindus ever came. We are Dravidians – we're the original people of India!"'

A secretary came in with some papers and while the bishop rapidly scanned them I gazed about the room. Behind me were twenty-odd plastic chairs, arranged in rows and facing the bishop's desk. One wall was covered with a massive poster of a Swiss alpine scene of the sort favoured by dentists, another by a poster of a tropical beach with swaying palms, golden sands and blue sea. A crook hung from a nail behind the bishop. There were no pictures of Christ, but there was a wall clock whose face was a soppy photograph of a kitten. As soon as the secretary left, another man appeared with a garland made of coloured paper and azure wool and a length of beautiful purple cloth. The bishop waved me to my feet, dropped the garland around my neck and draped the cloth around my shoulders. The three others, none of whom had spoken so far, clapped politely. 'Of course, I didn't buy this especially for you,' said the bishop. 'I didn't even know you were coming. But everywhere I go in the villages people give me cloth like this and they garland me.' He said he was always very touched. I said that I was too.

A tray of tea and biscuits appeared. 'I mustn't have sugar,' said Bishop Azariah, pushing the biscuits away and tapping his heart. 'I have had a heart bypass – no sugar, no fat.' He added that most *dalits* didn't suffer from heart disease, as they couldn't afford sugar or oil. However, his family had owned a little land and as a child he had eaten better than his *dalit* neighbours, or worse, depending on how you looked at it.

The most vivid descriptions I heard of the practical consequences of being a *dalit* came not from the bishop, nor from any other *dalits* I met, but from two Jesuit priests who worked for the

Indian Social Institute (ISI). A secular organization founded by the Society of Jesus in 1951 and based in Delhi, the institute was committed – in the words of its prospectus – to creating 'a just social order where every person can experience and enjoy true justice, equality, liberty and fraternity as is envisaged in the Constitution of India'. Fathers Josey Kunnunkal and Jose Kananaikil had spent much of their lives working among the poor of rural Bihar. The former, a keen smoker and cricket fan, had conducted a five-year study of the nature of untouchability. 'We felt that if we were going to be any help to the *dalits*,' he had explained when we met in Delhi, 'we had to understand precisely what it meant to be untouchable – how it affected their psyche as well as their social and economic status.' The research team was struck by the *dalits'* overwhelming feeling of anger – it was an existential anger, according to Father Josey – and by their total lack of self-worth. 'They'll always tell you, when you ask them how they see themselves, that they're amoral, that they're crooks, robbers, cheats, because that's the image that the upper castes have given them. Even now they live in fear in rural districts. It's said that one Rajput could walk into a village and control a hundred *dalits*. That's what fear does.' In many villages in Bihar the *dalits* occupied the southern districts, the places of death where they skinned carcasses and dealt with the village waste. 'You see,' said the priest, 'the wind always blows from the north, so the stench is carried away from where the high castes live. Imagine if you're a *dalit* child: right from birth you are on the fringe of society – that'll be with you all your life, whatever your economic status.'

Father Jose, who was also a Keralite, had helped to set up Bihar Dalit Bikas Samity, which was now a sizeable movement working for 63,000 *dalit* families in twelve districts. The *dalits*, explained Father Jose, had learned to live without justice. If their women were raped by upper-caste men – a common enough occurrence – or if their men were murdered, there was little point in going to the police or the courts. 'The courts are always controlled by the upper castes,' explained the priest. '*Dalits* don't expect justice, and they seldom get it.' However, over the past decade the ISI had helped the *dalits* to organize themselves and fight for justice whenever they were subjected to persecution. 'The lesson we are giving,' said Father Jose, 'is that you will get justice only if you take it. You must organize. The bigger you are, the greater your power to change things.' He added that although *dalits* generally had little or no respect for their own caste, they were very proud of their own families, and *dalit* women were psychologically more liberated than high-caste Hindu women.

While I was in Delhi I had also called on Dr James Massey, the general secretary of the Indian Society for the Promotion of Christian Knowledge, a Punjabi *dalit* and author of many learned works on the *dalit* issue. Dr Massey had translated the Bible into Punjabi and he told me about the difficulties of translating from Hebrew into other languages. There were, he said, six or seven words for 'poor' in Old Testament Hebrew; in English they were all translated by one word, 'poor'. *Dalit* was a Sanskrit word but the same root, *dall*, was found in Hebrew, where it was used to denote something more profound than being poor: it signified helplessness, low status and oppression. Dr Massey had discovered over fifty instances of *dall* and its derivatives in the Bible; he said that no other Scripture used the term. Bishop Azariah knew Dr Massey very well; indeed, he implied that he had been the person to alert him to the biblical use of *dall*. He knew both Greek and Hebrew and he had noticed that the term *dall* was particularly prominent in the Book of Isaiah.

Dr Massey talked at length about *dalit* theology and gave me several papers on the subject. I read these and I listened to others who were promoting *dalit* theology, but I was little the wiser about what it really meant. How could one formulate a theology – literally, a science of God – for or about one group of people? If it made sense to talk of *dalit* theology, did that mean that one could formulate a theology for the middle classes too or the landed gentry? The triumph of Christianity, surely, is its universality: it is a religion which reaches out to all nations and all peoples. Certainly, men can choose to reject the message of the cross, but that is their choice. In the words of St John, God gave his only-begotten son 'to the end that all that believe in him should not perish, but have everlasting life' (3:16). All, not some: not just the poor and persecuted, but tax collectors, bankers and politicians as well.

When I asked Bishop Azariah what he understood *dalit* theology to mean I anticipated a vague and convoluted answer, based more on emotion than on logic. 'Good news,' he replied. 'The good news that we are all relations. Now we can touch each other. I can touch you, you can touch me. That's *dalit* theology.' To me this made sense: stated another way, all are equal in the eyes of God.

~

'If you came to Madras at the start of the nineteenth century,' writes Jan Morris in *Stones of Empire*, 'you thought you were approaching a foreshore lined with Grecian temples: if you came at the end of the century, it was like sailing into some fantasy of orientalism.' The latter years of the nineteenth century saw a burgeoning of Indo-Saracen architecture, and the new buildings – Senate House, Chepawk Palace, the Post Office, the High Court – helped to create a 'marvellously airy and festive waterfront, floating there all pinnacles and bubbles in the southern heat above the surf'. None of which impressed Rudyard Kipling, who described the city as a withered beldame. The extravagant touches on the waterfront did nothing to alter the basic disposition of Madras: they were *maquillage* on the face of a crumbling diva. Madras was the oldest of the imperial cities – the Honourable Company took possession of the land in 1639 – but as an important economic and political centre it had long ago been eclipsed by Calcutta and Bombay. It remained, in Morris's view, an easygoing, overtaken, slightly disappointed place, more charming than decisive. If I were Madras, I would take this as a compliment. It has none of the flashy pretensions of Bombay, nor the abject misery of Calcutta, nor the cool arrogance of New Delhi. It does not even have a real centre, a heart pumping distinctive blood through the outerlying arteries of the city; in fact, it is not so much a city as a sprawling amalgam of settlements, and nowhere does one feel its fractured provincialism more keenly than in the district of Egmore, which is where I chose to stay.

My hotel was one of the better-class establishments on Kennet Lane, a narrow, ill-paved thoroughfare which ran from the grandly dilapidated Egmore station down towards the river Cooum, which slowly flushed the city's wastes out into the Bay of Bengal. Kennet Lane was one of the noisiest places in Madras: at any time of day or night there would be half a dozen or more buses revving up outside the hotel, honking at rickshaws and lorries which blocked their path and charging their roofracks with vast quantities of cargo. The pavements were the passengers' waiting-rooms and they felt like purgatory: lassitude and confusion, disappointment and elation – these were the emotions that flickered across the haggard faces of the waiting travellers.

When I embarked on my journey in Shimla, the pre-monsoon rains were beginning to sweep in from the south-west, albeit fitfully; by the time I reached Bombay they were in full flow. In Goa and Kerala there were a few violent storms, but these were the dying rages of the retreating monsoon. It was retreating, in particular, to Tamil Nadu, and scarcely a day went by in Madras when the city was not hit by a deluge; within a matter of minutes Kennet Lane was transformed into something more akin to a tropical stream than a roadway. It was a climate like this that gave malaria – *mala aria* in Italian or 'bad air' – its name, and with good reason judging from the memorials in the old British churches. Countless numbers of soldiers and Company members were 'victims to the fever', which most of the time meant malaria.

Some of the memorials are vague and only hint at the cause of death. For example, there is a marble tablet in St George's Cathedral which records the 'premature and sudden dissolution in a distant clime' of a thirty-three-year-old man. Perhaps gin rather than malaria was the cause of death in his case. Other memorials, like the one to Nurse Charlotte Andrews at the door of St Andrew's Kirk, are more precise. Born in Glasgow in 1876, she died in Madras in 1905. The memorial was erected 'in recognition of her devotion to duty in having volunteered her services during an epidemic of cholera to which she herself fell a victim'.

The architecture and iconography of the old British churches is exactly what you would expect. Many were modelled on churches back home – in St Andrew's case on St Martin-in-the-Fields in London – and the memorials and monuments were hewn out of marble by British sculptors in the styles which prevailed in Britain at that time. The British knew precisely how they wanted to depict Christ and the saints and precisely what sorts of building they wanted for their worship; there was an imperial confidence at work here. Indian Christians, by contrast, are still struggling to find a recognizably Indian way of expressing, in art, their faith in Christ. For every portrayal of Christ as dark-skinned in a *dhoti*, there are tens of thousands in which he is depicted, improbably, as a blond-haired Caucasian. Indian Christians are having similar difficulties in fashioning an architecture which might be considered indigenous. This is partly to do with the nature of Christian worship. Hindus tend to carry out their devotions individually, and their method of temple building, with its reliance on pillar and flat beam, creates an intimate environment which is perfectly suited to their purposes. The Christians, on the other hand, must rely on the arch to span the great spaces they require for communal worship, and this has inevitably led to the adoption of Western styles of architecture. Some efforts have been made to give an Indian flavour to church architecture – St John's at Merhauli in Delhi, for example, is a synthesis of Islamic and Hindu styles –

but most of the new churches in India are poor imitations of Victorian Gothic or an often hideous mishmash of Art Deco, modernist and classical styles. An Indian style of church building, and one of true merit, may emerge over the coming years. In the meantime we are left to marvel at those two great periods of church architecture on the subcontinent: Portuguese baroque and British neo-classical.

It was the sight of its spire pointing high above the roofscape of Egmore which attracted me to St Andrew's Kirk early one morning. I walked across the iron footbridge which traversed the rails at Egmore station, past the cinder park for commuters' bicycles and along a broad street which was lined with slum dwellings. The church was an immense neo-classical building, set back from the road in a large compound with some fine trees which were probably as old as the building itself. A magnificent Ionic-columned portico had the date – MDCCCXX – carved on the pediment below the Hebrew word for Jehovah. Above rose a stone spire of singular beauty, almost an exact replica of the one designed by James Gibbs for St Martin-in-the-Fields. The portico was clothed in bamboo scaffolding and as I approached I could hear the muffled sound of hammering coming from the interior. I was met at the door by a Sri Lankan who introduced himself as the church clerk and he accompanied me as I made a tour of the church. Sixteen fluted pillars supported a dome which was decorated like the night sky with silver stars on an indigo background. A mahogany pergola held the lights and fans which illuminated and aired rattan pews arranged to suit the curvilinear plan of the church. I was pleased to see that the organ came from my old home town of Huddersfield.

'We had a wonderful organist till recently,' said the clerk. 'He was called Handel. Handel Manuel.' He had played at St Andrew's for fifty-three years till his death the previous year. Fortunately, the new chap was a pupil of Handel and an excellent organist as well. St Andrew's Kirk was famous for its music, and this was one of the attractions for the 450 families who worshipped here. Another was the relative brevity of its services.

'One hour, five minutes maximum,' confirmed Rev. R. M. Dravyam when I went to see him at the Manse, a rambling building tucked away among the trees at the rear of the compound. A square-faced man with a letter-box mouth and thick, brushed-back hair, Rev. Dravyam had experienced the many flavours of Protestantism during his lifetime. He was baptized as a high-church Anglican by missionaries from the Society for the Propagation of the Gospel, but his family had moved around the state in his youth and he came into contact with the Australian mission at Madurai, with the Congregationalists of the London Missionary Society at Nagercoil and with the Church Missionary Society elsewhere.

While the Catholic missionaries went pretty much where they pleased in India, the early Protestant missions worked out a system which ensured that they did not compete for the same souls. During the nineteenth century matters were informally arranged – with the Basel Mission taking south Kanara, for example, and the Church Missionary Society central Kerala; with the Leipzig Lutherans taking Tranquebar and the American Lutherans a chunk of Andhra Pradesh – but as the number of missions increased, so did the need for a more formal system, and at the end of the century the Comity principle was established: missions were now allocated certain territories in which other Protestants were expected not to trespass. Place of birth has thus had more to do with an Indian Protestant's denomination than theology, although families and individuals who move around the country tend to dip into a variety of ecclesiastical traditions. 'So I had all these different backgrounds,' mused Rev. Dravyam, 'and then my first parish was Methodist.' His eclectic experience had stood him in good stead and he was evidently at ease with the Scottish system of church management which still prevailed at St Andrew's Kirk.

During the course of our conversations it became increasingly clear that St Andrew's had an uneasy relationship with the diocese.

I was expecting as much; the priest who was present during my meeting with Bishop Azariah had told me that the congregation at St Andrew's was élitist and had no sympathy for the *dalit* struggles in which he and the bishop were so involved. The kirk was a member of the Church of South India, explained Rev. Dravyam, but it joined only in 1959, twelve years after the CSI came into being and then on its own terms. Most CSI churches must give 60 per cent of their income to the diocese; St Andrew's does not, although in the past it has contributed generously to diocesan appeals. St Andrew's congregation also insisted that they be allowed to retain the kirk session. The congregation could not be described as élitist, said Rev. Dravyam firmly when I told him of the *dalit* priest's remarks about his church. The services were nearly always in English, but this was inevitable: it was the common language for the Keralites, Anglo-Indians, north Indians and Tamils who worshipped here. As far as the *dalit* issue was concerned, he was somewhat at odds with the bishop and his cohorts. 'What they don't tell you,' he said, 'is that social change is sweeping India, especially in the cities. We have *dalit* bishops in the church; the Port Trust chairman was a *dalit*; till recently the chief minister of Uttar Pradesh was a *dalit* woman. In our church you'll find *dalits* marrying non-*dalits*. There is a greater mingling of different castes now than ever before.' In St Andrew's Kirk they never talked of caste differences and they did not allow caste to affect the life of the congregation or its work in the wider community. 'Two thousand years back,' said Rev. Dravyam, 'the barriers were broken down. Slaves and masters, Greeks and Romans, Jews and non-Jews – all sat together to worship God. That is our tradition. There can be no going back.'

Rev. Dravyam added that he had worked in many different churches, but this was the only congregation which was actively involved in social work to help the poor. 'If they say we're élitist,' he said, 'they're forgetting that this congregation has built three village churches. This congregation has set up a day-care school for the slum children around the church – and they're 100 per cent *dalit.* It has set up leather-training schemes for girls from the slums, a school for the mentally disabled, a day-care centre in a leper colony. In the rural areas it's true that the *dalit* issue does matter, and St Andrew's has been working in the villages for the past twenty years. All the beneficiaries there are *dalits*, so there is no justification for the bishop and his people calling us élitist.'

The term *dalit* is far from precise and today is used to encompass more than the scheduled castes or the untouchables. For example, the Dalit Panther Movement of Maharashtra defines *dalits* as 'members of scheduled castes and tribes, neo-Buddhists, the working people, the landless and poor peasants, women and all those who are being exploited politically, economically and in the name of religion'. So, in the eyes of some, Brahmins and other high-caste Hindus can also be *dalits*: oppression and servitude are the defining parameters – in which case the definition of *dalit* could be broadened still further to include groups like the mentally handicapped and lepers, as they, too, suffer from rejection and poverty.

I arrived at Asha, the centre for the mentally disabled which occupied a purpose-built compound to the west of St Andrew's Kirk, just after morning prayers. The children were heading for their classes, some under their own steam, others with help from the staff. In an office which opened on to the central atrium Nalini Manuel, the petite and pretty project officer, was listening attentively to a garrulous little girl with Down's syndrome. 'We always start with prayers,' she explained once the girl had left for her class. 'They give the children a routine, which is important. The mentally disabled do understand the idea of God – the idea that there is something up there.' She said that only two of the children who attended Asha came from Christian families; most were Hindus, but their parents were very appreciative of the work done here at the church centre. 'They all tell me, "Besides our Hindu gods, we all believe in Jesus."'

Asha was founded in 1982 by St Andrew's Scottish presbyter,

Rev. Peter Millar. For the first seven years of its existence it acted as a placement centre, finding suitable jobs, medical care, mobility aids and so forth for the adult disabled. Then in 1989 the church decided to help the mentally disabled children of the neighbouring slums. 'We found that there were enough schools for the deaf, the blind and the mentally disabled,' explained Nalini, 'but parents had to pay for them. The people in the slums certainly couldn't afford to. In any case, most schools want children who are toilet-trained, who won't be messy. We'll take any child from the slums providing we've got space, however severe their disability.'

In 1989 Asha opened its doors to four children; now forty-five attend the centre from nine thirty to three thirty each day and they range in age from two and a half months to twenty years. 'The earlier you start with children, the easier it is to help them,' explained Nalini, 'but getting parents to accept that their babies are mentally disabled can be a real difficulty.' Superstition and ignorance were rife in the slums. 'You see, the parents believe in astrology and horoscopes. They think that if their child's behaving oddly, it's God's punishment for something that they've done; but when the bad times are over the child will be OK.'

The malign influence of astrologers had caused great distress to one of the pupils. 'You see that girl? The pretty one over there?' said Nalini, pointing to a thirteen-year-old in the next-door room. 'She was normal till she was two and a half years old, then she had brain fever and her mental age has hardly changed since then. Some years ago she suffered very severe bleeding and her mother wanted to have her womb removed. I agreed with her, but her father went to an astrologer who said: "This is a bad time, but soon your daughter will be all right and you will be able to marry her off."' When the girl reached puberty her father threw a huge party to announce that she would soon be ready for marriage. She was even dressed up as a bride. 'She's not even toilet-trained,' said Nalini in exasperation, 'and at the party she became violent. How could she understand what was happening?'

According to Nalini, most parents wish to keep their mentally disabled children at home rather than place them in permanent care – 'They love them,' she said simply – but lack of help meant that they were often forced to restrain them. 'You might have ten people living in a shack 8 feet square,' explained Nalini, 'and that space is your bathroom, kitchen, bedroom, everything. If you've got a hyperactive child, it might run around too much and cause trouble in the neighbouring shacks, so the parents will bind its legs together or tie it to a post.' This was happening less often in the slums around the church, thanks largely to the activities of Asha, and it was clear that the centre was having a good influence not only on the children but, equally important, on their families as well.

Before I left the centre, Nalini showed me around. Some of the children appeared to be only mildly disabled and the older ones were making office stationery from waste paper. The profits were divided among them, and some had even opened their own bank accounts. Others were suffering extreme forms of mental disability, but they were being expertly cared for and making much greater progress than they could ever have done had they remained in the slums. It was a measure of the centre's success that when the staff suggested to parents that they should pay a nominal fee of 1 rupee, many of the mothers, though very poor, said they wanted to give more. 'One gave 50 rupees,' recalled Nalini. 'Another 100, another 5. They said they could see that their children were benefiting from what we were doing here.'

The following afternoon Rev. Dravyam took me to see a leper colony on the outskirts of the city. On the drive out we talked about Asha. 'I've only been here a year,' he said, 'and I can't take any of the credit. Asha is the creation of the congregation. It's a people's project. It's the congregation who raised the money to run the centre and some of them are actively involved in its work.' It was also a member of St Andrew's, Mary Karkada, who had helped to establish the leper colony at Balaramapuram, although most of the work in recent years had been done by Catholic priests.

The very term 'leper colony' has a forbidding ring to it and I was expecting a grim medieval building, fortified as much for the sake of its inmates as for those outside. 'Sir, if only you will, you can make me clean,' said the leper to Jesus. 'Jesus stretched out his hand and touched him, saying, "I will; be clean"' Matthew 8:2–3). It was an unfortunate choice of words on the part of both men, for by implication it meant that lepers were dirty, defiled, polluted. That is precisely how they have always been treated in India, although the president of the Balaramapuram Leprosy Rehabilitation Society, Mr A. Prakasam, himself a sufferer, said that attitudes were slowly changing. Fifteen years ago no one would sit next to a leper on public transport; now most people realized that it was impossible to catch leprosy through bodily contact. All the same, they remained an outcast community and preferred to live together rather than face the vicissitudes of life in the world outside. There were 110 families here and most of the adults were missing fingers and toes and sometimes more than that. Consequently few could find work and there was an atmosphere of enforced idleness about the place. A group of men and women were playing dice in the shade of some trees in the small square outside the Catholic church; others were sitting about on their doorsteps and gossiping.

Balaramapuram was a beautifully planned village with some eighty modern homes neatly dispersed along a grid of spotlessly clean streets. 'It's much cleaner in here than outside,' whispered Rev. Dravyam approvingly as we made our way around. Each home contained three rooms; all were painted in bright colours, some had Rousseauesque murals on their walls and most had a little shrine tacked on to their flat gables. Ganesh and Shiva were popular among the Hindus, the Virgin Mary among the Christians. Altogether there were thirty Christian families, two-thirds of whom were Catholic, five Muslim families and some seventy Hindu families. Balaramapuram was a model of religious tolerance and everyone joined in everyone else's religious ceremonies and festivals. There were eleven leper colonies scattered around Madras; this, said the lepers I spoke to, was by far the best, in terms of both the accommodation and the treatment which was provided by the Catholic sisters in the clinic. They were also very pleased with the day-care centre which had been set up by St Andrew's Kirk: it looked after twenty-nine children between the ages of three and five. I was intrigued to see that one of the donors who had contributed to the clinic, and whose name was inscribed on the stone tablet, was a Mr Karl Marx of Germany. His namesake would certainly have sided with the *dalits*, as had the congregation of St Andrew's Kirk, whatever the bishop's views to the contrary.

CHAPTER 10

In the Midst of Life

I have forgotten her name, but I shall not forget her face, nor what she said, nor the manner in which she said it. She was thirteen, though she looked somewhat older, and she had jet-black hair, the darkest of eyes, a powerful nose and a fleshy and expressive mouth. She wore a pink dress the same colour as the *bindi* on her forehead and she spoke Bengali in a rasping voice, more like a boy's at puberty than a girl's. There were thirty other children crammed into the small upstairs room in Bowbazar – pictures of Ramakrishna, Tagore, Gandhi and Nehru on the walls – and to escape their screams and chatter we went out on to a narrow wooden balcony with one of her teachers. We closed the door on her classmates and from where we stood we could observe the restless stream of life in the ill-lit alley below. I was reminded of Gustave Doré's lithographs of the poorer districts of Victorian London. A tall building with crumbling balconies and sagging lintels loomed above a fruit stall like the stern of a rotting galleon. Smoke drifted up from charcoal braziers and women waited as still as statues for the early-evening trade, while cyclists and pedestrians swirled around them like shoals of passing fish.

The girl told me first about her daily routine, using the teacher as an interpreter. In the morning she went to school, then at midday she returned home, cooked lunch for her brother and sister and helped her mother with domestic chores. In the afternoon she did her school homework and then around four thirty she came to this class: she liked painting and drawing and playing with the other children, but most of all she loved the drama lessons. When the class finished, around seven o'clock, she would return home, watch television and go to bed. She didn't say what her mother would be doing when she got there: working, presumably, for the evenings were a busy time for Bowbazar's prostitutes.

Her teacher had told me when we stepped out on to the balcony that Calcutta's pimps liked to get hold of children when they were twelve or thirteen. He and his colleagues had arranged for this particular girl to stay at a hostel some distance from the red-light district, largely to protect her from the pimps, but she had missed her mother and her mother had missed her, so she had come back home again. He said they realized now that she was a headstrong girl and that she was in no danger of being inveigled into prostitution. So what did she hope to do with her life? I asked.

'I'd like to be a doctor,' she replied in a confident voice. 'I can't stand seeing all the poor lying around in the streets and dying without medical treatment. When I'm a doctor I'll open a hospital for the poor. I'll look after them.' All the children in this evening class were the offspring of prostitutes, but their economic situations varied greatly: some of them had relatively wealthy mothers, but many were very poor. Doctors carried out regular check-ups, but they had to be paid for their services. 'When I'm a doctor,' said the girl emphatically, 'I'll take care of them all for free.'

Even in the days when Calcutta was known as the City of Palaces, and long before Kipling more tellingly described it as the City of Dreadful Night, most visitors were shocked by its poverty. 'Find, if you can, a more uninviting stop than Calcutta,' wrote Sir George Trevelyan in 1863. 'It unites every condition of a perfectly unhealthy situation . . . The place is so bad by nature that human effort could do little to make it worse; but that has been done faithfully and assiduously.' Kipling put similar sentiments into awkward verse. Calcutta, in his view, was:

Chance-directed, chance-erected, laid and built
On the silt
Palace, byre, hovel – poverty and pride –
Side by side.

This was my third visit to Calcutta and I found myself, as always, in the grip of conflicting emotions. When I wandered among the early-evening crowds on Chowringhee as a red sun sank behind the angular bulk of Eden Gardens; when I walked across the Maidan in the early morning and saw a trail of cattle egrets flap slowly past the great white bulk of the Victoria Memorial; when I watched the gangs of children with their broken bats and battered balls playing cricket among the imperial graves of South Park Street cemetery: on these and many other occasions I was utterly beguiled by the city and by the exuberance of her people. But just as frequently I was overcome with disgust. I recall, offhand, walking down Park Street to meet a pastor at the offices of the Assembly of God. Shortly before I reached there I passed a man sprawling face down on the pavement. He was naked and a swarm of flies buzzed around his buttocks, which were smeared with excrement. There was an appalling stench and passers-by covered their faces with hands and handkerchiefs. No one, myself included, stopped to help him – I suspect he was already dead – and I suppose we all comforted ourselves with the knowledge that Mother Teresa's Sisters of Charity would eventually lift him from the pavement and take him to a home for the destitute or, more probably, to a crematorium.

Calcutta's poverty, suggests Geoffrey Moorhouse in his fine portrait of the city, *Calcutta: The City Revealed*, will one day be its undoing. Perhaps a medieval-style plague, he speculates, will kill vast numbers; then the real carnage will begin:

> While some people are counting their rising piles of dead, others will have become so maddened by their loss, and by their fury at the fates, that they will set out to destroy. They will rage

> through the city with torches, with knives, with bombs, with pistols, with axes and with bare hands. They will burn everything that can be put to the torch and they will smash everything that cannot be burned and they will kill and terribly mutilate anyone who gets in their way and even those who flee . . .

Or if plague does not presage the destruction of the city, predicts Moorhouse, then the revenge of the poor will: 'In this haunting horror, the night comes when every poor man in the city rises from his pavement and his squalid bustee and at last dispossesses the rich with crazy ferocity.' The rickshaw-wallahs will drag the rich from their cars and butcher them in the street and across Calcutta and over the river Hooghly in Howrah the poor will rise up to exact a terrible revenge for the suffering they have been forced to endure for so long. Why? Because, in Moorhouse's view, the time for compassion will be over.

It is more than twenty years since Moorhouse issued his apocalyptic warning. The poor are still there, seemingly in greater numbers than ever before, and they have not risen up, against either the rich or their own government. I reread Moorhouse's epilogue before I returned to Calcutta, a couple of weeks before Easter, in the hot and steamy month of April, and hoped that during the course of this stay I might be able to explain, to my own satisfaction if no one else's, why the poor had failed to fulfil Moorhouse's brutal prophecy. Were they less poor than they used to be, and if they were, then had Christianity had anything to do with it? Or was there some other factor which had prevented the plunge into barbarism?

~

'When I came to Serampore in 1990,' said Dr J. T. K. Daniel when I told him that I had just dropped by St Olaf's, 'that church was in a terrible state. Here in Bengal Christianity's so weak, you see. You wouldn't believe what people were doing. There were cattle in the garden and the church was even being used for night-time activities.' The squatters in the garden had also drilled holes in the church walls and wired lights up to the mains.

I had arrived in Serampore, a small town fifteen miles upstream of Calcutta, midway through the afternoon and an hour before I had arranged to meet Dr Daniel, the principal of Serampore College. My taxi-driver had searched unsuccessfully for the old Danish graveyard and we had found instead St Olaf's, an imposing building with a good classical façade and the date of its construction, 1805, carved on the pediment. The church was locked but I rattled the main door and after a while a workman appeared and let me in. It was in the process of being renovated and a thick layer of plaster dust coated the pews and the stone floor. The walls were unadorned save for a few marble tablets. One was a memorial to the three men who did most to introduce Christianity to this part of India: it recorded that William Carey, Joshua Marshman and William Ward 'gave their faithful and gratuitous ministrations to the congregation here assembled'. Another marble tablet had been erected to honour the memory of Lt. Col. Ole Bie, Governor of Fredericksnagar, as Serampore was known when it was in Danish hands, and disciple of the great C. F. Schwartz, who served for almost fifty years in the mission at Tranquebar, the Danish colony in south India. Bie had received and sheltered Carey and the other Baptist missionaries in 1799, and it was he who commissioned St Olaf's church, though he died before its completion.

It was less than half a mile from the church to Serampore College, the narrow road running for the most part along the east bank of the Hooghly. The broad river was grey and placid and sandpipers and mynah birds scurried about its muddy banks in search of food. We passed a sprawling jute mill with a squat industrial chimney and a neat little jetty with narrow-gauge rails which gleamed in the late-afternoon light. Beyond was the college, which was about to close for the day. On the grass playing field in front of the grand Ionic portico of the main building men were playing cricket, while on the steps and in the shade of scattered trees groups of students lounged about, chatting quietly among themselves.

I found Dr Daniel in a handsome building with its own fenced garden a little distance back from the river. He came to the door with his dog, a golden retriever, and we sat on low-slung chairs in a room the size of a small chapel. He was a lithely built man, in his fifties I imagine, with very dark skin – he was a Tamil from Madras – and a gentle, undemonstrative manner. He explained that this was the house where William Carey had lived and he told me about Carey and his colleagues and about the founding of the college on Danish territory.

Carey is sometimes called the father of modern mission, which is by no means the case, although he is one of the towering figures of recent Christian history. His beginnings were modest. A self-educated dissenting pastor in a Northamptonshire village, he supplemented his income by teaching and working as a cobbler. At the age of twenty-nine, in 1792, he published a treatise with the curious title *An Enquiry into the Obligations of Christians to use Means for the Conversion of the Heathens*. This was a study of Christian achievement in the world and a call to arms: the message of the cross had to be carried to heathens, wherever they were, for all could be saved if only they were reached in time. Expect great things from God, said Carey; attempt great things for God. He was a founder member of the Baptist Missionary Society and in June 1793 he sailed with his family to India, arriving at the mouth of the Hooghly on 11 November. Within months the Careys had run out of money and they relied for a while on the charity of a local Hindu, who lent them a house. The East India Company's anti-missionary policy led Carey to accept a position as manager of an indigo estate some distance inland and there the family resided for five painfully difficult years. One of the children died of dysentery; Mrs Carey gradually went mad. Carey translated the New Testament into Bengali, but when put to the test his translation was unintelligible. He scrapped it, became more familiar with the language and tried again.

Carey's fortunes were to change in 1799 when a new group of Baptist missionaries arrived in India. Among them were Joshua Marshman, a schoolmaster, and William Ward, a printer. Realizing that it would be unsafe to settle in Calcutta or in any other territory of the East India Company, they immediately headed for the Danish colony of Fredericksnagar. There they were welcomed by the devoutly Christian Lt. Col. Bie and within a short space of time they were joined by Carey. The Serampore mission was born and the three men were to work together, without interruption, until Ward's death in 1823. They are best remembered today not so much for their preaching, although they made many converts and ranged widely across Bengal, Bihar and Orissa, as for their work in the field of biblical translation. Over a period of thirty years the Serampore mission produced six translations of the complete Bible, Carey being responsible for those in Bengali, Sanskrit and Marathi. They also published translations of the New Testament in twenty-three other languages and parts of the Bible in a further ten. Carey's first efforts in Bengali may have been clumsy, but his eventual mastery of the language was such that scholars now claim him as the founder of Bengali prose literature.

Carey never wavered in his belief that there was no salvation except through Christ, but he made great efforts to understand Hindu culture and thought. The Serampore trio also recognized the importance of secular learning and the curriculum of the college is a testament to their claim, outlined in their statement of principles, that part of their work involved the 'forming of our native brethren to usefulness, fostering every kind of genius, and cherishing every gift and grace in them . . .'

'William Carey had a vision that religion should not be taught in isolation,' explained Dr Daniel, 'that it should be taught alongside all the other subjects. Christian mission is not just a matter of theological training – it's also about learning how the world works and about living in society.' In 1819 Serampore opened as a 'College for the Instruction of Asiatic, Christian, and other youth, in Eastern Literature and European Science' with thirty-seven students, eighteen of whom were non-Christians. Today it has over 2,000 students, approximately a hundred of whom are studying theology and will go on to serve as ministers in various Protestant Churches. The standard of excellence established by Carey continues to this day, and thirty-six theological colleges in India are affiliated to Serampore.

During his four decades in India – he died in 1834 – Carey witnessed many great changes, some of which he helped to bring about himself. Soon after his arrival he saw a widow being burned on her husband's funeral pyre and he was one of several prominent Europeans and Indians to campaign against *suttee*, which was eventually outlawed on Company territory in 1829. By then the Company had long since dropped its prohibition on missionary activity and Carey and his colleagues had established missions and schools in Calcutta, Nagpur, Delhi and the north-east. The Serampore trio were on good terms with the Anglicans, and the second bishop of Calcutta, Reginald Heber, suggested to Carey that there should be a reunion of the Anglican and Baptist Churches. When Carey arrived the only Christians in Bengal were the Europeans and Armenians who worked for the Company or were here on business. By the time he died an Indian Church was emerging and Christian leaders confidently anticipated the triumph of their faith. Lord Macaulay even went so far as to suggest that within forty years of his 1835 education reforms, Western knowledge would purge India of superstitious faiths – of Hinduism and Islam – and her people would all turn to Christianity. A few years later the fifth bishop of Calcutta, Daniel Wilson, pronounced at the consecration of St Paul's Cathedral that the new building claimed 'India as the Lord's'.

Critics of Christian endeavour in India – the most notable in recent times being Arun Shourie, author of *Missionaries in India* – have justly claimed that some Christians deliberately set out to portray Hinduism in the worst possible light. They highlighted barbaric practices such as *suttee* and ignored Hinduism's intellectual and philosophical qualities. For example, in 1805 Claudius Buchanan, chaplain to the East India Company, wrote: 'We shall not pollute the page with a description of the horrid rites of the religion of brahma. Suffice it to say that no inhuman practices in New Zealand, or in any other newly discovered land of savages, are more offensive to natural feeling, than some of those that are committed by the Hindoo people.' In similar vein, Charles Grant, the chairman of the Court of Directors of the East India Company, maintained that Hinduism led to dishonesty, social discord, sexual licence and cruelty to women and animals. I doubt whether Carey would have subscribed to this extreme view but in his *Enquiry* he did write that non-Christians were 'inveloped in ignorance and barbarism', and his colleague William Ward wrote a treatise whose aim was to establish in the minds of his readers the evils of Hinduism and the virtues of his own faith. Such critiques of Hinduism outraged many Indians, who felt that their religion was being deliberately misrepresented, and also caused disquiet within the Christian community. The missionary James Long wrote, 'Many of Mr Ward's remarks respecting the cruelties and immoralities among the Hindus are no more applicable to the body of the people than a description of Billings Gate and the Old Bailey, in London, would be to the inhabitants of the west end of town.' Sophistry and slander were the stock in trade of missionaries who vilified Hinduism in the last century; precisely the same weapons are used today by Christianity's more outspoken Hindu critics. There is a sort of Manichean inevitability about this and I am inclined to think that the belligerents of the two sides deserve one another.

In Bengal most local Christians were low-caste converts, many having come to the Church through mass conversions. However, the missionaries also sought to bring the Hindu intelligentsia into the fold and on those relatively rare occasions when they succeeded there was much rejoicing. One interesting case involved an ancestor of Rabindranath Tagore, novelist, poet, philosopher and Bengal's most famous son. Gyanendra Mohan Tagore was baptized at a church in Calcutta on 10 July 1851. According to the *Calcutta Christian Advocate* and the *Madras Native Herald*, the person whose writings influenced him most was a nonconformist divine, Dr John Pye Smith, who was my grandfather's great-grandfather.

I discovered this surprising piece of information not through painstaking research in some musty newspaper archive but while reading a weighty biography of my relative. John Medway's *Memoirs of the Life and Writings of John Pye Smith* were published in 1853, shortly after his death. They are written in the biographical style of the day, which is to say that they are verbose, pious and deferential. I doubt that I would have attempted to read the memoirs had I not embarked on this Indian journey, but I am glad that I did, not least because they provided an interesting portrait of the intellectual life of the nonconformist Church during the first half of the last century. Like Carey, Pye Smith was largely self-educated. His father was a Yorkshire bookseller and he apparently taught himself Greek and Hebrew by desultory reading in the family shop. He also taught himself Latin, in which language, by the age of twenty-one, he was delivering lectures to fellow students at the Rotherham Academy. In 1805 he became a Congregationalist minister at the Old Gravel Pit chapel in Hackney, and he combined his ministry there with his duties as theological tutor at Homerton College, where he served till 1850. Being a Congregationalist, he took a keen interest in the work of the London Missionary Society, but he also supported other nonconformist societies which were attempting to spread the gospel overseas. In 1842, on the occasion of its fiftieth anniversary, he was invited to address the Baptist Missionary Society (BMS) at the London Tavern. He used the occasion to attack Roman Catholic pretensions to an apostolic succession; he also affirmed the truths of the Book of Revelation, praised Carey and his followers and defined the BMS's role in Benthamite terms which may have been considered bland at the time: 'A Christian Mission is a plan, conceived and arranged methodically, but in as simple a manner as possible, for the communication of the greatest sum of happiness to the greatest number of our fellow-creatures.'

The Dictionary of National Biography is more critical of Pye Smith's achievements than the *Memoirs*, whose purpose was primarily to praise him. It suggests that he frittered away much of his time in ephemeral controversies – in his support of the Anti-Church State Society, for example, and on denunciations of this person's views and that – but it concedes that he did more than any other theologian of his time to reconcile the geological discoveries of the early nineteenth century with the Mosaic theory of creation. His family Bible, which I inherited along with a copy of the *Memoirs*, has a commentary which dates the creation of heaven and earth to precisely 4004 BC. Pye Smith realized that geological research challenged this belief and rather than refute science, as many church leaders had, he decided to become better acquainted with it. Indeed, it was his scientific acumen rather than his theological views that led to his becoming the first dissenting Fellow of the Royal Society. Scientific study prompted him to reinterpret the creation story to fit the facts and this, it seems, was what finally persuaded Gyanendra Tagore to embrace Christianity.

The *Madras Native Herald*'s description of his conversion was prefaced with the assertion that certain events had 'tended much to deepen the impression of the power of Christianity to vanquish Hinduism'. Twelve young men had renounced the faith of their fathers and five others were on the verge of doing so, although they were being restrained by the 'strong hand of force and confinement'. Most were Brahmins and all came from the middle or upper ranks of Indian society.

> The most important and striking case is that of Gyanendra Mohan Tagore, a relative of the late Dwarkanath Tagore, and only son of Prasannakumar Tagore, the well-known later Government Pleader in the Sudder Court, and for many years the intimate friend of Rammohun Roy. Being of an inquiring and philosophical cast of mind, and possessing ample leisure, his attention was directed to Christianity about ten years ago, whilst a Student in the Hindu College. Not being intimately acquainted with any Christian men, he was left to struggle alone with all the various objections and difficulties which fell in his path. After he had arrived at the conclusion that Hinduism, even in its more refined and philosophical form, was false, there seemed to be in Christianity itself serious difficulties which precluded its being true. Thus, at one time, the geological argument against the Scripture narrative of the Creation seemed to him insuperable, until he met with Dr Pye Smith's work on the *Relation between some parts of Holy Scripture and Geological Science.* At another time, the mystery attaching to the doctrine of the Trinity led him to profess Unitarianism, when he fell in with Dr Smith's *Scripture Testimony to the Messiah*, which fully established him in the Orthodox belief.

Gyanendra also read extensively from the works of French infidels, German rationalists and English and American sceptics, but their arguments were not compelling enough to dissuade him from becoming a Christian. 'We need not say,' continued the newspaper, 'how mighty were the obstacles to be overcome in taking such a step; loss of friends, displeasure of relatives, calumnies of the wicked and the misrepresentation of the ignorant. Happily, poverty was not added . . .'

Many members of the Tagore family were intimately involved with the Brahmo Samaj, a religious movement which advocated a monotheistic form of Hinduism, rejected idol worship and discarded the caste system. They wished to see Hinduism reformed, not vanquished, and they would have undoubtedly disapproved of Gyanendra's apostasy. However, Christianity – or at least, the life of Christ – did inspire the greatest of all Tagores, Rabindranath. One of his poems, 'Manab Putra' – 'The Son of Man' – is explicitly about Christ; many others have Christ's birth, life and death as their central theme. Christ, wrote Tagore, 'clearly perceived the true Kingdom of God not through the might of empire or wealth but through poverty'. Tagore also wrote religious songs, many of which are still sung in Christian churches in Bengal.

~

Calcutta is said to be India's most cultured city, and I suppose I should have spent my evenings in smoke-filled rooms listening to discussions about Tagore or Satyajit Ray, or watching the latest offerings of the Bengali theatre, or rubbing shoulders with bearded intellectuals in galleries specializing in the avant-garde. I did not do any of these things, and even if I had, I doubt whether I would have been any better entertained than I invariably was when I called in for a drink at the Fairlawn Hotel.

The Fairlawn was tucked away behind high walls midway along Sudder Street, whose pavements appeared to have been cleaned up since my last visit, presumably for the Wills Cricket World Cup, which had concluded a few days before my arrival in the city. A bald-headed man in a *dhoti* used to occupy the pavement opposite the Indian Museum, lolling about like a dejected Caesar among a motley platoon of dogs which he loved deeply and who loved him in return. They ate together on the pavement, slept on the pavement and appeared as much a fixture of Sudder Street as the chapel a little further on. However, he and the dogs had gone, and so too had the squabbling, procreating families who once lived below a faded sign which read 'Mass Feeding of the Poor on Sundays'. But beggars and taxi-drivers still milled about outside the gates of the Fairlawn and I was relieved to see that nothing else had changed in my absence. The green columns of the portico and the trees in the garden were still slung with coloured fairy lights, the waiters were still dressed like the sepoys in *Carry On up the Khyber* and the walls were still hung with portraits of Queen Elizabeth and Prince Philip, Diana and Charles and other prominent members of the royal family. Most important of all, Mrs Violet Smith was still there, sitting in a chair behind the small reception desk and gazing imperiously around her domain, while Fifi, a white poodle of great antiquity, sat obediently at her feet. She seemed to remember my face but I had to remind her who I was. She slapped me affectionately on the forearm and shouted over her shoulder to a waiter: 'It's an old friend! Bring him a beer.' Then, turning to me: 'Now you don't expect me to call you Charlie, do you? What sort of a name is that, for heaven's sake?'

While I waited for the beer to arrive we had a conversation, or rather Mrs Smith talked while I listened; her monologue, as far as I could recall, was almost an exact replica of the one she had offered two years earlier when I also dropped in at the Fairlawn, unannounced but dimly recognized. Mrs Smith was an Armenian, born in Dacca, but everything about her manner and aspirations seemed English, although she spoke scathingly of the snobberies of the old expatriate community, now long since gone. She reminded me that she had a grandson who had been to Charterhouse, that she and her husband spent several months in Europe each year and that she was seventy-something years old. She always looked the same: younger than her years, with clear skin, lovely brown eyes, beautifully manicured hands and a magnificent hair-do which was carefully tended, like a piece of exotic topiary, by someone who came in each morning. She also reminded me, waving a hand towards the framed pictures and newspaper cuttings on the stairs, that many famous people had stayed in her small hotel.

'Eric Newby, Tom Stoppard, Felicity Kendall,' she said, wagging a finger. 'And just the other month Clive Anderson of the

BBC came to see me. He had me interviewing Jyoti Basu outside the gates. Very slippery.'

Who was slippery? The Chief Minister?

'No, darling. Clive Anderson. When I interviewed him he was very tricky, very devious. I found it very stressful.'

The beer came and I drank it standing at the desk.

'And just today,' continued Mrs Smith, 'a girl came to see me here. Indian. Very pretty. Asked me to act opposite Richard Attenborough.' She looked hard into my eyes, nodding her head and tossing her eyebrows about, which was a habit of hers, while she waited for me to react to this astonishing piece of news.

'Well?' I said.

'The girl said: "You'll have to go to Ootacamund to do the acting." Well, I couldn't possibly, and I told her I couldn't!'

By now the small garden had filled up with evening drinkers and Mr Smith, a former major in the British Army, had come downstairs from the family living quarters to take Fifi for a walk. The dog's hair had been primped up as lovingly as Mrs Smith's, although it was going bald in places along the spine. Last summer, when the Smiths had taken their annual holiday in Europe – 'We always stay in the best hotels,' said Mrs Smith – they took the dog to Amsterdam to have her eyes done.

'She spent the whole holiday with you?' I asked.

'No, darling, she flew back with KLM. First-class.'

Mr Smith and the dog tottered out of the gates to take some air among the beggars and drug addicts and ne'er-do-wells of Sudder Street. It was an improbable sight, even by Calcutta's improbable standards.

'Why aren't you staying with us?' asked Mrs Smith.

I told her that I was staying at a guest house in Middleton Street; it was far cheaper than the Fairlawn and I could choose where to eat, which the Fairlawn's guests could not.

'Well, we've modernized everything,' she continued. 'A/c in all the rooms. Music in the garden every night. You know, pop music. Loudspeakers, that sort of thing. We're very modern now.'

The following evening I came again and when Mrs Smith saw me chatting to a couple who were sitting in wicker chairs in the foyer, she said, without so much as a glance at me: 'How do you know Charlie?'

They replied that we had only just met.

'If I'd known he was here,' she said as she turned to leave, 'I'd have thrown the bastard out!'

Later that week she suggested to a waiter that he should sprinkle arsenic in my beer, then led me to a table to meet a man whom she introduced as one of her dearest friends. He was about my age, with short hair and jeans and an aggressive air about him, and he was sitting with a group of people whom he had presumably been foisted upon by Mrs Smith. They were from Australia, though the younger of the two couples were Armenians who had been brought up in Calcutta. Mrs Smith's dear friend said that he was a narcotics agent and that he had been working in Calcutta and the Far East for the past twenty-three years. He looked and sounded English. I happened to mention that I had just come from the evening class for prostitutes' children in Bowbazar and I asked him if he knew the area.

'You're raping them,' he said.

'I beg your pardon?'

'You're raping them, I said.'

At most, I replied, I might be writing about the children and the people that were helping them. He ignored what I said and embarked on a lengthy diatribe in which he accused organizations which help Calcutta's poor of imposing the liberal values of the West on people who were struggling to avoid starvation. In Calcutta, he said, you could have sex with a two-year-old girl if you wanted or with a cripple. People had to make a living, and if a mother could sell her child for 300 rupees for sex, then that could feed the family for a week. Life was cheap in Calcutta, he continued, and there were people outside the gate at the Fairlawn who would blow him away for twenty bucks. That, he said, was why he never went anywhere without his gun. Later I overheard him telling the elderly Australian couple that he had helped a great many people in Calcutta. For all I know, he may have had a saintly streak in him, but he certainly did his utmost to hide it.

I had not intended to visit Calcutta's dwindling Armenian community, but the Armenian couple I met that evening invited me to accompany them to Park Circus early the following morning and there I met Charles Sarkies, vice-president of the Armenian Association and superintendent of the Sir Catchick Paul Chater Home, in which resided, at present, fifteen elderly Armenians. He came over to greet me while I was studying the small chapel in the grounds and led me up to his residence on the second floor of the old people's home. He was a man of great warmth and charisma and his looks suited his character: he was attractive in a rugged way with a large nose, humorous, hooded eyes and the complexion of a man who had spent much of his life outdoors. We sat at a table in his study and drank Kingfisher beer, into which he sprinkled some salt.

'In this weather,' he explained, 'you must always have salt in your beer. You know we were the first race in the world to embrace Christianity? When Archbishop Fisher came to Calcutta for the 250th anniversary of the Holy Church of Nazareth – that's on the other side of town – he said: "Armenia is a bastion of Christianity. You should be proud to be the first Christian nation in the world." '

Mr Sarkies had spent his childhood in Persia, but at the age of thirteen his parents had sent him to Calcutta to take advantage of the free education which could be had at the Armenian College. 'I arrived by ship in January 1935,' he recalled in a deep, gravelly voice. 'The only English I knew was "good morning" and "good evening", but I didn't know which one to use when. Next I learned to say "thank you".'

I asked him whether he used to return to Persia in the school holidays and he laughed. 'I never saw my mother again,' he said, 'and the next time I saw my father was in 1960, when I brought him out here for three months.' Financial considerations, he implied, had made the separation inevitable; many other Armenians who had been dispatched to Calcutta as children had had a similar experience. Anyway, Mr Sarkies completed his studies in Calcutta and became a mining engineer. In 1942, at the age of twenty, he began work in a British-owned coal mine in Bihar and he continued to work in the mines, which were nationalized after Independence, until his retirement forty years later.

When Mr Sarkies arrived in Calcutta there were over 3,000 Armenians in and around the city. Some worked on the railways; others were involved in the coal, jute and shellac industries and in the hotel trade. 'Now,' he said, 'there are just 103 adult Armenians left here – that's excluding the students who come from Iran – and in the last twenty-five years we have only had two Armenian weddings.'

There had been plenty of deaths, though, and Mr Sarkies had recently helped to establish the Christian Burial Board Funeral Service. 'You know, there's only one undertaker in Calcutta to look after all the Christians and they've got a hearse that won't even go five miles,' he said, his lips curling in disapproval. 'Even when a person dies they've got no peace. There's no one to clean them up, dress them properly.' If one of the old ladies died in the home during the night Mr Sarkies put her on blocks of ice and had her buried first thing in the morning in the Armenian plot in the cemetery next to the home. He expected matters to improve now: all the main Churches had come together to form the new Burial Board and an architect was presently designing a funeral parlour which was going to be built where the children played cricket in South Park Street cemetery. This was bad luck on the children, but Mr Sarkies thought that Christians could now look forward to a decent burial.

When we had finished our beer he led me through a gate in the garden wall into Lower Circular Road cemetery. It lacked the monumental grandeur of the more famous South Park Street cemetery, but it was an impressive place none the less, with over 10,000 graves spread across 350 acres of land. The 300 or so graves in the Armenian section were beautifully tended and Mr Sarkies had recently planted flowering shrubs along the neatly kept paths. 'We don't bother with lead lettering now,' he explained. 'The urchins outside just come and steal it.' Mr Sarkies had taken over responsibility for managing the cemetery a little over a year ago. One of his first acts was to increase the wages of the fifteen workers. 'Now they're expected to work,' he remarked dryly as we wandered down a brickwork path towards the main entrance. During the course of the last year the paths had been cleared, old graves which were buried by scrub and spoil had been unearthed and restored and Mr Sarkies's men had planted over 250 trees and shrubs; this year the target was 500. The brick wall which surrounded the cemetery had been raised by four feet and this had stopped vandals coming in from outside. Mr Sarkies was hoping to get the defunct crematorium back into working order – the Catholic archbishop had agreed that his people could now be cremated – and this would help to lengthen the cemetery's active life. 'If we cremate them,' said Mr Sarkies, 'I'll be able to fit six people into the same space that I need to bury one.' He was a great believer in simple graves and he scoffed at some of the more elaborate affairs near the entrance. One particularly ornate grave with a pretentious canopy would have looked fine in a Californian pet cemetery, but here it looked very out of place. Mr Sarkies put on his glasses to inspect the inscription. 'Anglo-Indians,' he said. 'And I'll tell you something. They never spent any money on the old lady when she was alive, so why spend 10,000 rupees on her now she's dead?' A little further on we came to the section where the British had been buried in the latter years of the last century. Two graves belonged to women who had had eight children each.

'Yes,' mused Mr Sarkies, 'nothing else to do, you see. That was the entertainment in those days.'

~

On one of my earlier visits to Calcutta I stayed at the Great Eastern Hotel, largely because of its proximity to BBD Bagh and the offices of the Municipal Sewage Authority, with whom I had business. Explore the hotel, suggested my guidebook, and you will discover marble floors, wood-panelled corridors and other architectural details of the 1930s. Apparently Mark Twain stayed here and so did Kipling, and the Great Eastern was famous for its belly-dancers and glamorous balls. It was not always such an inviting place to stay: a visiting civil servant in the 1850s described it as 'a large, stuffy, vulgar, noisy place permeated with a mixed odour of cooking and stale tobacco'. In those days it was privately owned; now it is run by the Communist government, which has restored it to its former inglorious state – which is to say that it is stuffy, vulgar, noisy and so on. During my stay the only other foreigners were Communist officials from Bulgaria and, if I remember correctly, North Korea. Presumably they were guests of the state government, which may also have been responsible for supplying the young women in chintzy dresses who entertained the visitors in their rooms and whom I occasionally passed in the gloomy corridors. The service was slow, although possibly not for them, the rooms dusty and the food ordinary, but the Great Eastern did have one virtue: there was much to see and do within walking distance.

Turn right out of the front door of the Great Eastern and within a matter of minutes you will reach St Andrew's Kirk and Writers' Building, once the headquarters of the East India Company and now the seat of government and a citadel to overmanning. Turn left out of the hotel and within a couple of minutes you will reach the Maidan, and if you feel inclined you can buy some nuts and feed the rats whose sprawling and overpopulated colony occupies the hole-pocked territory behind the squatting fruit-sellers. A hundred yards to the east is Government House, which was modelled on Adam's Keddleston Hall, and a little further on you will come to the old cathedral church of St John, which dates from the same period, the end of the eighteenth century.

St John's is my favourite church in Calcutta, although it is by no means the most beautiful. Like St Andrew's Kirk, it was modelled on St Martin-in-the-Fields, but the designer, Lieutenant James Agg, was forced to reduce the height of the spire for structural reasons and a few years after its consecration the main entrance was shifted from the east to the west; consequently, it looks as though it has put its trousers on back to front. Having visited the church several times when I was staying at the Great Eastern, I did not need a guided tour on this occasion, but the caretaker insisted on following me around. I asked him how the church survived, for it was clear that the cost of upkeep must be considerable. He replied that it relied partly on donations from the foreigners who came to see the tomb of Job Charnock, the merchant who founded Calcutta in 1690, and to admire the marble memorials and Johan Zoffany's magnificent *Last Supper*, which had originally been hung over the altar, but now looked down one of the aisles.

The person whom Zoffany used as a model for Judas was a Company official with whom he had had a dispute; a Greek priest modelled Christ; and a fervent opponent of Christianity, a police magistrate, stood in for St John. Were the spirit of the magistrate to wander around Calcutta's Protestant churches today, he would doubtless reflect with some satisfaction that his antipathy to Christianity – or, at least, to the institutions of Christianity – was shared by the vast majority of Bengalis. St John's, according to the caretaker, seldom attracted more than ten people to its one service of the week, which was held on Sundays. St Andrew's Kirk did slightly better, with forty or so regular communicants, and the morning service at St Paul's Cathedral attracted rather more.

However, St Paul's hangar-like nave was built to seat 800 and on the two occasions when I went to Evensong there were so few people – thirteen on Sunday, nine at a Lenten meditation in midweek – that the services were held in a small side chapel and I had to strain to hear the address above the sound of the whirring fans and the noise of the funfare across the road. Macaulay's claim that India would become a Christian nation before the end of the last century was always outlandish and the great empty spaces seemed to mock his memory now. The last census of west Bengal put the population at 77 million; of these fewer than three-quarters of a million were Christian.

One of my early calls in Calcutta was to Bishop's College, where I met Dr Timotheus Hebrom; like many of the Christians in the city, he seemed despondent about the present state of the Protestant Churches. Dr Hebrom was a member of the Santal tribe and a native of the district of Santalparganas in Bihar. Appreciable numbers of Santals had turned to Christianity after they had been defeated by the British in the 1850s: the defeat had shaken their belief in their tribal god, and when the missionaries arrived in the wake of the British victory they decided to embrace the faith of their erstwhile enemies. At a later period some of the converts went back to their old ways and now no more than 5 per cent of Santalparganas's 400,000 inhabitants were Christian. This may be more impressive than west Bengal's 1 per cent, but it is meagre when compared with the figure for Chota Nagpur, the hilly land in south Bihar, where over 40 per cent of the tribal population has embraced Christianity. Dr Hebrom deplored the way in which Christian organizations had concentrated their work, and their financial resources, on the cities rather than the countryside, where most Indians still lived. 'If the amount of money spent in Calcutta had been spent in the tribal areas,' he suggested, 'all would have been Christians now – and we'd have many good tribal leaders.'

The early missionaries often adopted a negative attitude towards the old tribal beliefs, explained Dr Hebrom. Some identified the tribal deity with Satan and his emissary with the serpent in the Garden of Eden, and many – the Scandinavian Lutherans being an obvious example – not only insisted that tribal converts abandon all their old beliefs, they also forbade drinking, dancing, singing and other traditional entertainments. 'Everything the tribals did they considered satanic,' explained Dr Hebrom. 'That was the wrong approach. They also encouraged the converts to think of themselves as super-tribals. That was wrong too, as it alienated all the others who hadn't converted to Christianity.' The Churches, he believed, needed to adopt a more enlightened and sympathetic approach to tribal culture if they were to expand and attract more new members in the future.

During the past few months there had been several reports in the newspapers of clashes between Christian missionary organizations and Hindus who opposed their activities. In some instances the authorities, most notably in Madhya Pradesh, had sought to proscribe missionary activity: for example, in March 1996 an eighty-year-old Belgian priest and a fifty-year-old Indian nun were sentenced to six months' rigorous imprisonment for converting a hundred tribals without informing the authorities. The RSS was also said to be behind unprovoked attacks on Christian groups in the central tribal belt. The BJP, which later in the year was briefly to assume political power in India, was instrumental in bringing to court the case against the Belgian priest and it was also spear-heading a 'reconversion drive' to turn tribals into Hindus. One BJP leader claimed that 50,000 tribals had been won back, a curious claim in view of the fact that they were not Hindus in the first place. The Christian community had good reason to feel aggrieved, and in certain places frightened, but there were occasions when missionary organizations seemed to go out of their way to court opposition. In November 1995 missionaries from a US-based evangelical group called Gospel for the Unreached Millions were told that they could not hold a public meeting in a village in Orissa for fear that they might cause a public disturbance. They went ahead regardless and sparked off a riot between tribals and police in which many people were injured. The missionaries, all but one of whom were Americans, were arrested and thrown into prison. They were later let out on bail and, as far as I know, some four months later they were still awaiting trial.

I often heard it said that the tribals found the evangelical, charismatic forms of Christian worship especially appealing. However, Dr Hebrom disputed this. 'The Pentecostals and the others are making few converts in the tribal areas I know,' he said. 'All their hallelujahing and witnessing – it's too noisy. It doesn't suit the tribal temperament.' But he conceded that the Assembly of God had established excellent schools in many tribal areas. Of the other main Churches it was the Roman Catholics, with their more liberal approach to tribal customs, who were having the greatest success in attracting new converts, especially in Chota Nagpur. In Santalparganas, he thought the RSS was probably making more converts to Hinduism than all the Churches combined were to Christianity. 'One of the big problems,' said Dr Hebrom, 'is that Christians have been left so much property by the foreign missionaries. They're too involved with administrative matters.'

When I was at Serampore Dr Daniel recalled how one of his friends, reflecting on the in-fighting among Christians in Kerala, had said to him: 'Christians are like manure – if they are together, they stink; if they're separate, then they're OK.' I am not sure how this analogy applies to Calcutta, and opinions about the cordiality, or otherwise, of relations between the various Churches seemed to vary. In Dr Hebrom's view, Christianity had failed to become a united force in India: 'We're very divided. There are so many different groups and it creates real confusion. It's a blessing in disguise for opponents like the RSS.' Madhu Singh, the secretary and manager of the Baptist Missionary Society, tended to agree: 'I'd like to see all the Churches unite and become one,' he said when I saw him one afternoon at the Baptist compound on AJC Bose Road. 'We're so weakened by divisions, by groupism. How can this possibly help?' There were even divisions within the Baptist Church itself, which had three provincial unions, one for north India, one for Bengal and one for Mizoram; power feuds within and between them had led to discord, according to Mr Singh.

There might have been a greater feeling of unity among the Protestants had the American Methodists joined the Church of North India. At the time of union, in 1970, there were approximately 600,000 Methodists and 600,000 members of the six denominations which did form the CNI. The Methodists' decision to remain independent had nothing to do with theology; they withdrew from negotiations at the last minute primarily because of disagreements over the episcopal arrangements for the new Church. The Methodists argued that they should provide half of the twenty-two bishops; the others disagreed. This was the explanation I received from Rev. Subodh Mondal, the young pastor of Thorburn Methodist church on Lenin Sarani, although a CNI bishop, formerly of Anglican persuasion, told me later that financial considerations also lay behind the Methodists' withdrawal. Their bishops were far better paid than the bishops of the other denominations and they would have had to accept a massive cut in salary had they joined the CNI.

India's Methodists have eleven regional conferences, the equivalent of dioceses, and they now number around 700,000. In some areas – Madras and Gujarat, for example – they are still making appreciable numbers of converts, but according to Rev. Mondal the Bengal Regional Conference was growing only biologically: virtually the only new members over the past thirty years had been the offspring of Methodist families. His church had actually seen its numbers decline sharply, but that was before his time and a result of emigration rather than loss of faith. Half a century ago it used to attract over a thousand people to its services; now just twenty families worshipped here. The Anglo-Indians and the expatriates who originally formed the bulk of the congregation had left Calcutta in droves after Independence.

Rev. Mondal felt that the Methodist Church, like the other mainstream Protestant Churches, had been too preoccupied with institutional matters over the past thirty years and had lacked strong spiritual leadership, but he was encouraged by the attitude of young people today. 'I know things won't be easy,' he said as he walked me out on to the main road after our meeting, 'but I feel the Church will begin to grow again. Many of the young members are involved in gospel outreach – they're not interested in the administrative side of the Church. They want to evangelize, and that's a good sign.' During the short period of time he had been pastor at Thorburn church the congregation had become much more active in looking after the venerable old building. They were mainly lower-middle-class, salaried people, he said – clerks, teachers and the like – and although they were not well off, they supported him and his family and they had agreed to contribute towards the support of a rural pastor too.

One of the reasons why many of the mainstream Churches in this part of India have seen their numbers stagnate is because they have lost members to the 'Full Gospel' Churches. Of these the largest and most influential are the Pentecostal Assemblies of God, of which there are now some 3,000 in India. The first Assembly I came across was in Madras, not far from St Thomas Mount. The church was a cavernous building the size of an indoor sports stadium and capable of seating 5,000 people. I was shown around by Sister Getzie Mohan, the wife of the leading pastor, who was in the United States at the time. In 1973 the Assembly in Madras was established in a thatched hut with seven members. By 1982 the congregation had grown to 2,000 and moved to the present premises; it now numbered over 9,000 and was growing so rapidly that there were plans to expand the church building. Sister Getzie estimated that 25 per cent of the members were Hindu converts;

most of the rest had been what she called 'nominal Christians', Catholics, Lutherans and members of the Church of South India. She attributed the growth of the Assembly mainly to the work of the 240 home cells – house churches – which met every Wednesday evening.

If success is measured solely in terms of conversions, then Calcutta's Assembly of God had not performed as spectacularly as Madras's. It had been here much longer – the founding missionaries came from Canada in the 1950s – but it had many fewer members. However, there was no denying that it has had a considerable influence on Calcutta's secular life. One of the Church of North India priests whom I met said that the Assembly reminded him of a multinational company, and I immediately understood what he meant when I first visited AG Towers, a high-rise building which loomed above South Park Street cemetery. The Assembly offices would not have looked out of place in Dallas or Washington. Pastor David Luke was tapping away at a lap-top computer and the air-conditioning was so sophisticated that I couldn't even hear it. The pastor told me a little about the history of the Assembly, then led me around. Behind AG Towers was the Assembly of God high school and nearby was the Assembly's 160-bed hospital. The Assembly also ran a feeding programme for over 20,000 people, some of whom were queuing along the wall of the cemetery opposite, waiting for the daily handout of rice and dal.

I was for ever being told by members of the mainstream Churches that there was always an ulterior motive to the social activities of groups like the Assemblies of God: they sought, by whatever means, to win new converts. I am not so convinced, at least not in the case of the Assembly in Calcutta. Were it true, then why do so many affluent Hindu families send their children to the Assembly school, and why do they so happily patronize the hospital? The answer is simple: good education and good health care with no strings attached, other than financial ones. They are paying for good service, not for indoctrination. Admittedly, the medical authorities do not allow Hindu priests to perform *pujas* for the patients, but there is no attempt to proselytize. As far as the school's religious life is concerned, students do have to attend morning prayers, but these are often broadly spiritual in nature rather than explicitly Christian. My Hindu landlady's teenage daughter had just completed her final exams at the Assembly of God high school and she said that she had enjoyed the prayers and morning talks: 'It's good moral teaching, and the pastors are good fun. They never try to convert, although some Hindus do become Christians.' She had appreciated not only the education but also the music and singing and other activities that the pastors encouraged. One of her friends, another Hindu, had attended both the Loreto school, which is run by Catholic sisters, and the Martiniere school, which is a Protestant institution. She said that the nuns at the Loreto school had never attempted to convert Hindus; she had felt genuinely close to the staff and appreciated their moral guidance. At the Protestant school, by contrast, she had found the staff remote and at times frightening; she added that pupils received no moral teaching and she thought this sad. Pastor David Luke insisted that the Assembly took great care not to deride other religious faiths in the school or chapel. He and the other pastors hoped to influence people by the example of their lives. Referring to those waiting in the food queues, he said: 'I am sure they see the compassion of Christ in action.'

Pastor Luke was unable to say exactly how many 'nominal Christians' had come over to the Assembly of God, but he thought they made up a good proportion of the 3,000 or so people who worshipped at Park Street. Some of the church leaders I spoke to accused the Assembly of 'sheep stealing', but when I used this expression in conversation with the CNI Bishop of Calcutta, Dinesh Chandra Gorai, whom I met in his palatial residence opposite St Paul's Cathedral, I received a sharp rebuke.

'I'm opposed to this expression,' he said, eyeing me sternly. 'It's not responsible. It makes me very angry, partly because it implies that numbers are all that matter. If anyone is getting spiritual enlightenment, that's to be welcomed.' He said that one of his CNI priests came to him some years ago with the news that a dozen members of his church had joined the Pentecostals. Apparently they liked the singing. The bishop told the priest to tell them to enjoy themselves: 'I said, "Don't strike their names off. Don't worry about their monthly contributions. Tell them they are welcome back any time."' He even suggested to the priest that he should invite the Pentecostal pastor to give a sermon in his church, and this he did. Two years later those who had left returned to the CNI. 'If we'd talked of sheep stealing, that would never have happened,' said the bishop. 'They'd have been alienated. As it is, they've come back and livened up the old church.'

Bishop Gorai admitted that the Church of North India was failing to attract the young as it had done when he was a youth. There were, he suggested, many more distractions for the young nowadays and this was one reason why they tended to become less involved in church activities. All the same, he thought that as a race the Bengalis were a very spiritual people; there was no danger of their forsaking their religious beliefs, whether they were Hindu, Muslim or Christian. I frequently heard complaints about the poor quality of leadership in the Church of North India, but Bishop Gorai was often cited as an exception. He had served as a moderator of the CNI and he was widely respected as an evangelist and Christian thinker. In the words of Dr Reeti Biswas, whom the bishop suggested I meet, he was a rare article, but then so too was Dr Biswas, the director of the Cathedral Relief Service (CRS).

Dr Biswas's appearance was at odds with his character. He was a small man with a bald head, a sallow complexion and heavy-rimmed spectacles; had I passed him in the street, I would have taken him for an accountant or perhaps a middle-ranking civil servant. His demeanour was modest and his looks unremarkable, yet he was a man of extraordinary vigour and passion. He reminded me, soon after we met in his offices beside the cathedral, of the closing words of the morning service: 'Let us go out in peace to love and serve the Lord.'

'And how many people really do that?' he asked. 'Hardly any. We're basically Sunday Christians. One of the problems is that few people are preaching the real Jesus. They don't see him as a revolutionary speaking out against aggressive structures, but that's what he was. Jesus came to do away with anything which degrades and debases.'

Dr Biswas was disappointed by the Church of North India's failure to take a stand on important issues, and he mentioned as evidence the lethargy of the local clergy. The CRS had recently helped organize an AIDS-awareness march in Calcutta and Dr Biswas had asked the bishop to send a letter to the forty or so CNI priests in the diocese requesting them to attend the march dressed in their cassocks. 'To show that they took the issue seriously,' explained Dr Biswas. 'And do you know what happened? Five thousand people came to the march, but there wasn't one CNI priest there. And not one person came from Bishop's College either.'

The CRS was set up in 1971 by the then vicar, Canon Subir Biswas, to help the victims of the Bangladeshi war and particularly the refugees who fled across the border and swarmed into Calcutta. The name is now a misnomer, for the Cathedral Relief Service no longer provides relief. Rather, it is involved in a range of development activities: it provides community health care in seventeen slums; it runs over a dozen schools for children who are not receiving any formal education; and it holds literacy classes for women. It has also established a network of training centres where women in the slums can learn such skills as tailoring and dressmaking. Dr Biswas estimated that around 150,000 people were in some way being helped by the CRS's projects and that at any one time about 1,500 women were taking the one-and-a-half-year training courses. The CRS also provided grants to a number of other organizations, one being Jabala, the group which was running the evening classes for prostitutes' children in Bowbazar.

When I asked Dr Biswas why the cathedral did not provide food for the poor, as the Assembly of God and Mother Teresa's Sisters of Charity did, he immediately bridled. 'With all the money she receives, Mother Teresa could really do something positive to help the poor,' he said. 'She could open vocational centres and factories, places where people could learn skills and earn a living. She could give life to people.'

Surely, I said, she was giving life to people, or at least she was helping them when they faced death?

He conceded that her homes did give comfort to the dying and the destitute, and that she had helped lepers too, but he maintained that the Sisters of Charity and the Assembly of God fostered what he called a culture of dependence. 'Many of the people who queue up for handouts of free milk powder or whatever go back to their slums and sell it or gamble with the money they make,' he said. 'I've lived in the slums for twelve years. I've seen it with my own eyes. And, you know, nobody has died of starvation in Calcutta. What we should be doing is helping people to find work, not doling out food.'

He asked me whether I had seen any food queues and I mentioned the Assembly of God distribution centre in Park Street.

'They're making animals out of people,' he replied curtly. 'Making them stand for hours in the sun. Where's the dignity in that? And the fact is that people don't respect what's given to them for free. Whenever we go into a slum where we haven't worked before the first question people ask is "What will you give us?" That's the attitude that stems from the handout mentality.'

When I visited the Muslim-dominated slum of Tiljala with Mrs Sumita Sen, one of Dr Biswas's colleagues, we came across one of the CRS's mobile health units. Around twenty women and children were being seen by a doctor and each paid a fee of 2 rupees for the service. The women and children who were attending the CRS's training and literacy classes also paid a fee. The fee might be small, said Mrs Sen, but it was significant: 'Doling out is no good for a human being,' she said simply. 'What we want to do is encourage self-reliance. In a small way, insisting that people pay a fee does that.'

The CRS received two-thirds of its funding from Christian Aid and Bread of the World, but this reliance on foreign charity worried Dr Biswas, and he was scathing about the reluctance of Indians to give to their own poor. 'It's a sorry state of affairs,' he said with an air of weariness. 'In Calcutta you have the very rich and you have the very poor. Calcutta's a city where both can survive, even the poor. But Indians – and especially rich Indians – haven't learned to give. They haven't learned to share.' Dr Biswas was also concerned about the casual and trusting way in which many Western donors gave to charities in India. He mentioned a Christian organization in Calcutta which was receiving large sums of money from the West but doing nothing with it, and he told me how schoolchildren in Warwickshire had raised 11 lakh rupees (£25,000) for an institution in north India which appeared to have been set up with the sole object of embezzling donations from abroad.

There was much else that Dr Biswas railed against – the uninspiring nature of most church services; the reluctance of Calcutta's doctors to treat the poor free of charge ('Just two hours a week. That's all I'm asking'); corruption within the church – and had he been no more than an armchair critic, I might have taken less notice of what he said. However, he was a man of action – he still did evening work in a TB clinic as a doctor in addition to running the CRS – and his 100-strong staff, most of whom were Hindus, were doing their utmost to improve conditions in the slums. 'The Church is desperately in need of spiritual renewal,' he said at one point. 'In India we Christians are spiritually dead, but at least we're going out to fulfil the social gospel of Christ.' That evening Dr Biswas gave the Lenten address at a poorly attended service in the cathedral. For his text he took Romans 12, in which Paul calls upon all Christians to put whatever gifts they have to good use. Live in agreement with one another, urges Paul; love in all sincerity; use good to conquer evil. And that was precisely what the staff of the Cathedral Relief Service were trying to do.

One of the many people I met in the Tiljala slum was Afroz Begum, who attended one of the CRS training classes. A serious young woman with a perpetual frown, she recounted her life story in a way that suggested that she had told it many times and become weary of telling it. When she was fifteen years old she was married to an alcoholic who frequently beat her. She became pregnant and bore his child; he continued to beat her. Eventually, she left her husband, divorced him and went to live with her parents. Not long afterwards a relative said that she had found another man for her to marry in distant Kashmir, so she set off for north-west India, leaving her child with her parents. When she arrived in Kashmir she discovered that she was not to be married; rather she had been sold to a Kashmiri Muslim. After much hardship, she managed to escape and she made her way across India and back to Calcutta. She now lived with her parents and child again. For the past year she had attended the tailoring classes in Tiljala and she could earn up to 300 rupees a month making clothes. This, she said, had made a big difference to her life: it meant that she had a degree of independence from her parents and was able to support her child.

A few yards down the street from the tailoring class thirty or so children were crammed into a small room which had nothing in the way of ventilation other than the open door and a small window. They were learning to read and write and each had a piece of chalk and a miniature blackboard. These were the children of the poorest people in the slum and many helped to boost their parents' meagre earnings by working themselves. One intermittent attender was Ashok Kumar Das. He was thirteen years old, but I would have put him nearer ten; he was thin and undernourished, although he had a strikingly beautiful face. He said that he came to the classes when he could and he enjoyed learning to read and write, but he also had to help his parents. He explained that his father didn't earn enough to support the family, so he often worked fourteen hours a day cutting leather patterns. If he cut 500 a day, he earned 5 rupees, and in a good week he made 30 rupees. Ashok did not appear to resent his situation or his parents' penury: this was the life he had always known and he was simply doing his best for his family. He said that he hoped one day to find a good job which would pay a decent wage. He was an admirable child: uncomplaining, upright and intelligent.

Like Ashok and Afroz, Ishrat Jahan, a handsome woman in her mid-twenties, had also been born in the Tiljala slum. Her parents were dead and as she had yet to marry she lived with her stepmother. When she was a teenager she did a training course in tailoring with the CRS and she now taught in the class where she had learned her skills. She said that there had been great changes in the slums since she was a child. She was referring not to the physical improvements – the streets were now paved and lit and Tiljala had been connected with the sewerage system – but to the behaviour and status of the women. Twenty years ago Muslim women would never leave their homes without wearing the *bharkha*, the traditional black veil. Now hardly any of the younger generation wore the *bharkha*. Furthermore, the women had learned to be more vocal, to speak out and stand up for themselves; they would even talk to strangers like me, something which was unheard of twenty years ago.

If you stand at the edge of a slum like Tiljala, either metaphorically or in person, you will see it as an agglomeration of nameless individuals. You may think that you understand it better if you have in your hand a sheet of paper with figures provided by the

World Bank or the World Health Organization or some other institution which panders to the modern obsession for statistics. You may read – and this is conjecture on my part – that 75 per cent of the slum dwellers are illiterate; that 80 per cent of children between the age of twenty-four months and fifty-nine months are physically stunted; that infant mortality is 98 per 1,000; that less than 10 per cent of the population has access to clean water. All of which may be true. But these statistics tell you nothing about specific individuals, about Ashok, Ishrat, Afroz or anyone else, and nothing about the feelings and emotions of the people. They also mask one of the most obvious truths, and one which I never fully understood till I talked to slum dwellers in places like Tiljala. Most human beings are incurable optimists: indeed, you probably have to be if you are to survive with your dignity intact in a Calcutta slum. Wherever there is hope there is industry, and wherever there is industry there will be progress: Tiljala is proof of that. This is not to deny that a quarter of its children are forced into child labour, that alcoholism is rife and crime common, but life is better, however you look at it, for the younger generation in Tiljala than it was for their parents. And this, I believe, is one reason why the poor have not fulfilled Moorhouse's prophecy: where there is hope there is the possibility of a future worth living. No doubt there are many other reasons why the poor have not risen up *en masse* to massacre the rich. Indeed, it is insulting to think of the poor as pack animals driven by some primal instinct and devoid of compassion, not just for themselves – and the words of the girl in the pink dress in Bowbazar ring in my ears – but also for those who live in more favourable conditions.

CHAPTER II

An Uneasy Triumph

In 1840 Welsh Calvinists founded a mission society and cast around in search of a place and people to evangelize. A Scottish missionary in Bombay suggested Gujarat; another from the London Missionary Society mentioned the Khasi Hills, which lie to the south of the Brahmaputra, the Manipur Valley further east and a remote region in central India. The eventual choice was determined by pecuniary considerations. The Welsh Calvinistic Methodists' Foreign Mission Society accepted the offer of a free boat passage to Calcutta, and as the Khasi Hills were the closest of the suggested mission fields to the port, the society's first missionaries made their way there. They arrived at Cherrapunji, which had recently been established by the British as their headquarters in the hills, on 22 June 1841. It is safe to assume that it was raining. In those days Cherrapunji used to receive over 42 feet of rain a year; 22 feet fell during August 1841, with over 30 inches being recorded on five successive days.

'It's a big problem, the rain,' said Rev. Overland Snaitang, shaking his head, as we peered through the glass panes of the locked door to the library in Cherra theological college. 'It's terrible for the books – they rot away in the damp.' The climate nowadays is marginally drier than when the missionaries came – the annual average rainfall has dipped to 35 feet, largely as a result of deforestation – but the weather had finally got the better of the college and dampness was one of the factors which convinced the authorities that it was time to move to somewhere drier and less remote: in December 1993 the staff and students were transferred to a college in Shillong, the state capital of Meghalaya. It seemed curious that the books were still here, for there was little else in the gloomy building save the hard wooden benches in the classrooms, a board with the names of the former principals and a large sign with the words SILENCE PLEASE above an austere fireplace in the William Lewis Hall.

The rain was not the only problem the early missionaries had to face: they also met with considerable hostility and would quite possibly have been martyred had it not been for the protection afforded them by the British. In 1853 Rev. William Lewis wrote in a report to the government of his 'trying labours among the superstitious denizens of the hills'. Three village schools established by the Welsh were virtually empty, although another at Shella was doing reasonably well and Rev. Lewis had identified ten 'hopeful candidates for baptism'. The Welsh were making more tangible progress at Nongsawlia, the main mission station on the flatter land just below the town of Cherrapunji, although it was to be another forty years before they built the theological college. During their first twelve years the missionaries made twenty-four converts, but they doggedly stuck to their task and their influence gradually spread to the Jaintia Hills and Shillong, which the British made capital of the region in 1874. In 1875 there were still only 514 Khasi Christians, but the pace of conversion quickened thereafter and by 1900 the Presbyterian Church, as the Welsh Calvinists now called themselves, had a membership of 15,885. Today there are over 700,000 Christians in Meghalaya, approximately half of whom are Presbyterian, and Christians outnumber non-Christians by a factor of more than two to one.

I had long resolved to spend Easter, the greatest of Christian feasts, in an area where Christianity thrived, and several months before I reached the north-east I applied for permission to visit Mizoram, where nine of out of every ten people are Christian.

The government declined to give me a permit, presumably because Mizoram, like many of the other states which comprise India's north-east, was periodically troubled by insurgency and civil unrest. Once I realized that I could not travel to Mizoram I turned my attention to Chota Nagpur, the stronghold of Bihar's Christian tribals. I even went so far as to book a train ticket from Calcutta, but after ten days in its fetid heat I longed for a spell in a temperate climate, far from polluted cities and preferably among a people who were at peace with themselves. With the elections approaching, as well as the monsoons, Chota Nagpur lost its appeal and I headed instead to Meghalaya, one of three north-eastern states which had recently dropped its restrictions on foreign visitors.

Meghalaya was neither as temperate nor as peaceful as I had anticipated. I arrived on Palm Sunday to be greeted by a cyclone. It was short-lived, but its brevity was matched by its violence and it stripped electric wires from pylons with casual ease, leaving the central part of Shillong in darkness for the rest of the night. The following day there was a riot near the main bazar: an initially peaceful march turned violent when demonstrators fired country guns at the police and the police returned fire. Two people were killed, many were injured and the state government declared a twenty-four-hour curfew over much of the town. The morning after the riot I telephoned the Presbyterian synod for the Khasi and Jaintia hills and spoke to its secretary, who explained that the mission was at the heart of the troubled area. The curfew was indefinite; there was no telling when it would be lifted and he suggested I look elsewhere for enlightenment about his Church. And so it was that I went in search of Rev. Snaitang, whose name I had been given by the principal of Serampore College.

The pastor lived in a pretty, tin-roofed cottage in the hilly district of Kench's Trace on the southern edge of Shillong, well to the south of the curfew-bound districts. I arrived to find his children playing cricket in a small garden which was splashed with colour: everlasting pea clambered over a low wall, pink bush roses grew beside the cottage and there were clumps of red poppy and white carnations at the batsman's end of the garden. Rev. Snaitang was evidently at work on a piece of machinery, for he came into the front parlour with hands smeared with oil and grease. He said by way of explanation that he had just returned from Serampore and there were practical things which had to be done. I offered to return later, but he insisted I stay for a tea and for the next couple of hours he talked about the Khasis and their enthusiasm for Christianity. A well-built man with the Mongoloid features of his tribe – the Khasis migrated to these hills from southern China many thousands of years ago – Rev. Snaitang spoke in a gently authoritative voice, choosing his words precisely and pronouncing them in a lilting accent. He was a serious man, but he laughed easily and it soon became obvious that the puritanism of his Church – he belonged to the Church of God, an offshoot of the Presbyterians – had in no way diminished his sense of humour or his ability to enjoy life to the full.

When I told him that I intended to visit Cherrapunji he offered to join me, and the following morning I hired a taxi and arrived at his cottage a little after seven o'clock. He greeted me pleasantly but it was clear that he was agitated; he explained that one of his wife's brothers had gone missing – in view of the riots, this was especially worrying – and that another member of the family had died during the night. The missing brother and the family of the deceased lived in the same village, which was a little distance off the main road south, and he wondered if we could take his wife there before proceeding to Cherrapunji. We arrived at the village to discover that the missing brother had turned up during the night. While the Snaitangs paid their respects to the four daughters of the dead woman, and our Manipuri driver carried out repairs on the taxi – 'Jesus Saviour pilot me' read an optimistic sticker on the windscreen – I strolled slowly about the village. It was a windswept place, a ribbon development of tin shacks scattered across a virtually treeless bit of moorland, and it reminded me of the bleak townships along the coast of north-west Scotland: all it needed was the smell of fish and seaweed and I could have imagined myself to be on the Isle of Lewis or on the coast near Ullapool. Before we left, Rev. Snaitang invited me into the barely furnished house and introduced me to the bereaved sisters. They wore the traditional Khasi dress, long skirts which reached to the ground and tartan shawls, and they were contemplating the loss of their mother with great dignity.

We took tea and cakes in the front room, then returned to the main road and continued on our journey to Cherrapunji. The countryside was varied and in places spectacular, with rolling hills giving way to great gorges whose pine-clad flanks were slashed by long waterfalls. We passed a taxi which had a sticker declaring, as the early British settlers had, that Meghalaya was the 'Scotland of the East', and besides the topography and the climate there was much else which reminded me, if not always of Scotland, then of Britain. When we stopped to relieve ourselves I studied some of the plants at my feet: there was coltsfoot and yellow tormentil and a grass that looked like Yorkshire fog, and far below, lining the lower slopes of the valley, the fields were rowed up ready for the planting of potatoes, a crop which the British introduced to the hills in the 1830s. A little further on, and shortly before we reached Cherrapunji, we passed through rugged country disfigured by drift mines whose narrow entrances were surrounded by heaps of spoil and pyramids of coal awaiting transport to Assam. The Welsh, I remarked to Rev. Snaitang, must have felt at home here.

I expected the wettest place in the world to be verdant and lush, but it was barren and forbidding and human efforts to civilize it seemed simply to have accentuated the hostility of the natural environment. Cherrapunji was dominated by a shrine to Dom Bosco and the Ramakrishna mission, while the ground below was largely given over to the Presbyterian mission at Nongsawlia and its schools. Once we had seen what there was to see at Cherra theological college, we inspected the church, a tin-roofed building with a detached bell-tower and a concrete monument erected in memory of Welsh missionaries who had served here between 1841 and 1967. The first was a Jones, the last a Barlow, and in between were several more Joneses, three Robertses, a couple of Evanses, a Parry, a Pryce, a Sykes, a Griffiths and a Hughes, all but two of whom had come with their wives. On the hillock to the north of the church was a damply atmospheric graveyard where the stone crosses of Christians were scattered among the burial obelisks to Khasis who had retained their tribal faith. One of the largest memorials was that of Rev. John Roberts, who wrote the Khasi national anthem. I asked Rev. Snaitang if he knew it and he sang it as we climbed to the summit, a cool drizzle sweeping in from the south and dampening our faces: it was to the tune of 'Land of Our Fathers'.

We climbed back into the taxi, drove past the Presbyterian high school and skirted around an industrial lime works to the village of Mawsmai, which had two churches, one Presbyterian and another Catholic, and a small community hall by a stream. Beside the hall were ten stone monoliths in a row, the largest of which was three times the height of a man. We had passed other groups of monoliths on the way, but none in such a concentration. Rev. Snaitang thought they were probably three hundred years old and he explained how they would have been erected: 'They were pulled into place by hand,' he said in his slow, thoughtful manner, 'using only the stem of a gourd. The people had to do it with great religious dedication. If their religious fervour was insufficient, then the stems would break.'

I asked if people still did this.

'No.' He laughed. 'If they did it now, they would need tractors!' He added that in some areas the Khasis' tribal faith was still strong; this was especially true in the remoter parts of Meghalaya where Christian missionaries had seldom ventured.

The Khasis came into contact with Hinduism long before

Christianity and the British arrived in the hills, but of the chiefs who ruled the twenty-five largely autonomous Khasi states only one became a Hindu. If I went to the Jaintia Hills, suggested Rev. Snaitang, I could visit Nartiang, the chief's village; at one time human sacrifices were offered there to the goddess Kali, but the locals were largely unimpressed and they retained their traditional beliefs, at least until the Christians arrived. In fact, their belief system had far more in common with Christianity than with Hinduism: it tended towards monotheism, although some clans had their own deities, and religious practice did not involve the worship of idols, as popular Hinduism does. Paradoxically, it was the dramatic upheavals in Khasi life following from the British conquest which created the ideal conditions for the Christian evangelists. 'It's hard to imagine the impact the British must have had when they arrived,' mused Rev. Snaitang as we studied the monoliths. 'Before they came the Khasis lived in a state of virtual isolation. Then there was the Anglo-Khasi war in the 1820s and before long the British had got all the chiefs to sign treaties. For the first time they came into contact with a mighty power and the impact was enormous.' The British came with an army to subjugate the people; they built roads and set up an administration system and a postal service. They brought in soldiers, engineers, civil servants. They introduced money, which the Khasis had never used before, and they even introduced a seven-day week to replace the eight-day one which then governed Khasi life and is still used in the markets. 'All this happened in a very short space of time,' continued Rev. Snaitang, 'and it caused a great trauma for my people. It was then that the Welsh missionaries appeared in the hills and they came with more than their faith; they came with an alphabet, with schools, with medicines, and I think they helped people to cope with the trauma.'

Early British visitors to the Khasi Hills were often disparaging about the manners and attitudes of the people they encountered. In his *Himalayan Journals* the botanist Sir Joseph Hooker described the men of Cherrapunji as sultry, intractable fellows who spoke a disagreeably nasal language; the Khasis, he wrote, displayed a most bloodthirsty and cruel disposition. A judge who was dispatched to the Khasi Hills to report on the region in the 1850s was impressed by the jail at Cherrapunji – 'The accommodation is good and the food is simple' – but not by the natives, who had 'become arrogant, deceitful and untrustworthy' following their contact with civilization. Neither of these gentlemen mentioned the most striking feature of Khasi society: it is matrilineal, and this has had a profound bearing on the development of the region. The matrilineal system affects everything: life in the clan and family most obviously, but also the way in which the Khasis relate to outsiders. One of the first things to strike the visitor to Meghalaya is the bold and attractive demeanour of the women, whose forwardness is a reflection of the high status they enjoy in Khasi society. Children take their mother's rather than their father's name; the family wealth is inherited by the youngest daughter rather than by the eldest son; and women exercise a considerable degree of control over the family budget. The Welsh missionaries were aware of the important role which women played in daily life, and while they were bluntly fundamentalist in their determination to make converts renounce most of their old beliefs and customs, they did not object to the matrilineal system. This was prudent. Rev. Snaitang believed that young Khasi women were among the first to challenge the traditional beliefs of their people and adopt the Christian faith; their acceptance of Christianity would undoubtedly have encouraged their menfolk to view the new religion with greater respect, even if they did not embrace it themselves.

Shortly before we took the road back to Shillong we went for a walk in a small park on the edge of a spectacular scarp which commanded magnificent views over the plains of Bangladesh. Among the few people there were some teenagers in T-shirts and jeans who were dancing around a cassette recorder. As we passed them Rev. Snaitang remarked that young Khasis much preferred Western to Indian music. There was, in fact, a widespread antipathy among the Khasis to anything emanating from mainland India, although contact with people from the plains had helped to foment what he called a masculinist movement. A growing number of Khasi men were challenging the old system: they wanted children to take their father's name and family wealth to be handed down to sons rather than daughters. However, everyone I met in Meghalaya was in favour of retaining the matrilineal system, and my only encounter with the opposition came in the letter columns of the perennially entertaining *Meghalaya Guardian*. In that day's edition a correspondent wrote: 'God commanded man to multiply and increase the world; in case there are no women at all, it is entirely God's look-out, not yours, since you are not authorized to do so.'

God also gave firm instructions that we should love our neighbours, however trying they might be. Sadly – and I say sadly as my time in Meghalaya was full of conviviality and entrancing encounters – there was conspicuously little in the way of brotherly love when it came to the Khasis' treatment of Shillong's *dalit* Sikhs, whose presence in the slum colony beside Bara Bazar had led to the demonstration and subsequent riot. Over much of India the tribal people are treated as second-class citizens by caste Hindus and the authorities; frequently they are driven from their forest homes to make way for development programmes from which they will garner few benefits, and many live in a state of permanent servitude on the plantations of the wealthy. However, in Shillong there was an unusual reversal of roles: this time it was the tribal people, the Khasis, who were doing the persecuting.

In 1881 Shillong's population was no more than 4,000; fifty years later it had risen to 26,500 and there are ten times that many people living in the town now. A sizeable minority are descendants of the plains people who came during the days of the Raj. They are racially different from the Khasis and they speak different languages; they are mostly Hindu and invariably patrilineal. They are also more astute when it comes to making money. 'Our culture is a village culture,' said Rev. Snaitang when we were discussing the racial tensions in the town. 'We like to gossip, to hold meetings. We don't have a history of doing business and you'll see that in the district where you're staying.' Rajasthanis ran the fax shop opposite my hotel, Sikhs the clothes shop beside it; a little further down the street a Gujarati Catholic and his half-Eritrean wife ran a sari shop, and the man from whom I bought cigarettes was a Bengali. None of these relatively well-to-do traders was involved in the riots, although their metal shutters came smartly down at the first whiff of trouble.

The *dalit* Sikhs who lived near the bazar belonged to the untouchable sweeper caste. Their ancestors were brought up to Shillong by the British at the turn of the century and they performed the menial tasks which the British, the Khasis and the caste Hindus refused to do. When they came they were settled in a colony on the outskirts of town and they still lived in the same area, but the town had expanded over the years and they now found themselves in its commercial heartland. For some time there had been a vociferous Khasi-led campaign demanding the removal of the colony. It was a slum, and it suffered all the familiar problems of a slum. Those who wished to see the colony moved claimed that some of its inhabitants were criminals, that prostitution flourished among its thread-thin alleys and that its proximity to the town's main bazar was bad for business.

A week before I arrived in Shillong 200 shacks in the sweeper colony were destroyed by fire, leaving over a thousand people homeless. The fire may have started accidentally – one newspaper suggested that it began in a cow shed – or it may have been the work of arsonists who wished to get rid of the slum. Whatever the cause, the partial destruction of the colony prompted five Khasi organizations to call their members out on to the streets and demand, once again, that the sweepers be shifted to the outskirts of town. The rally began peacefully enough but the police refused to allow the demonstrators to march on the state Assembly and *lathi*-charged them when they tried to. The crowds pelted the police with missiles, a few shots were fired, and the police retaliated, brutally by all accounts. The army was called in and the town sank into the quagmire of curfew, as the *Shillong Times* colourfully put it.

The only Christian denomination with a significant following in the sweeper colony was the Church of North India, which had two places of worship in Shillong, a modest tin-roofed shed on the edge of the colony serving the *dalit* Christians, and All Saints Cathedral, which was perched high on the hill to the south of Police Bazar, its physical elevation reflecting the social status of its congregation. With its wood-panelled altar, low-ceilinged nave and leaded windows, the cathedral had the intimate atmosphere of an old-fashioned gentleman's club. There were no grand memorials, just simple brass plaques recording the pitfalls of colonialism: Captain Herbert Brown was treacherously attacked and killed by Looshais; Robert Blair McCabe was killed in the earthquake which flattened Shillong and the original cathedral in 1897; W. B. Melville and J. O'Brien were murdered by Nagas in Manipur.

At early-morning communion the day after the riot the congregation consisted of four women, the vicar, Rev. Purely Lyngdoh, the headmaster of the church school, Rev. Presley Lyngdoh, and the Bishop of North-East India, Ernest Talibuddin, who on the conclusion of the service led me past the well-tended beds of snapdragons and mallows to his office and residence, Bishop's Kuti, where we were greeted by his servant, a Bengali girl, and his dog, a Yorkshire terrier. Silver-haired and approaching retirement, the bishop was warm and loquacious and I visited him several times, always unannounced, for he said that he liked to keep an open house. On this particular morning he was in a state of agitation about the sweeper colony. 'My argument is this,' he said, wringing his hands in *angst*, 'it's fair enough that the people want the sweepers to shift, but the government must give them proper houses. They should also realize that these people have an emotional attachment to that place. It's most unfortunate. Meghalaya is known as a Christian state, and then this sort of thing happens!'

The bishop had been in touch with the Church Auxiliary for Social Action in Calcutta and a lorry-load of relief – clothes, bedding, cooking utensils – was now on its way to Shillong. However, the riot had led to the closure of the main road to Guwahati and the aid was going to be delayed. This was by no means the first time that Khasis had agitated against people from outside, said the bishop, who was a native of Delhi; in recent years the Nepali and Bengali communities had also come under attack. He thought that the people of Shillong had a moral duty to help the sweepers in their hour of distress, not least because the town needed them: they performed the tasks associated with untouchability, and these the Khasis would not deign to do.

We were joined after a while by Rev. Aziz Massey, a dark-skinned Punjabi who had been brought up to Shillong many years ago to work with the sweepers, whose language and culture he shared. In 1962 he opened a primary school in the kitchen of Bishop's Kuti. He began with five sweeper children; now there were fifty children in the school, which was housed in a separate building, and many sweepers had converted to Christianity. Of the 200 families who lost their shacks in the fire, ninety-nine were Christians. Rev. Massey had visited them regularly since the fire, but the curfew prevented him from going there now.

All the church leaders whom I spoke to said that they were concerned about the misfortunes of the sweeper colony, yet none of the Churches made public pronouncements on the issue, and as far as I could see they were not doing much to help. When I mentioned this to a Catholic priest he nodded his head vigorously.

'I'm very upset about the sweepers, and about how little the Churches are doing,' he said. 'I'm preaching that we have a duty to help them. What would Jesus do? When I preach this, the congregation finds itself in a very uncomfortable situation.' The priest was from south India; the congregation was Khasi. 'I'm afraid it's entirely racial,' he continued. 'In the hills one is first a Khasi, or a Naga, or whatever, then you're a Christian. The tribe comes first, religion second.' Which probably explained the reluctance of church leaders to stick their necks out over the sweeper issue.

The priest was quick to add that there was much to admire about Khasi society and the town of Shillong, which he clearly loved. One afternoon we were walking along the narrow lane which led from his theological college to the main road when he took hold of my arm and swivelled me around in the direction of a Khasi house. It was no different from thousands of other dwellings in Shillong: modest in size, with many-paned windows, a tin roof painted russet, a veranda with pots of orchid and geranium and a carefully tended garden. 'Just look how beautifully neat and clean the Khasis are!' he exclaimed. He recounted that one of his brothers – whether blood or religious, I am not sure – recently came to visit him from Kerala. 'He thought he was coming to some primitive tribal area,' said the priest, laughing at the memory, 'but by the time he left he said the Khasis had given him an inferiority complex!'

Shillong was an expansive place, spread out across a collection of small hills and hemmed in to the south by rugged mountains which still had a few good stands of pine despite the recent encroachment. It was, without doubt, the cleanest town I had come across in India: the streets were not lined with litter, nor used as urinals, and the traffic was light, which meant that it was a very pleasant place to amble about on foot. The architecture was pleasing and unpretentious and the Khasis' love of flowers ensured that even the poorest dwellings were spattered with colour.

If their gardens suggested an exuberant spirit, then so did their names. When I asked Rev. Snaitang whether his Christian name had any special significance – I wondered whether he had been conceived or born while his mother was making a long journey – he replied that Overland was quite common among Khasis, who tended to choose names for their sound, for their bombast. Frequently children of the same family had names which rhymed: twins at the Catholic school run by the Salesians were called Efficiency and Sufficiency; their brother had been christened Graphite-stone. In the same area there was a man called Memory, next door to whom lived a woman called Forget, or perhaps it was the other way round. I heard of brothers called Shoulder and Moulder and young men called Milky Way and Mount Everest, and it was clear that educated people, fluent in English – at one time it was fashionable for Presbyterians to speak with a Welsh accent – were just as likely to provide their offspring with eccentric names as illiterate villagers who spoke little other than Khasi, although the latter were more likely to choose names which the priests felt obliged to change. Had a priest not intervened, a Khasi woman called Prosper would, I was told, have been christened Prostitute, which her mother liked the sound of. And if a Khasi ends up with a comical Christian name, then he or she can always reduce it to an initial, and I suppose that was why the Presbyterian pastor in Jowai introduced himself as Rev. P. A. Challam. He had been christened Peace Arrow, which struck me as an excellent choice of name for a Christian leader and showed some prescience on the part of his parents. He would, in name at least, have been the ideal emissary to send among the disgruntled and persecuted sweepers of Shillong.

~

'My dream, my hope and my prayer,' said Bishop Ernest Talibuddin when I dropped by to see him on Good Friday, 'is that the established Churches will collapse.'

I had heard such sentiments expressed on other occasions, but never by a bishop or a person of authority within a Church with an episcopal tradition. I must have looked suitably perplexed.

'Yes,' he continued, leaning forward in his chair, 'what I say is very biblical. Before AD 312, when Constantine made Christianity the religion of the Roman Empire, before then Christianity had no institutions – not as we understand them now. It was a suffering Church. All Christians were responsible for preaching the gospel. The more they were persecuted, the more Christianity spread. But after 312 everything changed.' The religion of idiots, slaves, poor women and children, as one early opponent had defined Christianity, was now the religion of emperors. Freed from persecution and obloquy, the suffering Church became an institutional Church. 'And people within the institutions began to compete with one another over who should run them,' continued the bishop. 'More and more institutions sprang up and at the same time evangelists became professionals.'

On Palm Sunday the bishop had preached at the morning service at All Saints Cathedral; there had been several hundred people there and every pew was taken. In the afternoon some fifty members of the congregation set off from Shillong in a convoy of thirteen cars to the residence of a family who were stationed at the Air Force headquarters in the hills to the south. 'And when we were there,' said the bishop, 'I could really feel the Holy Spirit moving while we prayed together, which is something I couldn't feel at the morning service. I believe – I hope – we're going to witness the collapse of the institutional Church and move to more and more informal ways of worship, in house groups like that one last Sunday.'

I asked the bishop what this would mean in practical terms. What would happen to the churches and to all the institutions which were run by Christians?

'Get rid of them,' he replied emphatically. 'Faith doesn't require great buildings or bank accounts. The institutions must wither away.'

In 1988 the bishop and his wife spent five days in Berlin and while they were there they went to see the wall, which had recently been breached. 'I went all over,' recalled the bishop. 'I touched this wall and at times I was crying with emotion. Even now I find it difficult to believe that the wall's been broken down. I thought it would be there until the end of the world. And the USSR, that too, that collapsed almost overnight. If that can happen, then by God's providence the institutions of the Church can also collapse overnight.'

And what about the servants of these institutions? I asked. What would become of the archbishops and bishops?

'Do we need bishops?' he asked in rather a whimsical voice. He conceded, with a wry smile, that he was on the verge of retirement and that he had enjoyed all the benefits, material and otherwise, of his position as a bishop. All the same, it was clear that his disillusionment with the institutions of the Christian religion was of long standing.

There have been a handful of Christian leaders in India who have shunned institutions and gone among the people, preaching the gospel under no other banner than that of Christ. The most famous of these itinerant preachers was Sadhu Sundar Singh, whom I mentioned in an earlier chapter. On one occasion, recalled Bishop Ernest, Sadhu Singh's ministry led him to the Ganges, along whose banks are some of Hinduism's holiest cities. In Varanasi he listened to a Hindu *sanayasi* delivering a discourse to a gathering on the river bank. He was astounded to hear that everything the *sanayasi* said accorded with the teachings of the New Testament, and when the crowd had dispersed he approached him and said as much. The *sanayasi* replied that he was a great believer in Jesus Christ. 'And what Sadhu Singh found,' said the bishop, 'was that there were thousands and thousands of hidden Christians. Outwardly they were Hindus, but inwardly they were Christians who didn't want to join hands with Christian institutions.' Sadhu Singh was a rare bird. No other independent preacher has made such an impression on the Indian people, and for the most part Christianity has been championed by evangelists working within specific institutions, belonging to specific denominations.

The bishop frequently talked about the Church emptying itself and divesting itself of wealth. I don't think he was decrying Christian achievements in the fields of health care and education, or its social work among the poor. I think he was reacting, rather, to two separate issues, though they have been historically related. The first concerns bricks and mortar: the problems associated with the ownership, maintenance and disposal of property have sapped the spiritual energies of the Churches, and especially the Churches of North and South India. The second relates to Christian disunity: in a religion whose two great commandments are to love God and to love one's neighbour, the enmities between different denominations are absurd. 'I believe a time will come,' said the bishop, 'when even what we call Christianity will disappear. I say that because we attach the word "Christianity" nowadays to institutions, not to the life of believers. One day the institutions will collapse and we shall see each other as we truly are.'

In the meantime we continue to see through a glass darkly, and the pure and humble religion which gently insinuated itself into the minds of men, which grew up in silence and obscurity, derived new vigour from opposition and finally erected the triumphal banner of the cross on the ruins of the Capitol – as Edward Gibbon famously described the Christian conquest of Rome – will continue for the foreseeable future to be a religion of denominations and sects. These are bewildering in their variety, and the north-eastern states appear to have been blessed, or cursed, with more than most. Mizoram is predominantly Baptist and Presbyterian, but there are eighty other denominations at work there. I am not sure how many were present in Meghalaya, but Rev. Snaitang was able to reel off a dozen without having to give the matter much thought. Beside the Presbyterians, there were the Church of God with some 50,000 members, the Church of North India with 10,000, the Church of Jesus Christ, the Church of God Ecclesia, a variety of Pentecostal groups, the Jehovah's Witnesses, the Seventh Day Adventists and several others which I had never heard of before. And, of course, there were the Roman Catholics, who now matched the Presbyterians in terms of numbers, with over a third of a million members. Most Catholics were poor or illiterate, and often both, but there was also an impressively cerebral side to their Church, as I discovered when Rev. Snaitang took me to visit the principal of the Sacred Heart Theological College, which was run by the Society of Don Bosco.

'When the Welsh came,' said Father George Kottuppallil when we were talking about the background of Meghalaya's Catholics, 'they insisted that only those who could read or write could be baptized. Well, we chaps were never too bothered about that!' And unlike the Presbyterians, who were staunch opponents of drinking and smoking, and the Church of God, which proscribed the theatre, dancing and betel-chewing, the Catholics adopted a relaxed attitude towards these simple pleasures. This was to prove a considerable attraction to Khasis who wished to become Christians without becoming puritans.

Father George was a Romo-Syrian from Kerala, the great breeding-ground for Catholic priests in India, and he had the dark complexion of a southerner and a relaxed, humorous manner. He had done part of his theological training at the Gregorian University in Rome, and like all the Salesian fathers who taught here he spoke many languages. However, he wore his learning lightly and he had the rare ability to turn what might have been an arid history, in this case of the Catholic incursion into the north-east, into a sort of religious soap opera full of intrigue and conflict.

Some 350 years after the Portuguese brought Catholicism to

the southern parts of India, Catholic missionaries made their first tentative steps into the north-east. They had to battle on many different fronts. The locals were frequently hostile – two priests from the Paris Mission were murdered as they tried to enter Tibet in the 1850s – the climate in the valleys was malarial and the religious orders made the task of evangelism all the more difficult by their own contrariness. The English Benedictines, for example, would take responsibility for the vicariate apostolic of Dacca, which included Assam, only if they were given sole access to the Khasi Hills, which they coveted both for their potential as a sanatorium and as a place for winning souls. The Vatican agreed, and this meant that an Italian priest who laboured for nineteen years among the scattered Catholics of the Brahmaputra Valley was allowed to enter Shillong only on condition that he did not attempt to baptize any of its citizens. As it happened, the Benedictines were infrequent visitors, and when news of their neglect of the Khasi Hills reached Rome in the 1880s the cardinals decided on firm action. The Khasis must be saved, but by whom? This remote corner of India held little appeal for most religious orders, who turned a deaf ear to the Pope's and the cardinals' entreaties. 'The Jesuits refused to go,' explained Father George, 'and so did the Capuchins, and the Milanese of the Pontifical Institute for Foreign Missions, and the Fathers of the Holy Cross. They had heard about the wild people and the malaria and the wild animals, and they felt uncomfortable, to put it politely.' It was around this time that Bismarck clashed with the Catholic Church in Germany. He suppressed the religious orders and a number of priests interested in foreign mission made their way down to Italy and founded a new order. 'The Pope needed them,' explained Father George, 'and they needed somewhere to go and evangelize.' In 1890 the Salvatorians arrived in the Khasi Hills and a year later, on 8 December 1891, Anna Nongum and her daughter became the first Khasis to convert to Catholicism.

Being Germans, the Salvatorians were perfectionists and they often made their Khasi catechumens wait an inordinately long time before they would baptize them. This was bad for business, but progress was also hindered by the outright opposition of the Welsh ministers of the Presbyterian Church. When Catholic missionaries paid a visit to the town of Jowai in the Jaintia Hills they looked for accommodation at the DAK bungalow. '"No, sorry, full up." That's what they were told,' said Father George. 'And that was the doing of the Welsh.' The Salvatorians, however, did make converts – including some *ot-bang*, those thrown out of the Presbyterian Church for drinking or whatever – and the Welsh decided to counter what they saw as an increasingly serious threat by publishing a pamphlet in Khasi called the *Christian Leader*. It ridiculed the Catholics for venerating the Virgin Mary, attacked the papacy and listed other aspects of Romishness that the Protestants deplored. The Catholics retaliated with the *Catholic Leader*, which attempted to answer the calumnies of the Presbyterian pamphlet.

In the early years of the century the Catholics moved into the field of education. Irish sisters opened the Loreto school for girls and shortly afterwards St Edmund's school for boys was founded. The European and Indian élite, many of whom were Protestants, sent their children to these schools and Catholics became, in Father George's words, socially important. By the time the Salvatorian priests were interned by the British at the beginning of the First World War there were over 5,000 Khasi Catholics. The Salvatorians were replaced by Jesuits from Bengal and the Jesuits by the Society of Don Bosco, the Salesians, who have been here ever since. When the latter arrived here in 1922 there were 5,488 Catholics in Assam; eleven years later there were 24,000. The number of Catholic primary schools rose from thirty-one to 280, of churches from six to twenty-four and of priests from six to twenty-eight. By the end of the Second World War there were three times as many Catholics, and the Church has continued to grow more rapidly than any other.

Father George attributed the success of the Catholic Church, in part, to its religiosity. 'The Khasis feel comfortable with us,' he said. 'In the villages most people are illiterate and they love the cult of Mary; they love the rosary, the holy waters, the scapular . . .' I was reminded of Abbé Dubois and his contention that the Catholic Church, with its rituals and celebrations, its love of colour and tradition, was far more appealing to Indians, or at least to wavering Hindus, than the Protestant Churches would ever be. 'For most of our Catholics,' continued Father George, 'religion is about faith; it comes from the heart. I think the Khasis have to make a bigger leap if they have to go from their tribal faith to the Presbyterians than they do from their tribal faith to us.'

Rather than attend any one service on Good Friday I drifted into several, and the social and intellectual differences between the denominations were vividly apparent. There were around 300 people packed into All Saints Cathedral, with another thirty or so on wooden benches outside the main door, and behind them a dozen or so chauffeurs, whispering among themselves and smoking. The women were beautifully dressed, some in saris, others in summer frocks, and most of the men wore suits and ties or tweed jackets and cavalry twills: it was the sort of turn-out, socially speaking, that you would encounter at a church garden party in Wiltshire or Dorset: not exactly the ruling class at prayer, but the educated middle-class attending a rite which was as much social as religious.

Further down the hill, past the Shillong Club and Ward's Lake, a similar number of people had gathered in the Presbyterian church and I stopped briefly to listen to a snatch of the sermon. Here, as at All Saints, the congregation was English-speaking and educated but the atmosphere was very different. This was Christianity stripped of its rituals and theatricality. There was nothing pretty or diverting to distract the believers' attention from the only thing which mattered, the word of God: no priests decked out in fine robes, as there were at All Saints; no paintings depicting

Eve offering Adam the apple, or the expulsion from the garden, as there were at the Catholic cathedral on the hill above. No statues of saints along the walls; no Christ on the cross even. Just a big shed of a building with a tin roof, a serious congregation soberly dressed and a pastor who wanted to hold their attention.

By now the curfew had been lifted, but the streets which led to the main bazar were still lined with armed soldiers and police. I walked past the Presbyterian mission compound on Mawkhar Road, past houses whose windows had been shattered by soldiers who had decided, the day after the riot, to impose the curfew with a show of terror, and along the winding lane to a Catholic church. It was capacious and colourful, its main façade painted a creamy green and pink, which made it look like a pistachio-and-raspberry ripple. There were at least 600 people inside and almost as many in the square outside. Many of the young men arrived in gangs and were spivvily dressed in shiny suits; a few had pony-tails and earrings and some had raffish hairstyles and looked like young James Deans. There was much swaggering to impress the girls, who looked demurely attractive in their Sunday best. The service, relayed through loud speakers to those outside, was in Khasi: it was ritualistic and devotional and the sermon was brief, at least by Presbyterian standards.

A few days later I mentioned to one of the priests at Sacred Heart College that the most brilliant sermon I had heard in India had been delivered by a Catholic, as had the most stupid and disgraceful. He nodded his head and laughed. 'You know,' he said, 'a couple of days after the riots we were supposed to go to a mass on the other side of town. It meant breaking the curfew and as we didn't fancy getting beaten up by the police, we didn't go. Later, when we saw some of the other priests who'd attended the mass, they said, "Why didn't you come? Were you frightened of the curfew?" No, we told them, it wasn't the curfew we were frightened of, it was the sermon!'

I dropped by Sacred Heart College on several occasions, dined with the priests and talked to some at length. Our conversations touched on a great many subjects, ranging from the practical to the sublime. Father Sebastian Karotemprel, an elegant, youthful-looking man who divided his time between Shillong and the Urban University in Rome, where he was Professor of Missiology, told me about the tribal research centre which was currently being built on the campus; he also talked about Salman Rushdie's latest novel and Gibbon's views on the spread of Christianity, of Cardinal Newman and the influence of American culture on Hindi movies. Father Zephyrinus, a dark-skinned, long-haired priest from Chota Nagpur – he was a member of the Oraon tribe, I think – told me about his work among the labourers of the Assam tea plantations. He said that over much of India the tribal people were treated no better than slaves; the Khasis were an exception, and I shouldn't see their situation as comparable with that of the tribes in Bihar or most other regions of India. Another priest, reading in the common room about the ransacking the previous day of a church in Bengal by a mob of vandals, remarked that had such an outrage been committed against a mosque or a Hindu temple, there would have been an outburst of communal violence. Unlike the Muslims, Christians tended to react to such events with sadness rather than anger. In Shillong, where Christians were the major force, they were more assertive: it was not unknown, said one of the priests, for Christian youths to lob rocks at the Hindu temple in town. The Hindus of Meghalaya also had to countenance the slaughter of cattle: the sacred was edible, and I ate beef for the first time in India when I was with the Salesians.

I liked the priests' lack of piety – no lengthy graces before meals, as there invariably were with the Protestants, especially those of an evangelical persuasion – and I liked their easy laughter, their fondness for debate and the way they talked of friendship. 'Without love, we'd be neurotic,' said Father George when we were discussing celibacy and how the priests had to sublimate their sexual energy into a broader love, for each other as well as for the boys in their charge. But what I admired most about the theological college was its catholicity. There was a library here with 90,000 books – 'We're part of the University of Rome,' explained Father George as he showed me round, 'so intellectually we have to be as good as they are – but there was also an intensely practical side to the Christianity which was practised here. Father George had set up a clinic to treat children with rickets, and Father Sngi Silvano Lyngdoh practised a form of healing which attracted villagers from all over the hills.

On one of my last mornings in Shillong I arrived at the college while the priests were having breakfast. A long queue of villagers waited quietly outside the door of Father Sngi's study and I waited with them. At exactly eight o'clock the priest appeared, unlocked the door and motioned me to follow him inside. I asked if my presence would be off-putting, either for himself or his patients. 'No,' he said, 'come in, come in. It's public. It's nothing special.' He called to the queue outside and three women came through the door. He greeted them pleasantly and waved them towards the chairs in the middle of the room. The oldest of the three, a handsome woman with sharp features and weathered skin, stared blindly ahead and her companions and the priest guided her into a chair. The women were thin and dressed in the traditional Khasi manner, with colourful shawls and long wrap-around skirts. Father Sngi shared their Mongoloid features, but he was constructed along different lines; he was small and squat and he wore a voluminous cassock, scuffed shoes, a thick woollen pullover and a turban which was loosely piled on his head like a carelessly whipped meringue. While he discussed matters with the women in a soft voice, I glanced around his study. The desk was covered with books, old medicine bottles, ancient files and a cardboard box which I later discovered to be full of commentaries on the Bible, written by Father Sngi in Khasi. Beneath the desk was a wastepaper-basket whose contents were spilling over the side like boiled milk and a half-eaten banana, which had turned black.

There were also several candles on the floor and some battered old suitcases covered in dust. On the shelves beside me were books in various languages: Khasi, English, Italian, Hebrew, Greek. Most were about Christianity, but I noticed Virgil's *Aeneid* sandwiched between the Bible and a copy of Alan Paton's *Cry, the Beloved Country*.

Father Sngi suddenly took the head of the sightless woman in his hands and spoke to her in a louder voice. She began to tremble and the other women watched apprehensively. He said a prayer, then he withdrew his hands and slapped her several times across the cheek, quite hard, and spat at her forehead. This action was accompanied by more indignant, insistent speech. He then picked up the plastic jug from his table and hurled handfuls of holy water at the woman's face. She bowed her head, but Father Sngi pulled it up again and splashed more water into her eyes. By the time the woman left five minutes later her eyes were beginning to focus. She was able to make out the shape of the water jug, held up for her to identify, and to count Father Sngi's raised fingers. He blessed the other women as well, less dramatically, holding their heads and splashing them with holy water, and then the three left together.

'This is most interesting,' said Father Sngi as he came to stand beside me, his voice lowered again to a gentle whisper. 'This woman – she's a very good woman – her husband has committed adultery and the shock has blinded her. You see, the Khasis believe that adultery will bring sickness and sometimes blindness. It's all psychological. But now she's beginning to see again. Soon she will be fine.'

'You're not saying this is a miracle?' I asked.

'Of course not,' replied Father Sngi, laughing gently. 'It's religious psychiatry. I sent the guilt out of her, and I've told it to go to her husband.'

He called for the next patient and a morose young man skulked into the study. He described his ailments to Father Sngi, clutching his stomach, and the priest turned to me and said, 'We have a lot of depression in the twentieth century. How is it in your country?' He prayed for the young man, slapped him a few times, doused him with holy water and sent him on his way, a broad smile having replaced his funereal frown. 'I've driven the depression out,' said Father Sngi simply.

Another young man appeared. He hadn't eaten for many days and he looked gaunt and weak. The same process was repeated, and Father Sngi explained: 'What he told me was "Food doesn't like me." So I prayed for him and I was very stern with food. I said, "Food, you must like him. That's what you're here for."' Before the young man left he handed the priest an empty gin bottle, and the priest filled it with holy water. 'Now he'll be fine,' said Father Sngi.

I asked the priest whether this healing, or religious psychiatry as he called it, was Khasi or Christian in origin.

'It's both,' he replied. 'First, I talk in a language they understand. By that I don't just mean in Khasi, but in terms they understand. But Christ is there, of course. It is Christ who drives out their fears, their ailments.'

Others came and went: a small boy who had had a shock; a teenage girl who dreamed of the dead; a woman who had passed out on a riverbank and believed that she had been attacked by water devils. 'If I denied that water devils exist,' explained Father Sngi, 'then she'd never believe me. She wouldn't have faith in what I do. So I don't deny it. I go along with it, and then pray to Christ to drive the devil out.' A few minutes later the woman left the room with an expression of deep peace on her face: it was, I suppose, the peace of God which passeth all understanding.

Bishop Ernest Talibuddin was longing for the day when the established Church would collapse, when its institutions would wither away. In my memory, they have already begun to do so.

I remember the cathedrals and churches as monuments to a certain age and a certain tradition rather than as places of worship: in fact, I can scarcely recall a single word I heard from the pulpit, and the act of communion, the central unifying act of Christian worship, could equally well have been conducted in a forest or cattle shed. When I think now of Christian India I see Father Sngi praying for a traumatized woman and the transcendental peace which descended upon her face; I hear a Hindu doctor in the slums of Delhi talking of his duty to go after the lost sheep, the lost sheep being both battered children and abusive parents; I hear the squabbling and laughter of the prostitutes' children in the upper room of Bowbazar; and I see the serious faces of the Muslim women of Tiljala who were learning to sew and read. I remember the conversations I had with priests and nurses, with slum workers and historians, about everything from sex to salvation, from the price of whisky to whether St Thomas came to India. And as I listen to the voices of those I met, I can hear the sounds which went with the voices – of birds singing in the banyan tree outside the vicarage; of engines backfiring and a drunk swearing; of singing in a classroom and fishermen's chanting – and I recall too the smells that went with the sounds: the stench of the sewers in Calcutta, the enticing smell of good spicy food in the Catholic seminaries, the tangy odour of fish and rotting vegetation in the harbour at Cochin. I have written much about the conflict between different denominations and different castes, but it is a triumph of sorts that the Christian religion is able to appeal to such an extraordinary diversity of people. The gulf between the Syrian Christian of Kottayam with his neatly tended feet and thriving gold business and the illiterate *dalit* who works as a coolie on the roads of Madras is as great as that between emperor and slave, and yet they are united by belief, by the message of the cross, with the half-starved fishermen of Vizhinjam and the down-at-heel Anglo-Indians of Calcutta, with the tribal Christians of Bihar and the wealthy Catholics of Bombay, with the recent convert who dares not admit to his new beliefs for fear of persecution and men and women who trace their Christianity back to a few years after the death of Christ.

On Easter Day I was invited to lunch with the bishop. 'It will just be you and me and a very old priest,' he said as we came out of the service at All Saints Cathedral. I arrived at his residence at the same time as the old priest, who had doubtless seen the bishop kissing many of the women who had attended the service. As we entered the house he touched the Bengali servant lightly on the shoulder and carefully explained, in English, 'I am afraid I'm not the kissing type. I'm from a different generation, but I love you all the same.' I don't think the girl understood a word of what he said, but she smiled broadly and was probably astonished to have been greeted at all. When we were having lunch the priest said he had recently met a Christian fundamentalist who told him that he would go to hell, presumably because he was not a born-again Christian: 'So I said to him, "You may have a greater faith than me, but I have love, and I love even you who condemns me."' The priest added that one of the defining moments in his spiritual life occurred when he was a young man, a recent convert from high-caste Hinduism. C. F. Andrews, a leading Christian thinker, leaned over his shoulder and scratched on his notebook the famous words from St Paul's first letter to the Corinthians (13:13). 'There are three things which last for ever: faith, hope and love; and the greatest of these is love.'

I cannot think of a better creed.

Selected Reading

On my first visit to a theological college in India I was shown into a library to look at the books on Christian India. To my horror, there were not a few hundred, as I had anticipated, but many thousands. Indeed, there were whole shelves dealing with Christianity in states which had hardly any Christians. I doubt whether I have read even a hundredth of what has been written on the subject. The books listed below are those which I have found especially useful or entertaining, and sometimes both.

Alexander Mar Thoma, Metropolitan, *The Marthoma Church: Heritage and Mission*, Tiruvalla, Mar Thoma Church, 1985

Appasamy, A. J., *Sunder Singh: A Biography*, Madras, CLS, 1985

Areeparampil, Mathew, *Tribals of Jharkhand: Victims of Development*, New Delhi, Indian Social Institute, 1995

Azariah, M., *Witnessing in India Today*, Madras, United Evangelical Lutheran Churches in India, 1983

Brockington, John, *Hinduism and Christianity*, London, Macmillan, 1992

Brown, Leslie, *The Indian Christians of St Thomas*, Cambridge, CUP, 1982

Chadwick, Henry, *The Early Church*, London, Penguin, 1967

Chatterton, Eyre, *A History of the Church of England in India*, London, SPCK, 1924

Davies, Philip, *The Penguin Guide to the Monuments of India*, Volume II, *Islamic, Rajput, European*, London, Penguin, 1989

de André, A. Pereira, *The Apostle St Thomas in the City of Mylapore*, Madras, St Thomas Cathedral, 1972

Dubois, Abbé J. A., *Letters on the State of Christianity in India*, New Delhi, Asian Educational Services, 1995 (reprint of 1823 edition published in London by Longman)

Fernandes, I. P. Newman, *St Francis Xavier and Old Goa*, Panjim, Koinia Publications, 1994

Firth, C. B., *An Introduction to Indian Church History*, rev. ed., Madras, Christian Literature Society, 1976

Francis, T. Dayanandan, and Israel Selvanayagam (eds.), *Many Voices in Christian Mission*, Madras, Christian Literature Society, 1994

Furer-Haimendorf, Christoph von, *Tribes of India: The Struggle for Survival*, Delhi, OUP, 1989

Gibbon, Edward, *The Decline and Fall of the Roman Empire* (first published 1776–81), London, Penguin, 1985

Gorai, Rt Rev. D. C., *New Horizons in Christian Ministry*, Calcutta, Diocese of Calcutta, 1993

Griffiths, Bede, *Return to the Centre*, London, Collins, 1976

Hazarika, Sanjoy, *Strangers of the Mist: Tales of War and Peace from India's Northeast*, New Delhi, Viking, 1994

Holcomb, Helen H., *Men of Might in Indian Missions*, London, Oliphant, Anderson & Ferrier, 1901

Hooker, Joseph Dalton, *Himalayan Journals*, London, Ward, Lock, Bowden & Co., 1891

Hrangkhuma, F., and Sebastian C. H. Kim, *The Church in India: Its Mission Tomorrow*, New Delhi, CMS/ISPCK, 1996

Johnson, Paul, *A History of Christianity*, London, Penguin, 1990

Jones, Kenneth W. (ed.), *Religious Controversy in British India*, New York, State University Press, 1992

Kanwar, Pamela, *Imperial Simla*, Oxford, OUP, 1990

Karotemprel, Sebastian, *The Impact of Christianity on the Tribes of North-east India*, Shillong, Sacred Heart Theological College, 1994

Karotemprel, Sebastian, *The Catholic Church in North-east India 1890–1990*, Shillong, Vendrame Institute, 1993

Kollaparambil, Jacob, *The Babylonian Origin of the Southists among the St Thomas Christians*, Rome, Pont. Institutum Studorium Orientalium, 1992

Kottuppallil, George, *History of the Catholic Missions in Central Bengal 1855–1886*, Shillong, Vendrame Institute, 1988

Livingstone, E. A., (ed.), *The Concise Oxford Dictionary of the Christian Church*, Oxford, OUP, 1977

McGavran, Donald, *Understanding the Church in India*, Bombay, Gospel Literature Service, 1979

Massey, James, *Indigenous People: Dalits*, New Delhi, ISPCK, 1994

Mateer, Samuel, *The Land of Charity: A Descriptive Account of Travancore and Its People*, New Delhi, Asian Educational Services, 1991 (reprint of 1870 edition published by John Snow, London)

Mayhew, Arthur, *Christianity and the Government of India*, London, Faber & Gwyer, 1929

Medway, John, *Memoirs of the Life and Writings of John Pye Smith*, London, Jackson & Walford, 1853

Moorhouse, Geoffrey, *Calcutta: The City Revealed*, London, Penguin, 1974

Morris, Jan, *Stones of Empire*, London, Penguin, 1994

Neill, Stephen, *A History of Christian Missions*, London, Penguin, 1990

Polo, Marco, *The Travels*, London, Penguin, 1958

Rowlands, J. Helen, and Hridesh Ranjan Ghose (compilers), *Sermons and Sayings of Sadhu Sundar Singh*, Shillong, published privately, 1924

Shourie, Arun, *Missionaries in India*, New Delhi, Voice of India, 1994

Snaitang, O. L., *Christianity and Social Change in North-east India*, Shillong, Vendrame Institute, 1993

Thapar, R., *A History of India*, Volume I, *From the Discovery of India to 1526*, London, Penguin, 1966

Thomas, Anthony Korah, *The Christians of Kerala*, Kottayam, published by the author, 1993

Thorogood, Bernard, *Gales of Change: The Story of the London Missionary Society 1945–1977*, Geneva, WCC Publications, 1994

Sister Vandana, *Social Justice and Ashrams*, Bangalore, ATC, 1982

Voice of India, *Arun Shourie and his Christian Critics*, New Delhi, Voice of India, 1995

Watson, Francis, *A Concise History of India*, London, Thames & Hudson, 1974

Webster, John C. B., *The Dalit Christians: A History*, New Delhi, ISPCK, 1994

During my travels I gathered many academic papers, pamphlets, brochures and magazine articles which contributed in one way or another to my understanding of Christian India. It would be tedious to list them all, but I must make special mention of the papers – many unpublished, as far as I know – given to me by the church historian in Shimla, Dr K. N. Thakur Das. I found his work on the Himalayan Mission especially useful.

Index